THE
SOCIAL CONSTRUCTION
OF SEXUALITY

Third Edition

Recent Sociology Titles from Norton

The Cosmopolitan Canopy by Elijah Anderson

Social Problems, 2nd Edition by Joel Best

The Family: Diversity, Inequality, and Social Change by Philip Cohen

You May Ask Yourself: An Introduction to Thinking Like a Sociologist, 3rd Edition by Dalton Conley

Gender by Myra Marx Ferree and Lisa Wade

The Real World: An Introduction to Sociology, 4th Edition by Kerry Ferris and Jill Stein

Essentials of Sociology, 5th Edition by Anthony Giddens, Mitchell Duneier, Richard P. Appelbaum, and Deborah Carr

Introduction to Sociology, 9th Edition by Anthony Giddens, Mitchell Duneier, Richard P. Appelbaum, and Deborah Carr

Mix It Up: Popular Culture, Mass Media, and Society by David Grazian

The Contexts Reader, 2nd Edition edited by Douglas Hartmann and Christopher Uggen

The Society Pages: Color Lines and Racial Angles edited by Douglas Hartmann and Christopher Uggen

The Society Pages: Crime and the Punished edited by Douglas Hartmann and Christopher Uggen

The Society Pages: The Social Side of Politics edited by Douglas Hartmann and Christopher Uggen

When Sex Goes to School by Kristin Luker

Doing Race edited by Hazel Rose Markus and Paula M. L. Moya

Readings for Sociology, 7th Edition edited by Garth Massey

The Sociology of News, 2nd Edition by Michael Schudson

Sex Matters: The Sexuality and Society Reader, 4th Edition edited by Mindy Stombler, Dawn M. Baunach, Wendy Simonds, Elroi J. Windsor, and Elisabeth O. Burgess

Cultural Sociology: An Introductory Reader by Matt Wray

American Society: How It Really Works, 2nd Edition by Erik Olin Wright and Joel Rogers

Norton Critical Editions

The Feminine Mystique by Betty Friedan, edited by Kirsten Fermaglich and Lisa Fine

The Communist Manifesto by Karl Marx, edited by Frederic L. Bender

The Protestant Ethic and the Spirit of Capitalism by Max Weber, translated by Talcott Parsons and edited by Richard Swedberg

To learn more about Norton Sociology, please visit:
wwnorton.com/soc

THE SOCIAL CONSTRUCTION OF SEXUALITY

Third Edition

STEVEN SEIDMAN

STATE UNIVERSITY OF NEW YORK–ALBANY

W. W. Norton & Company
New York • London

To Alan. Thanks for the gift of
Eros in its many forms

W. W. Norton & Company has been independent since its founding in 1923, when William
Warder Norton and Mary D. Herter Norton first published lectures delivered at the People's
Institute, the adult education division of New York City's Cooper Union. The firm soon
expanded its program beyond the Institute, publishing books by celebrated academics from
America and abroad. By mid-century, the two major pillars of Norton's publishing program—trade books and college texts—were firmly established. In the 1950s, the Norton
family transferred control of the company to its employees, and today—with a staff of four
hundred and a comparable number of trade, college, and professional titles published each
year—W. W. Norton & Company stands as the largest and oldest publishing house owned
wholly by its employees.

Copyright © 2015, 2010, 2003 by W. W. Norton & Company, Inc.
Printed in the United States of America

Editor: Karl Bakeman
Associate Editor: Nicole Sawa
Editorial Assistant: Lindsey Thomas
Production Manager: Andrew Ensor
Composition: Achorn International, Inc.
Manufacturing: Maple-Vail Book Group

Library of Congress Cataloging-in-Publication Data

Seidman, Steven.
    The social construction of sexuality / Steven Seidman. — Third edition.
        pages cm
    Includes bibliographical references and index.
    ISBN 978-0-393-93780-0 (pbk. : alk. paper)
    1. Sex—Philosophy. 2. Gender identity. 3. Social role. 4. Heterosexuality.
5. Homosexuality. 6. Sexual ethics.   I. Title.
    HQ16.S45 2015
    306.7—dc23

                                                        2014030827

W. W. Norton & Company, Inc., 500 Fifth Avenue, New York, NY 10110
wwnorton.com
W. W. Norton & Company Ltd., Castle House, 75/76 Wells Street, London
W1T 3QT

2 3 4 5 6 7 8 9 0

Contents

Introduction

FEW OF US WOULD LIKELY question the idea that sex is natural. Like our parents and probably their parents, most of us take for granted that humans are born sexual or that we are, in a manner of speaking, programmed to be sexual. This should not come as a surprise; it is what we have been taught to believe. If you are traditionally Jewish or Catholic, for example, you will likely have been taught that God equipped men and women with an innate drive to procreate. If you are of a liberal religious or a nonreligious background, sexologists such as Masters and Johnson or psychologists such as Freud have most likely shaped your beliefs about sex. Such scientists view sex as an evolved biological instinct or drive. Sex is said to be as deeply rooted in human nature as the need to eat or sleep. But is this belief true?

Consider that it was not too long ago that most of us thought that race was natural. Nature was said to create various racial types. Indeed, throughout most of the nineteenth and twentieth centuries, many Americans were unshaken in their belief that humans were naturally divided into distinct racial groups—whites, blacks, Asians, Indians, and so on. Every individual was said to belong to a specific racial group. An individual's racial identity supposedly revealed something basic about her or his core self. For example, many white people believed that blacks were emotionally, morally, and socially inferior. Blacks were thought best suited for social roles and jobs that primarily required physical strength and endurance, roles that just happened to be low in pay and prestige. We have come to see that such ideas are false stereotypes that contribute to racial inequality.

Today, most scholars believe that race is a social construction. The *idea* of separate racial identities and groups is a social creation. Many historians believe that it was not until the eighteenth century that some European societies began to classify individuals by their racial identity. Such classifications are the products of power struggles among groups, including nations. Establishing racial divisions is a way to create and justify social inequalities. For example, scholars argue that European Americans labeled darker-skinned peoples "Negroes" and defined them as inferior to justify slavery and white social privilege.

For another example, consider that for many centuries most Americans and Europeans, including educated folk, believed that gender differences were natural. Some of us still think that infants are born either female or male and that the two sexes have different psychological, intellectual, and social aptitudes. These natural differences are said to inevitably result in distinct gender identities and roles. For example, many people believe that nature equips women with empathizing, nurturing, and caretaking aptitudes that make them better parents than men. Many of us still think that most military leaders, corporate executives, and political rulers are men because nature has furnished men with "leadership" traits, such as aggressiveness and decisiveness.

But scholars today argue that beliefs about natural gender differences have little factual support. In America and elsewhere, infants are classified as either male or female and treated differently. For example, females are taught and pressured, sometimes coerced, into adopting so-called feminine behaviors and social roles. It is true that women on average are smaller and less muscular than men, but many women have the ability to perform traditionally male activities. In addition, physical strength is irrelevant to most blue- and white-collar jobs. Most occupations require social and intellectual skills, such as discipline, planning, analytical reasoning, and social cooperation, all of which can be learned by most men and women. There is nothing about women's bodies or brains that prevents them from becoming engineers, iron workers, accountants, principals, executives, or heads of government. If women are underrepresented in these occupations, it is either because men have refused to give them a chance or because women have been taught not to aspire to these positions.

Not very long ago, conventional wisdom held that race and gender differences were creations of nature. Today, however, many of us recognize that such beliefs are mistaken. We suspect that such beliefs may be ideological and contribute to creating racial and gender differences and inequalities. At a minimum, the new conventional wisdom views race and gender as shaped as much by social factors as by nature. Is it possible that the same is true for sexuality?

In fact, in the past two decades a virtual revolution has occurred in the way scholars understand sex. A vast body of research and knowledge has accumulated that highlights the social character of sexuality. What does it mean to view sex as social?

It is useful to distinguish a weak and a strong version of the claim that sex is social. The weak version holds that individuals are born with a sexual nature. For example, this perspective would say that most of us are born heterosexual and are biologically driven to engage in procreative behavior. However, social factors shape when (age), with whom (their race, class, or religion), and how (which acts) we engage in heterosexual behavior. The strong view holds that we are not born with a sexual nature. We are born with bodies that have enormous potential to experience sensual stimulation. Society teaches us which bodily sensations and experiences are sexual and their meaning. For example, heterosexual behavior is common throughout history, but only in some societies is this preference the basis of a distinct sexual identity. Social factors determine which desires are sexual and which serve as identities, which desires and identities are acceptable, and what forms of sexual intimacy are considered appropriate.

Approaching sex as social has made possible new historical and sociological perspectives on sex. For example, until recently it was assumed that the homosexual was a separate sexual and human type that has always existed; the only variation in history was how different societies responded to this sexual minority. In contrast, the new social approach has led scholars to document considerable changes in the very meaning of homosexuality. Historians of the United States have shown how homosexuality changed from a behavior (sodomy) in the nineteenth century, to a deviant individual identity (homosexual or lesbian) in the early twentieth century, to a positive social identity (gay or lesbian) today.

But, you might reasonably ask, does it matter to ordinary citizens whether we view sex as social or natural? Is the debate over whether sex is natural or social just an academic one that lacks any broader social and political significance? I think this debate should matter a great deal to the general public because in many societies, such as in the United States or the United Kingdom, *the idea of nature is used both to help us understand sexualities and to serve as a standard of sexual morality.* Sexual desires, acts, and identities that are defined as natural are often considered good, right, or normal. The authority of the government and other institutions is enlisted to support natural or normal sexualities. The notion that there are natural and normal types of sexuality assumes that there are also unnatural and abnormal sexual desires and acts. Unnatural sexualities are considered bad and immoral (sinful, perverse, sick) and, accordingly, should not be tolerated; individuals whose sexuality is labeled unnatural may be punished. For example, they may be subject to criminal sanction or denied rights and respect.

Most Americans likely consider heterosexuality to be natural. Several theories have been advanced to defend the notion of the naturalness of heterosexuality—for example, that it is an innate reproductive or family instinct, that it is the basis of the survival of the species, or that it expresses the natural fit between the bodies and psyches of men and women. These accounts of the naturalness of heterosexuality assume that homosexuality is unnatural. Homosexuals cannot reproduce or ensure the survival of the species, and, according to this view, the bodies and minds of two men or two women do not mesh. Accordingly, homosexuality has often been viewed as perverse, abnormal, and perhaps a social threat. From this point of view, society has an interest and a right to promote heterosexuality (through laws, culture, social policy, education) while repressing homosexuality and punishing homosexuals. So, whether a specific sexual act or identity is viewed as natural or not matters a great deal. Sexual behavior that is defined as natural may be celebrated and assigned all sorts of rights, resources, and benefits; unnatural desires are condemned and may be harshly punished.

The idea of a natural order of sexuality has been compelling to many of us precisely because it both explains our sexuality and furnishes a basis for distinguishing good and bad sexual behavior. But there are problems with this idea. The notion of nature is an unreliable moral guide. Our idea of what is natural and unnatural changes and is often the focus of conflict. For example, throughout most of the nineteenth century many Americans, including the most educated, condemned masturbation, interracial sex, and sex outside of marriage as unnatural and a social danger. Today, we may not all agree about the morality of these sexual practices, but few of us would judge them to be unnatural or abnormal. Another problem is that appealing to nature to judge what is moral seems too cut-and-dried. Either a sexual desire or act is natural and therefore good, or it is not. But there are many sexual desires and acts that seem to fall into a moral gray area. Is premarital sex, homosexual behavior, or using pornography to enhance pleasure good or bad? Finally, classifying sexualities as good or bad depending on whether they are natural or not is socially divisive and harmful: it creates a world of sexual pariahs and outsiders.

Serious doubts, then, can be raised about the value of a natural view of sex as a basis for understanding sex and as a moral guide. But can a social view of sex provide us with a moral compass? I think so, but it can offer only rough moral guidelines, not hard-and-fast rules of right and wrong. Rough guidelines mean living with considerable moral ambiguity. Understandably, this may be disconcerting to some; I think it is one of the chief strengths of the social view when it comes to sexual and intimate life.

Consider the case of heterosexuality. Let us say that you want to defend heterosexuality as a social preference but that you cannot appeal to nature or to religious doctrine. In other words, let us assume that the norm of heterosexuality is a social convention, underwritten neither by nature nor by God. How would you defend this norm? You would have to make an argument. You might reason that heterosexuality better preserves clear gender roles, which is a positive social value; or you might propose that historically heterosexuality has proved to be a solid basis for establishing families and providing social stability; or you might argue that heterosexuals will always have a deeper investment in raising children than will homosexuals because of biological ties; and finally, you might claim that heterosexuals are, psychologically speaking, healthier human beings—that is, better adjusted, happier, or less likely to engage in self-destructive behavior.

Notice: when you cannot appeal to nature to justify your preference, you must offer arguments. That is, you must give reasons for your value preferences; you must consider the potential social consequences of your position (What is the effect of viewing homosexuals as perverse or abnormal?); you must listen to opposing viewpoints; and you must consult the available research. In short, you must stake out a position, which then can be challenged on moral or empirical grounds.

The same would be true for advocates of homosexual equality. They could not just declare that homosexuality is normal or good because it is natural. Advocates would also have to make arguments, in the first instance against the claims of the superiority of heterosexuality. They might appeal to historical and social research to challenge the view that heterosexuality provides a more stable basis for family and society than homosexuality; they would surely wish to examine the methods and results of psychological studies comparing the mental health of homosexuals and heterosexuals; they would challenge the view that distinct and opposing gender roles are necessarily healthy or promote well-being; and they would look to research to contest the claim that biology necessarily makes heterosexuals better parents. The point is that if a social view of sex were the norm, the moral and social status of heterosexuality and homosexuality would be argued: there would be appeals to research, evidence, social consequences, social values, and so on. In principle, many voices, including those of gays and lesbians, would have to be heard.

A social view encourages a public discussion of the morality and politics of sexuality that includes all interested citizens. True, it cannot provide clear rules of right and wrong. If we cannot appeal to nature or religious doctrine to provide a sufficient rationale for our judgments, we are forced to make arguments, and arguments are rarely conclusive. In short, a social view forces us to live with considerable moral uncertainty about sexual behavior. But this ambiguity has a positive side. It means that we will be cautious and deliberate in our sexual judgments. This is a good thing because ignorant or misinformed beliefs about sexuality, especially as they become public opinion and social policy, often have harmful effects on people's lives. If we believe that homosexuals molest children or that prostitutes spread disease and moral disorder, we may feel justified in ruthlessly punishing these so-called deviants. A social view does not protect us from ignorance or stereotypes; it does, though, make us mindful of the real social consequences of our beliefs and may encourage more tolerance of sexual variation, especially when there are no obvious victims.

Today, a social view of sex is most influential among scholars. Because I believe that a social view promotes a more humane sexual and social world, I would like it to become more widely available. This book is written with that hope in mind.

PART I

THEORIZING SEX

Chapter One
THE SCIENCE OF SEX:
SEXOLOGY AND PSYCHOANALYSIS

IN THE LATE NINETEENTH and the early twentieth centuries, an influential body of writing viewed sexuality as a fact of nature. Paralleling the sciences of economics, political science, sociology, and criminology, a scientific approach aimed to discover the laws of sexuality. This science has come to be called sexology.[1]

Who are the sexologists? Among the more famous are Richard von Krafft-Ebing, Havelock Ellis, and Magnus Hirschfeld. While few today have heard of these nineteenth-century pioneers of sexology, many have heard of Alfred Kinsey, Masters and Johnson, and perhaps John Money. Sexologists produced research that has influenced the way many of us think about sex, in part because their work has been stamped with the imprimatur of science.

What are the key ideas of sexology? First, sexology claims that humans are born with a sexual nature, and that sexuality is part of the biological and genetic makeup of all individuals. Sexologists emphasize the physiological aspects of sexuality. For example, in *Human Sexual Response*, Masters and Johnson focus almost entirely on the physical basis of sexuality. They discuss sexual stimulation, biologically based sexual dysfunctions, the physiology of orgasm, and so on. In short, sexuality is understood as essentially a matter of biology and physiology.

Second, sexology views sexuality as being at the core of what it means to be human: our sexual drive is no less basic than our need to eat or sleep. Sexuality is not a superficial or minor part of being human; it is basic to who we are. Humans are fundamentally sexual beings.

Third, sexology views sexuality as a driving force in human behavior. It influences all aspects of our lives, from the physical to the psychological. It motivates much of human behavior.

Fourth, sexology states that the sexual instinct is by nature heterosexual. There is said to be a natural attraction between men and women. In the past, many sexologists thought that the chief purpose of sexuality was to procreate. Today, sexologists are less inclined to believe that human sexuality is programmed to be procreative. Yet most sexologists continue to think that heterosexuality is the natural and normal form of sexuality. Alfred Kinsey, the controversial chronicler of American sexual mores, reported in the 1940s and 1950s that homosexual behavior was widespread among Americans. Yet he still assumed that heterosexuality was the preferable form of sexuality. Indeed, the aim of Kinsey's research was to help make marriage stable and successful by raising the level of heterosexual knowledge and skill of adult Americans. So, while sexologists have often gone against conventional wisdom—for example, by claiming that women are sexual beings equal to men—they have rarely challenged the norm of heterosexuality.

Sexologists aspire to discover the laws of sexuality. Like the disciplines of physics and biology, sexology has championed a vigorously scientific approach. Facts, not beliefs, are to guide this science. The truth of sexuality is to be discovered by means of the case study method. Like physicians and psychiatrists, sexologists use intensive interviews and observation to uncover the true nature of sexuality. The details of human sexual desires, fantasies, and practices are recorded for the purpose of revealing the laws of sexual instinct. On the basis of scientific case studies, sexologists elaborate classifications of sexual types and detail the range of normal and abnormal forms of sexuality.

Sexology has always had a social purpose. In the nineteenth and early twentieth centuries, its goal was often to enhance tolerance for different forms of human sexuality by emphasizing that sexuality is natural. Some sexologists saw their work as contributing to the creation of a healthy, fit population. Often this meant that sexology was aligned with a belief in racial purity and improvement. There was a time when sexologists were aligned with a eugenics movement that discouraged active sexual behavior by so-called inferior races and the sexual intermingling of races.

As racist ideas lost favor during the twentieth century, sexology often became allied with the mission of promoting a natural view of sex to strengthen the institution of marriage. Many sexologists have argued that sex is at the core of love and marriage, and that a stable, happy marriage requires a mutually satisfying sexual relationship. Individuals should not be burdened by guilt; they should be sexually knowledgeable and skilled. Sexologists aimed to create sexually enlightened and skillful citizens who would marry and stay married, in part because of a mutually satisfying sex life.

Sexologists also have been outspoken critics of the sexual policies and laws of their nations. For example, in the late nineteenth and early twentieth centuries, Karl Heinrich Ulrichs and Magnus Hirschfeld of Germany and Havelock Ellis of Great Britain advocated the decriminalization of homosexuality by claiming that it is natural. Ulrichs argued that homosexuality is a kind of sexual inversion: homosexuals have the body of one sex and the "soul" of another. Thus, male homosexuals were described as having male bodies but a female psychology. Because this condition is congenital, it should not be punished. Similarly, Kinsey sought to convince Americans that homosexuality is a normal part of the sexual instinct by documenting its widespread occurrence among ordinary individuals, much to the surprise of his readers.

Although their writings are highly technical and often quite tedious, sexologists shaped Western sexual culture. By the early decades of the twentieth century, their ideas were popularized by an army of sex advice writers, such as Marie Stopes (*Married Love*), Alex Comfort (*The Joy of Sex*, which sold millions of copies), and Dutch writer Van de Velde (*Ideal Marriage*).

IN VIENNA, the pioneering sexologist Richard von Krafft-Ebing had a colleague who shared his interest in the science of sexuality. Eventually breaking away from sexology, establishing his own science of sexuality, and outlining a general theory of human psychology, Sigmund Freud outshone Krafft-Ebing and changed our conception of humanity and sexuality. Freud's perspective became known as psychoanalysis.[2]

Freud accepted many of the ideas of the sexologists. For example, he never doubted the biological basis of sexuality. Similarly, Freud insisted that sexuality is at the root of many of our feelings and actions. Like the sexologists, Freud thought that there is a normal course of sexual development that corresponds to specific stages of psychological development. Accordingly, Freud also believed that there are abnormal sexual expressions and sexual identities. The defining feature of sexual abnormality to his mind was deviation from genital-centered, intercourse-oriented heterosexuality based on love and monogamy. In many ways, Freud's vision of the normal sexual self was not very different from that of his sexologist colleagues.

However, although Freud viewed sex as a kind of biological energy that seeks expression, he believed that the sex instinct does not have a single purpose. Whereas sexologists defined the sexual instinct as reproductive and naturally heterosexual, Freud argued that the sexual instinct is oriented to pleasure. Moreover, humans get pleasure not only from sexual intercourse but also from kissing, touching, caressing, looking, and sometimes dominating and being dominated.

Freud argued that the body has many erotic areas and that there are many ways of experiencing sexual satisfaction. Accordingly, he held that enjoying nongenital pleasures is not necessarily abnormal. For example, it is normal to enjoy the range of pleasures that are today called *foreplay*. Freud viewed sexuality as even more basic to the individual than did the sexologists. In Freud's view, sex is at the core of the self, and it is the drive for erotic pleasure that places the individual in conflict with social norms of respectability and self-control. Sexuality is not only a type of pleasure but also a major focus of psychological and social conflict. The fate of the individual and society rests to a large extent on how the sex drive is managed. According to Freud, too much sexual expression leads to perversions and psychological and social instability. However, excessive social control results in psychosexual blockages and a rigidity that brings personal unhappiness and social malaise.

Viewing the sexual instinct as a drive for pleasure blurs the line between normal and abnormal behavior. To most sexologists, any sexual expression that deviated from a heterosexual reproductive aim was abnormal. However, according to Freud, the sex drive is a pleasure-driven instinct. Freud allows for a wide range of normal sexual expression beyond heterosexual intercourse. Deviation from heterosexual intercourse is not abnormal per se; sexual desires become abnormal only when they are exclusively pleasure oriented or fixated on one specific act or pleasure. For example, it is normal for individuals to feel pleasure from looking at someone or from touching the possessions of someone they desire or love, just as it is normal to feel pleasure from kissing and touching the person. It is abnormal, though, when these secondary pleasures replace the primary aim of heterosexual intercourse.

Freud had a much deeper social understanding of sexuality than did the sexologists. Although the sexual instinct may be somewhat flexible in its purpose, it is society that shapes its form and meaning.

Freud's ideas about sexuality changed over time. Freud's most influential idea is the stage theory of psychosexual development. Freud believed that a child goes through stages of sexual development. Individuals are said to be born polymorphous perverse. Infants experience many parts of their bodies as sources of excitement, and they seek out objects in their environment for stimulation and pleasure. These objects can be animate (animals or men or women of any age or type) or inanimate (food, clothes, or household things). In other words, at birth humans are driven to sexual expression, and these drives are amoral. Infants will seek stimulation from almost anything or anyone.

Initially, children are oriented to oral pleasure. Infants are notorious for putting all sorts of objects in their mouths. To Freud, thumb sucking was a kind of sexual act. You can see why Freud's ideas have often caused public outrage. Gradually, as the child matures, the "oral phase" is replaced by the "anal stage." Eventually the child arrives at the "genital stage." Freud believed that the genital stage marks the beginning of adult development, as the individual is no longer self-stimulating but is oriented to other individuals. In effect, the genital stage symbolizes the child's entry into the social world, as he or she now must negotiate social interaction to obtain sexual satisfaction. In fact, Freud argued that the way an individual manages the socialization of the sex drive is the key to adult psychological health.

Genital satisfaction is a difficult achievement because of its dependence on other individuals and because society is much less tolerant of immoral behavior among people at this stage. Freud believed that as a child seeks genital satisfaction, he or she is embroiled in a major, life-defining conflict—the Oedipal complex in boys and the Electra complex in girls. Because traditionally women have been the primary parents in most families, the child identifies the mother as his or her chief object of sexual desire. This is where trouble begins. The mother is off-limits both because of the incest taboo and because she is already sexually claimed by the child's father. Thus, the child's Oedipal desire is frustrated. Moreover, because this desire is forbidden, it is a source of guilt and shame. The healthy child must resolve this conflict in a way that does not leave him or her emotionally crippled.

The Freudian path to a normal adult self is somewhat different for girls than for boys. For girls, the bond to their mothers must be weakened in order to achieve a socially approved heterosexual status. But this is not easy. Whereas society directs women to men, in most societies the father is often a distant figure and less engaged in parenting. The mother-daughter bond, however, is tight and erotically charged. How does the girl manage to substitute her father for her mother as the source of her sexual desire? The explanation is complex, but one event is crucial for a girl to develop into a feminine heterosexual adult: her discovery that she lacks a penis. Freud believed that it is not unusual for young girls to see boys' genitalia—perhaps that of brothers or friends. Because boys have a penis and because they are associated with the powerful figure of the father, the girl experiences her lack of a penis as indicative of her social inferiority. She comes to devalue her mother. The girl's sense of inferiority turns into an envy of boys, symbolically experienced as "penis envy." The girl wants the status the boy has and seeks it symbolically by desiring a child. This desire for a child is initially associated with the father. However, if the Electra complex is satisfactorily navigated, the girl will transfer her romantic attention to a man who exhibits many of her father's characteristics.

Boys also orient toward their mothers as their primary sexual and romantic focus. However, boys do not have to renounce their mothers to conform to a norm of heterosexuality, though they also are subject to the incest taboo. Indeed, the romance between mother and son is heightened both because of the norm of heterosexuality and because the mother often substitutes the boy for the physically or emotionally unavailable husband.

Why and how do boys renounce their mothers to achieve healthy adulthood? While girls discover that only boys have a penis, boys realize that girls do not have a penis. As a result, whereas girls might develop penis envy, boys experience castration anxiety. They fear that their desire for their mothers might result in their feminization. Specifically, in the Freudian interpretation boys fear that their fathers will castrate them for wanting their wives. Faced with these fears, boys give up their mothers as love objects and identify with their fathers. Gaining masculine social power compensates for renouncing their mothers as a focus of sexual desire. The normal boy thus ends up with a masculine heterosexual identity. He substitutes women who have motherlike qualities for his mother, though this adjustment is disguised in order to avoid the fear and guilt attached to his Oedipal desire.

Freud's work is important for three reasons. First, sexuality is understood as pertaining to more than genital intercourse for purposes of reproduction. Sexuality is a drive for pleasure. Second, Freud insists that normal sexuality includes a wide range of desires and acts beyond procreation. By framing sexuality as a diffuse drive for bodily pleasure, Freud presents a very modern view of sexuality. Third, although he saw sex as rooted in biologically based drives and physical pleasures, Freud approached sexuality as a social phenomenon. Family dynamics, especially the relationship between child and parent, shape the individual's sexuality in fundamental ways. The sexual drama is a family—and therefore a social—drama. Finally, Freud proposed that sex is as much about fantasies and wishes as about physical sensations. We attach to our physical or sensual behavior a desire for power or for love. To Freud, sex was a matter of the mind and the body, and the mind is shaped by social dynamics.

Freud opened the way to thinking about sex as a fundamentally psychosocial reality; however, Freud never abandoned the sexological view that sex is natural. His successors in psychoanalysis were divided between those who developed the biological aspects of his ideas and those who explored the interpersonal context of psychosexual development. It was not psychoanalysts who developed a consistent social perspective on sexuality. Rather, such perspectives initially emerged out of three of the great social and intellectual movements of the twentieth century—socialism, the women's movement, and the lesbian and gay movement. These gave birth to three great social theories of sexuality—respectively, Marxism, feminism, and social constructionism.

Chapter Two
SOCIAL THEORIES OF SEXUALITY: MARXISM AND FEMINISM

ONE OF KARL MARX'S great insights was that human nature is shaped by society and changes historically. From this point of view, sexuality can also be understood as something that is social and historical.

Marxists argue that the economy is the most important social force shaping human society. Every society is organized around a specific economic system. From this perspective, a particular type of economy shapes a specific sexual culture. I will illustrate this perspective by turning to an analysis of the relationship between capitalism and sexuality.[1]

A capitalist economy is oriented toward profit and economic growth. Marx believed that profit is based on exploiting labor; growth occurs by reinvesting profits back into an enterprise. Marxists distinguish two phases of capitalist development in Europe and the United States. Throughout the nineteenth century, a market-based capitalism was dominant; since the early twentieth century, capitalism has been shaped by large corporations. The social organization of modern sexuality reflects this development of capitalism.

In the market capitalist phase, the chief economic challenge is to produce enough goods to meet the needs of the whole population. The answer to the problem of production is discipline.

In order for capitalism to flourish, a disciplined labor force must be created. Individuals are trained to adapt to the rhythms of a system of mass production that progressively strips work of individual imagination and skill. Ideally, capitalists would like to see laborers become almost machinelike. Anything that interferes with maximizing production, such as emotional or erotic feeling, is an impediment to efficient production. In short, in the market economy of the nineteenth century, capitalists tried to desexualize laborers and fashion their bodies and physical movements to the machinery of production.

Just as workers are made into industrial laborers, business owners become capitalists. They learn to defer spending and to avoid personal indulgence so their businesses remain competitive. Although capitalists may flaunt their class status with acts of conspicuous consumption, their lives are fraught with anxiety. The market is unpredictable, and competition is fierce. This drives capitalists to become economically and socially disciplined.

In a market economy, therefore, a repressed personality type is prominent. This kind of person is performance- and success-oriented and exercises tight internal controls over emotions and sensual desires. To this type of person, sexual impulses and desires are potentially disruptive of discipline; sexuality needs to be rigidly controlled. Accordingly, in market economies the pressures of industrial production and discipline shape a sexual culture that values self-control and the avoidance of sensual pleasure. Erotic play and pleasure are viewed as dangerous.

If work occupies half the laborer's life, the family is at the center of his or her nonwork life. However, the spirit of the labor process shapes the family by making workers into producers of children. Sexuality is valued only if it is confined to marriage and its aim is to create a family. The definition of legitimate sex is narrowed to intercourse for the purpose of procreation. According to Marxists, this procreative sexual ethic reflects capitalism's need for a large, mobile supply of laborers.

In the market economies of the nineteenth century, a sexual culture took shape that associated sex with marriage and children. Only genital-centered, procreation-oriented sex in marriage was acceptable. Sex oriented to pleasure, sex outside marriage, autoerotic sex, sex in public, nonheterosexual sex, and nongenital sex were unacceptable and deviant. These forms of sexuality, Marxists argue, were at odds with capitalism's need for disciplined, work-oriented, productive workers.

Between the nineteenth and twentieth centuries, capitalism shifted from a market to a corporate economy. The huge corporation replaced the small business as the major economic institution. This development brought about changes in modern sexual culture. By the early twentieth century, new technologies and a scientific approach to the labor process solved the problem of producing enough goods and services. A new problem confronted capitalism: how could it ensure that the vast sea of goods now being produced would be consumed?

Many corporations looked to international markets and enlisted the support of the government to gain access and control over Africa, Asia, and Latin America. In addition, capitalists sought to expand the domestic market by bringing commerce into areas of daily life such as leisure, recreation, and entertainment. For example, every aspect of sports, from clothes to equipment to the game itself, has gradually been commercialized. Capitalists also tried to convince individuals to want and consume more goods. But how did this shift from production to consumption affect sexuality?

Marxists argue that the new consumer economy weakened the Victorian culture and its emphasis on privacy, self-control, and the desexualization of the body and intimacy. Whereas Victorians wished to keep sex a private matter, consumer capitalism brought sexuality into the public world of commerce. To create higher levels of consumption, advertising gained a new importance. Sex is now used to sell commodities; the result is that images and talk of sex have gone public with a vengeance.

The commercialization of sex challenged Victorian culture in another way: capitalism placed a new value on sex as a source of pleasure. As sex was used to sell commodities and sex businesses flourished (porn, sex toys, phone sex), sex was no longer just a procreative or loving act but a form of pleasure and self-expression. From a Marxist perspective, business owners want one thing: to make money by selling their goods. If sex can be marketed as pleasure or championed as an authentic form of self-expression or identity, then sex becomes a valuable marketing resource.

Some Marxists have emphasized the role of sexual fantasy in marketing goods. To understand this dynamic we need to grasp a change in the nature of commodities. Marxists argue that a commodity has a "use value" and an "exchange value." Use value is related to a commodity's utility, whereas exchange value concerns its price. Capitalism tries to produce commodities that people want. There is an emphasis today on producing commodities of various materials, colors, textures, types, and models (such as with cars or clothes). The commodity is not just a material object; it carries social meaning as a marker of class or cultural identity, for example. The symbolic aspect of goods creates enormous marketing potential. Many of us buy things to present a certain public identity or to indicate a particular lifestyle. A style of dress, grooming, or body piercing can communicate who we are or how we want others to think of us. Our sense of self, Marxists say, becomes tightly connected to the goods we buy. Today, some of our deepest wants and needs—to be considered powerful, sexy, and attractive—are closely connected to the goods we purchase and display. Businesses deliberately market goods and services by selling fantasies of beauty, sexual potency, romance, and social power. In short, Marxists make the compelling point that corporate capitalism creates a highly seductive and sexualized world in which impulse reigns. Accordingly, a new personality type steps forward: hedonistic, expressive, impulsive, and highly sexualized.

Corporate capitalism promotes a culture that values sexual pleasure. Sexuality is now viewed as a natural and positive basis of self-fulfillment. The conventional wisdom assumes that too much self-control produces psychological and social problems. To most Marxists, however, this pleasure-oriented sexual culture does not promote real sexual freedom. A culture that celebrates a superficial drive for pleasure leads not to fulfillment but to an aimless, unhappy search for gratification. Moreover, sexuality focused on technique and performance comes to resemble work; accordingly, it loses much of its tender, intimate, and caring qualities. Finally, Marxists argue that as we search for personal happiness, the gross inequalities between the rich and poor go unchallenged. There can be no real sexual freedom until there is real individual freedom, which is impossible under capitalism.

Marxists argue, then, that a consumer-oriented economy has decisively shaped contemporary patterns of sexuality. Consumer capitalism promotes a view of sex as natural, brings sex into the public arena, creates new sex industries, and champions sexual choice and pleasure. A capitalist sexual culture promotes tolerance, but it wants to make sex more open and acceptable solely so that sex can be used to sell goods, to attach the individual to consumerism, and to turn people's attention to personal fulfillment rather than class inequality and political action.

Marxists have developed a powerful social theory and a political movement that has altered the social landscape of many societies. Another social theory that has resulted in considerable social change is feminism, which provided the ideas and inspiration for the women's movement.

Many feminists have been sympathetic to both the ideas and the political goals of Marxism. They have, though, created their own powerful social point of view. At the core of feminism is the idea that individuals are defined not only by their class position but also by their gender status. Feminists point out that all of us are introduced to the world as men or women, regardless of the economic system. Gender identity is not a superficial part of our lives; it shapes our personality and social life in important ways.

Feminists argue that we are not born men or women; we acquire these gender identities through a social process of learning and sometimes coercion. Feminists believe that our sexual desires, feelings, and preferences are deeply imprinted by our gender status.

To the extent that feminists view the division between men and women as a product of social processes, they approach sexuality in social terms. Feminists propose that individuals acquire a sexual nature as they develop a gender identity.

What exactly is the relationship between gender and sexuality? Feminist perspectives range from the assertion that the relationship between gender and sexuality almost overlap to the view that there is considerable slippage between gender and sexuality. In *The Reproduction of Mothering*, Nancy Chodorow offers a psychoanalytical feminist view that claims a tight link between gender and sexuality.[2] She argues that in societies in which women do the chief parenting work, the patterns of self-formation are different for boys than for girls. According to Chodorow, these gender differences shape sexuality in profound ways. For both boys and girls, their mothers are the primary sources of love and the chief objects of their desires. However, girls sustain an intimacy with their mothers throughout their maturation; boys have to separate from their mothers at an early age to acquire a masculine identity and learn to be men. This difference shapes the psychosexual character of girls and boys.

Chodorow argues that due to the intense intimacy between mothers and daughters, girls develop a psyche that has porous ego boundaries and is relationship oriented. Accordingly, women tend to connect sex with intimacy and value it as a means of sharing and caring. Women will also tend to be less genital- and pleasure oriented and more person- and emotion oriented than men. Women tend to approach sex more as a means of communication and intimacy than as a vehicle for erotic pleasure. Because boys typically break sharply from their mothers at an early age and rarely establish an intimate bond with their fathers, they have rigid ego boundaries and are more goal oriented. Accordingly, their sexuality tends to be more pleasure- and performance oriented. Men can, of course, experience intimacy, but they will likely express sexual love differently than do women. For example, men might approach love primarily in terms of the giving and receiving of erotic pleasure or orgasmic satisfaction. Furthermore, because women connect sex to intimacy, they will tend to be more monogamous than men, who are on average more psychologically disposed to disassociate sex from intimacy.

Yet most girls and boys become heterosexual because modern societies are organized around the norm of heterosexuality. Chodorow thinks boys and girls take different paths to heterosexuality. For boys, their primary love relation with their mothers creates a strong heterosexual desire. Moreover, boys are pressured to identify strongly with the masculinity of their fathers, which is associated with heterosexuality. By contrast, girls' intimate ties to their mothers make the accomplishment of heterosexuality more complex. Although girls are encouraged to shift the focus of their desire from the mother to the father, he is often a remote figure. Accordingly, girls' heterosexual identification may be emotionally weak. Women will likely be more open to bisexuality and homosexuality and approach sexual identity as more of a choice than will boys.

Chodorow's perspective is important because she assumes that sexuality emerges in the course of individual development. The family plays a crucial role in the making of the sexual self. Also, she insists that our gender identity shapes our sexuality in profound ways. As boys and girls experience different parent-child dynamics, they will have somewhat different sexual values and orientations.

Other feminists have also tightly linked gender and sexuality. In an influential essay, "Compulsory Heterosexuality and

Lesbian Existence," Adrienne Rich argues that we are all taught and coerced into adopting conventional gender identities.[3] Moreover, in most societies, being a respectable man or woman means being heterosexual. Shaping individuals into men and women who are also exclusively heterosexual is a complex social process. Individuals become heterosexual not only through positive inducements, such as economic incentives and the cultural romanticizing of heterosexuality, but also through punishments, such as ridicule, harassment, and violence toward gender rebels and non-heterosexuals. However, Rich believes that the social pressures that create a gender-divided, compulsory heterosexual order are concealed by ideologies that assert the naturalness of heterosexuality. For example, many Europeans and Americans hold to the belief that humans are naturally divided into men and women, that there is a biological attraction between the sexes, and that men's and women's bodies and minds are naturally complementary. Accordingly, heterosexuality is understood as an extension of a natural order composed of two distinct human types: men and women.

However, Rich argues that throughout history, there have always been women who have chosen to remain single or who have challenged gender norms. In particular, there have been women who have organized their lives around other women. Rich makes the controversial claim that women who choose to create lives around other women are lesbians. Lesbianism is not fundamentally a sexual desire or identity. Rather, Rich says that being a lesbian means choosing to make a primary social and emotional commitment to women. Becoming a lesbian is a political act, as it declares women's independence from men. The lesbian is a woman who defines her own wants and desires and makes other women the focus of her life.

Building on the work of Chodorow, Rich, and other feminists, Catherine MacKinnon also insists on the tight binding of gender and sexuality.[4] Specifically, MacKinnon views sexuality as a product of men's power, and sex as a means by which men control women. Indeed, sex is said to be the very basis of male domination. To the extent that men have the power to define what desires, feelings, and behaviors are sexual, they have the power to define women's sexuality in a way that gives them control over women. For example, in male-dominated America, so-called normal women are supposed to be oriented toward vaginal intercourse with the ultimate aim of procreation. This view of sexuality defines women as essentially heterosexual and as motivated, by their very nature, to be mothers.

Such feminists as Rich and MacKinnon approach sex as fundamentally social and political. In particular, they claim that the very essence of what is called sexuality—desires, fantasies, pleasures, acts—reveals the male wish for control and dominance. Sexual desires and behaviors in male-dominated societies are said to be related to gender struggles. From this perspective, feminists criticize the notion that women's sexual liberation is about women claiming the freedom to do as they please, an approach that expresses men's view of sexual freedom. Instead, women's sexual liberation would involve women fashioning a sexual life that reflects their own needs, feelings, and desires. The point is not to liberate sexuality from social control, which could lead to more violence or unwanted pregnancy, but for women to claim the power to define their own sexual desires and fashion their own sexual-intimate lives.

Some feminists, such as anthropologist Gayle Rubin, have objected to the view that sexuality is a direct expression of gender. Rubin argues that this perspective ignores considerable variation within women's and men's sexualities. Rubin tries to understand sexuality as connected to gender, yet as also having its own dynamics. This suggests that the concept of gender cannot be the basis for a comprehensive theory of sexuality.

In "Thinking Sex," Rubin makes the case that sex is fundamentally about erotic desires, fantasies, acts, identities, and politics—none of which are reducible to gender dynamics. "It is essential to separate gender and sexuality analytically," she writes. "This goes against the grain of much contemporary feminist thought, which treats sexuality as a derivation of gender. For instance, lesbian feminist ideology has mostly analyzed the oppression of lesbians in terms of the oppression of women. However, lesbians are also oppressed as queers and perverts, by the operation of sexual, not gender, stratification."[5]

In Rubin's view, all societies create sexual hierarchies that establish boundaries between good and bad or legitimate and illicit sexualities. Societies classify certain desires, acts, and identities as normal, respectable, good, healthy, and moral; other forms of sexuality are classified as unhealthy, abnormal, sinful, and immoral. Societies support and privilege "normal and good" forms of sexuality and punish those defined as "abnormal and bad" through law, violence, ridicule, or stigma. This system of sexual regulation applies to both men and women. American society considers heterosexuality, monogamy, marriage, and reproductive sex to be good and normal; it defines and treats S/M (sadism and masochism), commercial, public, and multiple-partner sex as bad. There are, of course, many sexualities that

fall somewhere in between—for example, promiscuous heterosexuals and gays and lesbians in long-term monogamous relationships. It may be less socially acceptable for a woman than
for a man to have multiple sex partners or to engage in S/M
because of a gender order that associates femininity with purity
and maternal feelings; still, these behaviors are disrespected for
both men and women. Those who engage in such behaviors, regardless of gender, will be stigmatized and subject to ridicule
and at times criminalization. Rubin's point is simply that gender influences patterns of sexuality, but there is still a great deal
about the organization and dynamics of sexuality that cannot be
grasped solely through the lens of gender.

Chapter Three
SOCIAL CONSTRUCTIONISM:
SOCIOLOGY, HISTORY, AND PHILOSOPHY

MARXISM AND FEMINISM have challenged biological and narrow psychological approaches to sex. They have also been influential in shaping new social approaches to sex, in particular through the work of sociologists, historians, and philosophers who have pioneered the rethinking of sexuality.

Sociologists have been at the forefront of researching sex from a social perspective. Since the early decades of the twentieth century, sociologists have studied patterns of heterosexuality. They have researched the role of religion, gender, class, race, and social values in shaping patterns of premarital, marital, and extramarital sex. Ira Reiss, a major sociologist of sexuality in the 1960s and 1970s, charted cultural and behavioral shifts among American youth during a time when sexual morality that associated sex exclusively with marriage gave way to one that permitted sex in a context of affection.[1] Reiss believed that this cultural change was related to women's increasing economic and social power. In this regard, he observed the decline of a double standard that had permitted men to have sex outside of marriage while it labeled women who engaged in the same behavior as "bad girls." The work of Reiss and many other sociologists was important because it documented the social character of sexual conduct. However, sexual practices that were not heterosexual or were not oriented to marriage were often treated as deviant; few sociologists investigated the social factors that explained why some behaviors or identities were viewed positively and other ones were seen as deviant. Moreover, they did not inquire why certain feelings, desires, acts, and identities came to be viewed as sexual at all.

Some sociologists and social scientists argued for a more thoroughly social view of sexuality. In the United States, John Gagnon and William Simon proposed a "script" theory of sexuality.[2] Instead of understanding humans as being born sexual, they argued that sexuality is socially learned. In the course of growing up, we are taught by society what feelings and desires count as sexual and what are the appropriate scripts for sexual behavior. Sexual scripts tell us where, when, and with whom (based on age, race, or class) we are supposed to have sex, and what it means when we do. Gagnon and Simon suggested that sexuality is not an inborn property but a product of social labeling.

In Britain, sociologist Ken Plummer further developed a labeling perspective. In *Sexual Stigma*, he argued that individuals are not born homosexual but learn to be homosexual.[3] An individual may feel desire for or attraction to people of the same sex, but he or she must learn that these feelings are sexual and that they indicate a homosexual identity. People learn this in the course of interacting with both the straight and gay worlds. For example, a high school student hearing derogatory comments about "fags" and "dykes" may begin to associate homosexuality with a stigmatized identity. This same individual may eventually be exposed to a gay subculture that champions a view of homosexuality as natural and good.

One of the pioneers of a sociological approach to sexuality was British sociologist Jeffrey Weeks.[4] He introduced the ideas of "essentialism" and "constructionism." Essentialism is the notion that sexuality is a basic and essential part of being human.

Constructionism states that sexuality is a learned way of thinking and acting. Weeks proposed a strong view of the social character of sexuality:

> First . . . we can no longer set "sex" against "society" as if they were separate domains. Secondly, there is a widespread recognition of the social variability of sexual forms, beliefs, ideologies, and behavior. Sexuality has . . . many histories. . . . Thirdly . . . we must learn to see that sexuality is something which society produces in complex ways. It is a result of diverse social practices that give meaning to human activities, . . . to struggles between those who have power to define and regulate, and those who resist. Sexuality is not given, it is a product of negotiation, struggle.[5]

Weeks not only proposed social constructionism as a theory but also researched the role of medical and scientific ideas in creating the idea of the homosexual as a distinct social identity.[6]

As Weeks was researching sexual identity as a social and historical event in England, American historians wished to explain the rise of a homosexual identity in the United States. This research paralleled the rise of gay and lesbian movements in America and in most European nations. In the 1970s and 1980s, the conventional view among gay activists was that homosexuals have always existed, but, because of homophobia and heterosexism, they have never been acknowledged. Activists and scholars sought to document homosexuals' existence throughout history and their contribution to civilization. If homosexuals have been valuable contributors to Western culture, should they not be accepted? The new history of sexuality challenged this approach. Historians argued that the very meaning of same-sex behavior has changed throughout history. A lesbian or gay identity is a historical, not a natural, fact.

Today there is a large body of historical research offering varied interpretations of homosexuality. Independent scholar Jonathan Ned Katz produced two pioneering books, *Gay American History* and the *Gay/Lesbian Almanac*, in which he documented the changing meaning of homosexuality in the United States.[7] He found that between colonial times and the 1970s, the meaning of homosexuality changed from a behavior (sodomy) to a type of gender deviance (invert) to an abnormal personality (the homosexual) and finally to an affirmative social identity (gay/lesbian).

In a path-breaking article, "The Female World of Love and Ritual: Relations between Women in Nineteenth-Century America," historian Carroll Smith-Rosenberg made a powerful case for a historical approach to sexuality.[8] She documented that the lives of most (white, middle-class) Victorian women were very similar. Their lives were focused on household and domestic tasks; they raised children and took responsibility for maintaining the religious piety and moral well-being of the family. As a result, these women often formed close ties with one another. These intimate bonds sometimes developed into romantic relationships that were public and celebrated as complementary to marriage. Although we cannot be sure if these "romantic friendships" were sexual in the modern sense, they were often lifetime committed bonds.

Building on the work of Katz and Smith-Rosenberg, Lillian Faderman crafted pioneering histories of sexuality.[9] In *Surpassing the Love of Men*, Faderman studied romantic friendships between women, which were common in Europe for centuries. Faderman also wrote the first history of lesbianism in the United States, *Odd Girls and Twilight Lovers*. Both Smith-Rosenberg and Faderman make the unexpected argument that, between the late nineteenth and early twentieth centuries, tolerance for intimacy between women actually decreased. As women started to attend college, work outside the home, and demand equal rights, those women who also chose to live independently of men were at times stigmatized as lesbians.

Building on this growing body of historical scholarship on sexuality, John D'Emilio offered the first detailed analysis of the rise of homosexual politics in the United States. In *Sexual Politics, Sexual Communities*, he analyzed the social forces that shaped homosexuality into an identity, a community, and a social movement.[10] For example, D'Emilio argued that World War II played a key role in shaping an awareness of homosexuality and in creating homosexual bonds. During the war, many soldiers were, for the first time, exposed to individuals who thought of themselves as homosexual. Moreover, the intense closeness among the men and women in the military encouraged some sexual experimentation. After the war, many of these men and women with homosexual feelings settled in Chicago, New York, San Francisco, and Los Angeles. It was in these cities that the first major gay and lesbian political organizations initially took shape. D'Emilio traces the rise of gay liberationism in the late 1960s.

By the 1990s, an impressive body of historical research on sexuality had accumulated. Historians have continued to refine their conceptions of the sexual past. One significant revision is George Chauncey's *Gay New York*.[11] Whereas historians and sociologists had come to believe that the modern homosexual emerged in the early twentieth century and was immediately closeted, Chauncey argues that in working-class New York, individuals were classified not as either heterosexual or homosexual, but as either "normal men" or "fairies." The former were masculine men; the latter were effeminate. In other words, the homosexual indicated a type of gender deviance. A masculine man who had sex with effeminate men was not necessarily considered a homosexual. Gender expression, not sexual preference, defined who was a homosexual. Moreover, rather than being closeted, gay life flourished openly in bars, taverns, speakeasies, restaurants, ballrooms, and parks.

Sociologists and historians have produced an impressive body of scholarship that documents changes in the meaning and social patterns of homosexuality, changes that have shifted the way we think about sexuality. But the work of philosophers is equally central. By far the most important theorist of sexuality has been French philosopher Michel Foucault.[12]

If there is one main idea in Foucault's writings, it is that "sexuality created sex." Foucault challenged the view of sexologists and psychologists that sex was something fundamentally biological and natural. We recall that these scientists claimed to have charted the true nature of human sexuality. Foucault proposed that it was the very idea—or, in his term, the discourse—of sexuality that created what we today know as sex. In other words, we are not born sexual; rather, we learn to be sexual beings; this occurs only in societies that have created the idea of "sexuality."

But when did this idea of sexuality originate, and why? Foucault's explanation begins with the early Christian practice of confession. The Christian duty to confess sinful desires compelled individuals to approach their erotic feelings as having moral meaning. Individual Christians began to analyze their sensual desires and pleasures as a path to self-knowledge and moral purity.

If Christian confessional practices provided the initial impulse to think of our erotic feelings as a separate sphere invested with moral significance, the birth of the science of sexuality in the nineteenth century was the crucial modern event. Scientists aimed to discover the hidden truth of human nature by uncovering the secrets of the sexual instinct. These scientists wished to lay bare the basic principles of sexuality—its normal progression and its pathologies. Sexologists charted the physiology of sexual desire and its varied practices while psychiatrists listened to their clients confess a shadowy world of sexual fantasies, and demographers surveyed human fertility. But these researchers did not discover an uncharted territory of sex; they fashioned human pleasures, excitations, and acts into a new object of knowledge and social regulation: human sexuality. Foucault is not saying that the feelings and behaviors associated with the body are created by these discourses. Rather, as a result of these new discourses, these bodily experiences are now viewed as expressions of human sexuality—as indicating a sexual type and a normal or pathological sexuality. In other words, the science of sexuality organized and unified our diverse somatic experiences into a coherent entity called *sexuality*.

Why did a discourse of sexuality appear and what was its social importance? Foucault advanced a twofold answer. First, he argued that these discourses are part of the rise of what he called a disciplinary society. In the military, churches, hospitals, factories, and schools, a type of social organization developed that exercises strict control over our bodies, aims to carefully manage those bodies in space and time, involves a great deal of surveillance and supervision of bodies, and uses judgments about what is normal to control individuals. Disciplinary control relies less on the power

to censor and silence individuals than on the power of normalizing ideas to shape individuals into productive and controllable
agents. Sexuality is at the core of disciplinary control. Controlling
people's sexual feelings, behaviors, and identities makes possible a
great deal of social control over their bodies and actions. Foucault
thought that sexuality had become a crucial part of the way modern societies control their citizens.

Second, Foucault believed that the modern state and other
social institutions had good reasons to want to control people's
sexuality. Between the seventeenth and nineteenth centuries, in
many European nations, large numbers of people were migrat-
ing to cities; there was an increasing need for mass literacy and
schooling and a growing dependence of national power on economic prosperity. These developments created a strong political
interest in gaining accurate, detailed, and useful information
about human bodies—how they reproduce, stay healthy, react
to different external stimuli, and can be made more productive,
efficient, cooperative, and so on. For example, as cities became
social and economic centers, governments and other institutions
responsible for keeping order and for the care of the needy and
indigent sought information about nutrition, health, migration
patterns, and fertility rates. This growing need to understand
and control bodies helped to create the idea of sexuality. A society that can control sex can manage the behavior of individuals
and whole populations.

Foucault believed that patterns of sexual control have changed
in modern societies. In the seventeenth and eighteenth centuries, marriage was the focus of social regulation. Sex outside of
marriage was proscribed and the emphasis within marriage was
on procreation. Social institutions aimed to channel individual

sexuality into marriage and families. This focus changed during the course of the nineteenth and twentieth centuries. Social institutions no longer concentrated solely on sex in its relation to marriage; they took an interest in a wide range of sexual behavior—in young people's sexuality, in homosexuality, and in heterosexual behavior outside of marriage. Furthermore, whereas the state and the family were the key agents of social control in the past, today medical and scientific institutions, the criminal justice system, and the mass media play key roles in regulating sexual behavior.

Foucault's perspective helps to explain why many Europeans and Americans are preoccupied with their own sexuality and that of their friends, neighbors, and public figures. Sex has become something we think of as basic to self-identity; it is often understood as the hidden truth of who we are.

Did Foucault give up the notion of sexual freedom? He wrote during a period of sexual rebellion in which many individuals and movements believed that a new era of sexual freedom was beginning. Sexual liberationists of all types saw the past as a dark period of repression due to ignorance. They declared that, in contrast, we had become more enlightened; for them, the present was full of possibilities for sexual freedom. Sexual liberation had two aspects. The first was a negative freedom—escape from unnecessary control, so people might exercise sexual choice. The second was a positive freedom—the right to express one's true sexual nature and identity.

Foucault agreed that expanding individual choice and promoting sexual variation were good things. In this regard, he supported the fight for gay rights. But gay rights is not liberation. It does relieve individuals of a horrific stigma and frees them from social discrimination. Yet it leaves in place a system of sexuality that sexualizes people's desires and feelings, forces them to declare a mutually exclusive sexual identity, and divides sexual feelings and acts into normal and abnormal. For all the good it has done, the gay rights movement has reinforced a system that forces individuals to declare themselves either straight or gay, and it potentially makes bisexuality into a deviant sexual identity. Moreover, a gay movement has its own ideal of how a gay person is supposed to look and act. In other words, the gay movement exercises control over its members, pressuring them to identify exclusively as gay and to act in ways that are recognized as gay.

If sexuality is today tightly linked to a system of social control, then, ironically, sexual liberation might involve freeing ourselves from the idea of sexuality. This would mean approaching our erotic desires and acts not as expressions of sexuality but as simply feelings and acts that give pleasure, create social ties, or act as a source of cultural creativity. Foucault advocates a politics against sexuality—against sexualizing selves, identities, and acts. Why would this be a good thing? If society did not assign a moral meaning (either normal or abnormal) to adult, consensual sexual desires and behaviors, individuals would be subject to considerably less social regulation. For example, instead of reversing the stigma of homosexuality by championing a normal gay identity, according to Foucault we might approach homosexuality simply as a desire and as a source of erotic pleasures, new relationships, and cultural expressions. Instead of celebrating the sexualization of the human body and all of its feelings and sensations, perhaps it would be more liberating to desexualize pleasures, focus on nonsexual pleasures, learn to enjoy a wide range of sensual pleasures, and be free of controls that rely on notions of normality. To the extent that sexuality is tightly intertwined with social control—for example, with advertising or with judgments of good and normal character—to be against sexuality is to support individual freedom. Foucault has shaped the field of sexual studies in far-reaching ways. Yet his work has also been challenged. In particular, critics believe that Foucault did not go far enough in analyzing sexual identity. Although Foucault argued that sexual identities are social and historical, he did not address the way sexual identities vary by gender, race, class, and age. For example, in male-dominated societies the social pattern of homosexuality differs between men and women; accordingly, lesbians may have a somewhat different history than gay men. Furthermore, the varied histories of gays and lesbians are further differentiated by such factors as race or class. Historians and sociologists have begun to sort out these factors. Foucault is also criticized for failing to explain how sexual identities are created and sustained in everyday life. He assumed that discourses of sexual identity are somehow brought into social institutions and mainstream culture, which in turn shape individual identities. How exactly individuals create sexual identities and what social forces exact pressure to sustain these identities are key questions left unaddressed by Foucault. These questions became a focus for scholars in the 1990s as attention turned to questions of identity and politics.

Among those who have thought hard about the question of identity, perhaps none has been more influential than philosopher Judith Butler. In *Gender Trouble*, Butler proposed a "performative" theory of gender identity that has proven to be very useful for analyzing sexual identity.[13]

The idea that nature has created two distinct, opposing genders—men and women—has been basic to modern Western culture. This notion is promoted in law, science, and popular culture, and it is part of the common beliefs of probably most Americans and Europeans. But where does this belief come from? Is this idea true?

Butler holds that the idea that nature has created two distinct, opposing human types should not be uncritically accepted. We have come to believe this view, she says, because we live in a society organized around heterosexuality, marriage, and the nuclear family. Viewing men and women as naturally different and complementary makes heterosexuality—and therefore also marriage and the heterosexual family—seem like the natural, normal, and right way of living. This explains why there is so little tolerance for men who act feminine or women who act masculine. Men and women who challenge gender roles threaten the norm of heterosexuality and the primacy of marriage and the nuclear family.

A system of compulsory heterosexuality may help to explain why societies divide individuals into two gender types, but it does not explain how gender identities are created and sustained daily. Feminists have explained the making of gender identity as socially learned or forced upon individuals. Butler asks us to consider gender in theatrical terms as a kind of performance.

Growing up in a society that classifies feelings, behaviors, and social roles in gender terms, as appropriate either for men or for women, we learn not only what our gender is supposed to be but also how to act in gender-correct ways. Through a mostly unconscious learning process, and by means of a system of rewards and sanctions, each of us learns to present him- or herself as either a man or a woman. We come to know, almost without thinking, what gestures, styles of dress and grooming, and ways of walking and talking are considered normal for men and women. If a male acts "masculine"—if his posture, talk, friends, dating, and jobs conform to masculine norms—his gender identity as a man will be taken for granted. If a male acts "feminine," he will still be viewed as male but he may be considered an "abnormal" man. Furthermore, Butler argues that as we conform to gender norms, others will likely interpret our behavior as expressing a core gender identity. For example, most of us would probably assume that a male who looks and acts like a man (for instance, is aggressive, competitive, and decisive) is a man and that this status is basic to his identity. In other words, his masculine actions are understood as expressing a deeply rooted gender identity. However, Butler suggests that there is no core gender identity that drives our behavior. Rather than viewing our gender performances as expressing an inner gender identity, she says that these behaviors are modeled after images of what it means to be a woman or man that we learn from our families and other institutions. The illusion of core feminine and masculine gender identities conceals the social and political forces that shape us into gendered and sexual beings. Similarly, the ideology of a natural gender order conceals the role of gender in the perpetuation of heterosexual dominance.

The idea of gender as a performance has been used by researchers of sexual identity.[14] Rather than approaching gay, straight, or bisexual identifications as stable, core identities that motivate our behavior, a performance approach emphasizes sexual identity as a process. We fashion and project our identities by our actions. Accordingly, researchers analyze the microdynamics of identity formation. For example, they try to explain which behaviors and objects (such as clothes, cars, homes, furniture, and eyeglasses) come to be signs of sexual identity and why. How do individuals acquire the skills to read one another's behaviors in terms of sexual identity categories? A performative approach to sexual identity should not be interpreted as saying that identities are freely chosen or that they are somehow not real because they are produced through a performance. They are quite real as we experience them and in terms of their personal and social consequences. In addition, although they may be performances, they are not freely chosen; a system of compulsory heterosexuality exerts enormous social pressure on each of us to "perform" the appropriate gender and sexual identity. Deviance from gender or sexual norms carries serious risks and dangers, from being denied respect to being the target of harassment or violence.

TO SUMMARIZE PART I, there has been a revolution in the way many scholars think about sexuality. Until recently, it was believed that humans were born with a sexual nature and that the natural order created a series of sexual types: heterosexuals, homosexuals, masochists, pedophiles, and so on. Scientists thought that a science of sexuality would reveal the nature of the sexual instinct, its normal and abnormal expressions. The idea of sexual normality would serve as the standard to judge and regulate sexual behavior.

Today, the leading edge of scholarship views sex as fundamentally social. We are born with bodies, but it is society that determines which parts of the body and which pleasures and acts are sexual. Also, the classification of sex acts into good and bad or acceptable and illicit is today understood as a product of social power: the dominant sexual norms express the beliefs of the dominant social groups. If we are supposed to grow up to be heterosexual, and if we are expected to link sex to love, monogamy, marriage, and family making, that is not because nature dictates this moral order but because of complex social dynamics. Beliefs that there are natural and normal ways to be sexual are understood as ideologies. How we come to have such beliefs as well as their personal and social consequences are important questions for the study of sexuality. Indeed, the question of who gets to define what is sexual and which institutions are responsible for regulating our sexualities are key political questions. In the coming chapters, I will illustrate this social perspective by addressing the politics and ethics of sexuality.

PART II

THE SOCIOLOGY
AND POLITICS OF
SEXUAL IDENTITY

Chapter Four
HETEROSEXUALITY: FROM BEHAVIOR TO IDENTITY

APPROACHING SEX as a social fact means understanding that, whether or not we are actually born with a sexual nature, the meaning of our desires and acts, the way they are organized, and which sexual expressions are socially approved and which are stigmatized are products of social factors. We will pursue this social view of sexuality by considering the relationship between sexuality and identity.

Today, most Americans take for granted that sexuality, like race or gender, is an identity. Individuals not only define themselves but also let others know that they are straight, gay, or bisexual, for example. For gays and lesbians, this disclosure—called coming out—is often deliberate and difficult. Heterosexuals typically reveal their sexual identity by simply talking about their girlfriends or boyfriends or expressing their attraction to people of the opposite sex. Because many of us view sexuality as at the core of our identities, we are preoccupied with our own and others' sexuality.

However, sexuality is not a basis of identity in all societies. Scholars make a distinction between sexual behavior and identity. Humans have always acted in ways that we call sexual, but not all societies interpret this behavior as self-defining. In some societies, sex is simply a behavior.

In a similar way, consider how many of us approach eating. Hunger, even more than sex, is a basic drive and need, a requirement of survival. Yet most societies today do not classify individuals by what they eat. For example, Americans do not categorize individuals by their preference for fish or hamburgers. True, we might say someone is a vegetarian, but vegetarians are not thought of as being different in any fundamental physical, psychological, or social way from meat eaters. To take another example, although we might label individuals by whether they are right- or left-handed, and we might even think it odd for someone to be left-handed, we do not define an individual by this trait. We do not allocate jobs or the right to marry according to whether individuals are meat eaters or vegetarians, right- or left-handed. In many societies—for example, Ancient Greece or nineteenth-century America—the same could be said of sexuality. Sex might be considered important because it is closely associated with procreation and the making of families, but not all societies have considered it a core, defining part of the individual.

In this part of the book, I want to illustrate a social approach to sexuality by exploring the topic of sexual identity. In this chapter, I discuss heterosexuality. However, heterosexuality is not merely one sexual identity among others; it is, in many societies, the norm and the ideal. Where there is a norm, there is often resistance. In subsequent chapters, I turn to the gay, lesbian, and bisexual movements to further illustrate the politics of sexual identity.

THE MAKING OF A HETEROSEXUAL IDENTITY

Most Americans would, if asked, likely say that heterosexuality is natural, that it is a basic human drive that makes life possible. They would be right, of course, in the sense that without heterosexual behavior humans would have become extinct, at least before recent technologies, such as artificial insemination. Heterosexual behavior has always existed. However, the meaning and social organization of heterosexuality has varied considerably throughout history. This is obvious if we think of the immense social variation in patterns of intimacy, marriage, and the family. Today, heterosexual intimacy can involve living together or apart, marriage or cohabitation, single-parent or multiple-parent families, nuclear or extended kinship units, or relationships based on rigid gender roles or on a companionate, egalitarian ideal. These variations in intimate arrangements are a product of social factors, such as the economic status of men and women, the role of the government in promoting marriage or certain types of families, and the influence of mass media and popular culture.

Have there always been heterosexuals? This question might sound foolish. Does nature not produce heterosexuals, just as it produces males and females or right- and left-handed people or green- and blue-eyed individuals? Is heterosexuality not a necessity for human survival, and therefore have there not always been heterosexuals?

Let us examine this issue a bit closer. What does it mean to say that a person is a heterosexual today in the United States? Most Americans would probably say that the term refers to individuals who are attracted to persons of the opposite sex. We need to be careful and precise. To be heterosexual in contemporary America means simply to exhibit sexual attraction toward the opposite sex. We do not say that to be heterosexual an individual has to be motivated to marry or to have a family. We simply say that heterosexuals are individuals who feel sexual desire for someone of the opposite sex—regardless of whether the aim is pleasure, procreation, love, or marriage. Moreover, Americans approach heterosexuality today as an identity. Many of us declare ourselves to be straight in the same way we would identify as Jews or Latinos. So, in contemporary America, to be heterosexual means that you are sexually attracted to the opposite sex and that you claim a distinct sexual identity.

Historians tell us that this notion of heterosexuality was not necessarily shared by our ancestors.[1] For example, in nineteenth-century America, scientific and popular writers believed that individuals were born with a sexual instinct. This instinct was a kind of genetic program to procreate. The male and female sexual instinct was *heterosexual and oriented to procreation*. In other words, the sexual instinct was a reproductive instinct. To be sexually normal meant to be oriented to reproduce in the same way that hunger means to be driven to eat. I want to underscore this point: heterosexuality indicated a reproductive drive, not simply a sexual attraction, and it was a drive or behavior, not an identity. Accordingly, Americans who sought only sexual pleasure in the opposite sex were considered abnormal. In other words, what we today call heterosexuality, a sexual desire for the opposite sex, was considered by our Victorian ancestors a potential perversion like sodomy or adultery. Moreover, there was no notion of the heterosexual as a type of person to be contrasted with the homosexual. The concept of the homosexual was foreign to nineteenth-century America. Without that concept, there could be no notion of the heterosexual as a distinct identity.

The term *heterosexual* first appeared in scientific and medical literature in the 1890s. It was defined as an identity based on sexual attraction for the opposite sex. The key point is that heterosexual desire was uncoupled from procreation. Normal sex was defined as heterosexual erotic attraction; abnormal sex was homosexual erotic attraction. In other words, the concept of "heterosexual" took shape and meaning in relation to the concept of homosexual. Both terms indicated a sexual desire unrelated to reproduction that was the basis of personal identity. By the early twentieth century, many writers and ordinary citizens defined an individual's sexual identity according to whether he or she was attracted to the same or the opposite sex.

We can see this change in the meaning of heterosexuality in Freud's writings. Unlike his nineteenth-century colleagues, Freud, you might recall from Chapter 1, viewed the sexual instinct as oriented to pleasure, not to reproduction. Furthermore, he held that sexual satisfaction can involve many different acts with varied goals in mind, such as pleasure, self-expression, love, or procreation. In Freud's writings, the modern heterosexual steps forward: this is a type of person defined solely by his or her sexual attraction to the opposite sex.

Why did the meaning of heterosexuality change from a reproductive instinct to a sexual desire and identity? One perspective holds that there was a crisis of gender identity in the early twentieth century.[2] Throughout much of the nineteenth century, men and women occupied different social roles. Men dominated the public world of work and politics, while women's place was in the private world of home and family. This division of labor was thought to reflect essential differences between men and women. Men were viewed as intellectual, rational, aggressive, and goal oriented, whereas women were defined as emotional, nurturing, empathic, and maternal. Marriages were based on the complementarity of gender identities and roles. Men supported and protected the family, while women provided a moral and loving environment.

This social arrangement began to break down in the early decades of the twentieth century. Women started to attend college, enter the workforce, organize for their rights, and take active roles in social reform. At the same time, men's work was gradually shifting from farm and blue-collar labor to white-collar jobs. White-collar workers in corporations or the government had little power and were increasingly reliant on what were often seen as "feminine" skills, such as being likable, cooperative, and agreeable. During this time in history, many people believed that women were becoming more "masculine" while men were becoming more "feminine." The gender division between men and women, which many thought to be the basis of a stable social order, was collapsing. The sense of crisis was heightened by the fact that many women were choosing to stay single, divorce, or marry and remain childless.

One response to the blurring of gender identities was a new emphasis on the norm of heterosexuality as a way to reassert gender difference and the normality of dichotomous gender roles. By emphasizing the naturalness and rightness of heterosexuality, people could view the differences between men and women as natural and good. That is, if heterosexuality was natural and essential for survival and a stable social order, men and women should continue to occupy different roles. Asserting a clear heterosexual identity became a way to flag a normal gender identity. Heterosexuality came to be associated with a person's core self-identity and its meaning was centered on being sexually attracted to the opposite sex.

Another result of this emphasis on a heterosexual identity was the creation of a culture of homophobia. As heterosexuality became an important way to demonstrate a normal sexual and gender identity, homosexuality represented a deviant status. Not only was sexual attraction to a person of the same sex stigmatized but gender deviance was disapproved of as a sign of homosexuality. The result was that men and women feared exhibiting any gender traits that deviated from norms of masculine men and feminine women. A sexual system that aggressively enforced heterosexuality as a norm aimed to shore up a fragile gender order.

PROJECTING A HETEROSEXUAL IDENTITY

Let us shift our focus somewhat from the history to the sociology of heterosexuality. If establishing a heterosexual identity became an important way to project a normal, respectable gender identity, how is a heterosexual identity achieved in everyday life? In other words, how do individuals convince others that they are heterosexual?

Keep in mind something that I mentioned previously about the sociology of identity. Our identities are established in relations of contrast. Being a woman, in part, involves establishing that one is not a man. An individual fashions a normal identity as a woman by not exhibiting masculine traits, such as extreme aggressiveness, competitiveness, or sexual assertiveness. Of course, there are different versions of what it means to be a woman. They may conflict with one another, but all involve contrasts to some notion of manhood. If a woman exhibits certain masculine qualities, such as an intense interest in sports or a single-minded pursuit of career success, she might still be able to command respect as a "good woman," but only if she is emphatically heterosexual.

Accordingly, individuals establish a heterosexual identity in part by distancing themselves from any associations with homosexuality. Such distancing has often involved engaging in anti-gay behavior. Homophobic conduct not only announces that one is heterosexual but declares that heterosexuality is good and homosexuality is bad.

British researchers studied how high school students used homophobic practices to establish a public heterosexual identity.[3] They found that students, especially boys, were eager to avoid any suspicion that they might be gay. The high school culture the researchers studied had its own conventions for defining sexual identity. For example, boys who were good students, hard-working, gentle, quiet, or unathletic were sometimes labeled gay. Students anxiously interpreted one another's behavior as signs of their sexual identities.

In response to such anxieties, students regulated their same-sex friendships so that any intimate expression that might be construed as sexual was excluded. Similarly, many of the boys would avoid any interaction with students who were suspected of being gay. Finally, boys would engage in aggressive public displays of homophobia: harassing, threatening, and sometimes assaulting students believed to be gay. This behavior allowed boys to publicly establish a respected heterosexual identity.

As well as needing not to appear gay, these boys felt an additional pressure to project a clear, emphatic heterosexual identity: gender anxiety. Presenting a seamless aggressive heterosexual self was seen as essential for maintaining a credible status as a masculine boy.

In *Fraternity Gang Rape*, a study of U.S. college fraternities, anthropologist Peggy Sanday explored how gender anxieties pressure individuals to act aggressively heterosexual.[4] Such behavior protects a man from gender anxiety, an anxiety that is driven in part by fears of being shamed if he is viewed as less than a consistently masculine man. Sanday showed how fraternity boys fashion a sense of a masculine self that leans heavily on aggressive heterosexual behavior that at times leads to violence.

Sanday studied a phenomenon known as "pulling train," in which fraternity boys successively rape a woman who is typically drunk or drugged. Frat boys report feeling enormous pressure to participate; resistance is taken as a sign of a faltering masculinity and possibly homosexuality. To rationalize this violence toward women, which at times involves coercion, the boys define the women as wanting and deserving this treatment because they are "whores," "sluts," or "bad girls."

Analyzing how the fraternity brothers talked about sex, Sanday observed a preoccupation with sexual conquest. What mattered was accumulating sexual partners; the higher the number, the more prestige the boys accrued. Of course, this meant that a normal, respected masculine status involved reducing (some) women to sex objects. Sex itself was narrowly viewed as intercourse, with the man clearly in control. Heterosexual sex was seen as a way to display masculine power. In this regard, frat boys were expected to make their conquests public, to brag about their sexual prowess by revealing details of their dominance. For some, the pressure to exhibit a certain masculine style led them to rape women, with the aid of alcohol, drugs, or verbal coercion.

Sanday believes that this norm of aggressive heterosexuality fosters the intense homosocial bonds among fraternity brothers. By organizing rituals of male bonding around heterosexuality, any trace of homoeroticism is suppressed.

"COMING OUT" AS HETEROSEXUAL

It was not too long ago that most Americans could simply assume that their fellow citizens were heterosexual. Until fairly recently, most Americans had very little exposure to openly gay or lesbian individuals. Homosexuality was far removed from the lives of ordinary straight Americans, and homosexuals could be approached as if another species.

But all that changed in the 1990s. As gays and lesbians exited from the closet, straight Americans have had to deal with them as co-workers, clients, celebrities, politicians, service providers, and as friends and kin. For the first time in U.S. history, it can be said that gays and lesbians are truly everywhere and increasingly can be seen and heard. Today, many Americans are more or less compelled to deal with gay and lesbian individuals as real people, not just abstractions. These close encounters between straights and gays present a challenge *to straights*: what does it mean to be straight, and how does one project heterosexuality if it is no longer acceptable to engage in public homophobic behavior? If establishing a heterosexual identity has relied heavily on publicly stigmatizing homosexuality, how is a public straight identity staked out when homosexuality is considered a natural and normal part of the human condition?

A few years ago, I researched this question.[5] I found that as gays and lesbians become more visible and vocal, and are integrated into everyday life, heterosexuals approach their sexual identity in a much more deliberate manner. Of course, for people who do not accept the changing social and moral status of gays and lesbians, they may continue to rely on homophobic practices to establish their heterosexual identity. However, what about those individuals who accept the "normal" status of being gay or lesbian? How do they assert their heterosexual identity without stigmatizing homosexuality?

I found that some of these individuals sought nonhomophobic ways to establish boundaries between being straight and gay. For example, I interviewed a twenty-year-old African American woman by the name of Natasha. She lived in New York City and was something of a party girl. As a large athletic woman who counted lesbians and gay men among her friends, she was often assumed by others to be a lesbian. Despite a religious upbringing that stigmatized homosexuality, Natasha accepted lesbians and gay men as ordinary, normal individuals. At the same time, she did not like that she was sometimes perceived as a lesbian. She was, as she told me, straight. So, I asked her why it mattered if some people perceived her as a lesbian. She said that she wanted people to know her for who she really is. She believed that being misrepresented could interfere with her social life and her academic interests in sports. It also seemed clear to me that Natasha, like many other straight-identified Americans, wished to be publicly recognized as straight because it is still a normative and socially privileged status.

So, Natasha struggled with how to project a straight identity without demeaning gays and lesbians. She decided that if someone asked her if she was a lesbian she would say she was not but that she would make it clear that she is accepting of gay and lesbian people. Also, Natasha decided that in conversations in school or with her family or peer group, she would find ways to reveal her heterosexuality. She said, "I talk about men, and I let it be known that I'm into men." She also mentioned that while she has some friends who are lesbian, she would generally avoid going "clubbing" with them to avoid being identified as a lesbian. Although Natasha's strategies for projecting a straight identity do not include public homophobic behavior, it seems clear that part of the reason she wants to be seen as straight is the sense of privilege and respect still associated with heterosexuality.

As being gay and lesbian is normalized and tolerated in American society, individuals will still be motivated to identify as heterosexual. But, more and more Americans will look for nonhomophobic ways to establish a boundary between being straight and gay. Some straight individuals will restrict their contacts with gays; others may lean even more on conventional gender norms to project a straight identity; while still others will flag their heterosexual interests and prowess to authorize an unambiguous straight identity. As long as heterosexuality is normative and "institutionalized," Americans will continue to feel the need to establish clear boundaries, and for most individuals this will involve a more deliberate approach—a kind of "coming out" process.

Chapter Five
GAY, LESBIAN, AND BISEXUAL POLITICS IN THE UNITED STATES

LET US BEGIN by clarifying what we mean by sexual politics. As we have seen, sex is not merely an individual desire or act but a social fact. Laws, institutions, mass media, and social policies shape and regulate our sexuality. Social forces also create sexual hierarchies. That is, certain sexual desires and acts are respected, valued, and supported by laws, custom, and institutions while others are stigmatized, criminalized, and punished. Every society has a system of sexual stratification. *Sexual politics is about the making and contesting of these sexual hierarchies.*[1] Struggles occur around the distribution of respect, social benefits, and material privileges across the spectrum of sexuality.

No one is free of sexual politics, because sexuality is not just one thing. It is not just about which sex acts you prefer or the gender of your partner. Sexuality also includes when and where you have sex, the number of partners, the type of intimate arrangements you prefer, whether you are monogamous or not, whether you intend sex for pleasure, love, reproduction, expression, fun, or power, and so on. Society regulates our sexuality in all of these ways.

In short, our sexualities are regulated by means of a very dense network of social norms and rules. *We are all potentially sexual outsiders.* If you are heterosexual, you have a privileged identity status. If your heterosexual practices are oriented to intercourse, connect sex to intimacy and love, and restrict sex to one partner with the expectation of marriage and a family, your choices will be respected. However, if your heterosexual desires favor rough sex or cross-dressing or nonmonogamy, you may be subject to ridicule, disrespect, or the loss of your job, family, and even your freedom.

Although our sexualities are regulated in many ways, not all forms of sexual deviance are equally socially significant. For example, if you are adulterous, you may experience social disapproval, but your job or freedom will likely not be threatened (unless you are a public figure). If your sexual taste for fetishes is exposed, you may experience shame or ridicule but, again, your job or family will likely not suffer. If you prefer a nonmonogamous lifestyle, you may be criticized, but you will not be subject to criminal sanction. However, if you force someone to have sex, or if you have sex with a minor, you are engaging in a criminal act and the state will prosecute you. In many societies, there is a great deal of public attention given to an individual's sexual identity. If you are not heterosexual, you may face criminal punishment, social isolation, ridicule and violence, and public disrespect; if you are heterosexual, you will likely be the beneficiary of all sorts of privileges, from the right to marry to public respect and celebration.

Identity politics refers in the first instance to the unequal way societies treat people based on who they are. In addition, identity politics indicates a type of social conflict that results when identity-based groups that are disadvantaged (for example, gays, bisexuals, blacks) struggle against the laws, media representations, and practices of harassment, violence, or residential discrimination that enforce their inequality.

As shown earlier, heterosexuality is not just one identity among many; in the United States and elsewhere, it is the norm.

Heterosexuality is assumed to be the natural, correct, and healthy way of being sexual. Accordingly, heterosexuals are granted privileges that are denied to homosexuals. For example, heterosexuals have full civil and political rights: their unions and families are recognized by the state and other social institutions. In advertisements, theater, art, literature, music, television, movies, and even in medical and scientific knowledge, being heterosexual, pursuing heterosexual romance, getting married, and being part of a heterosexual family are social ideals. In short, heterosexuality is more than a sexual preference or act; it is an *institution that organizes national life*. It shapes individual lives and institutions from schools and mass media to the criminal justice system and the government.[2]

Societies sustain heterosexuality in part by depicting homosexuality as unnatural, abnormal, and dangerous. Homophobia has been and continues to be an integral part of a society organized around the norm of heterosexuality. Until recently, many societies have supported the denial of rights and the harassment, physical assault, shaming, and social isolation of sexual minorities such as gay men and lesbians because of the belief in the naturalness and superiority of heterosexuality. It is true that some societies—such as Denmark, France, Canada, the Netherlands, and to a degree the United States—no longer tolerate blatantly homophobic practices. Still, in most states in America gays and lesbians cannot marry and do not have equal rights under federal law; many lesbians and gay men continue to live in fear of losing their jobs and families if their sexual identities are exposed.

It is hardly surprising then that gay, lesbian, and bisexual people have been in the forefront of challenging the institution of heterosexuality. They have the most to gain from challenging the compulsory status of heterosexuality.

Even though heterosexuality has always been the norm in the United States, there has not always been a pro-homosexual politics. Remember that throughout the nineteenth century homosexuality and heterosexuality were not viewed as identities. Americans did not think of themselves as heterosexual or homosexual. In fact, historians report that it was not uncommon for women, at least middle-class white women, to have "romantic friendships."[3] Same-sex intimacies were often conducted in an open or public way and were valued by kin and friends. We do not know if these relationships were "sexual" in the contemporary sense, but they were affectionate and involved passion and often a lifetime commitment. Typical is the loving bond between Sarah Butler Wistar and Jeanne Field Murgrove. They met when Sarah was fourteen and Jeanne, sixteen. A friendship formed during the two years they spent together at boarding school. Even after Sarah married and became a mother, their relationship remained deeply romantic and loving. Sarah writes to Jeanne: "I can give you no idea how desperately I shall want you." And Jeanne could hardly be restrained: "Dear darling Sarah, how I love you. . . . My darling how I long for the time when I shall see you." Although they lived far from each other, Sarah and Jeanne continued to be emotionally bonded for nearly fifty years.

Make no mistake, however; openly homosexual behavior was not tolerated. Individuals caught engaging in homosexual acts were punished, but in the same way that adulterers and rapists were punished. It was the specific behavior that was condemned, not the type of person. In fact, homosexual behavior was classified under the category of sodomy, which included adultery, fornication, oral-genital sex, and sex with animals.

Here is my point: before there can be a politics advocating the rights of homosexuals there have to be individuals who are defined as "homosexual." Furthermore, prejudice and discrimination against homosexuals must be judged unjust. These conditions were absent in America until the twentieth century.

The idea of the homosexual as a distinct sexual type appeared sometime between 1890 and 1920. Newspaper reports and court trials during this time suggest that people who engaged in homosexual behavior were gaining public attention in large cities. In New York City, homosexually oriented individuals often shared social spaces (bars, restaurants, clubs) with their heterosexual counterparts. There was a fairly robust public working-class gay culture that revolved around clubs, bars, ballrooms, and certain streets. There was also, especially among middle- and upper-income groups, informal socializing among homosexually oriented individuals in private homes.

How did mainstream society respond to this new homosexual visibility? In the first instance, Americans sought to make sense of these sexual beings; homosexuality began to be interpreted as the basis of an identity.[4]

Influenced by European sexologists, American doctors and scientists fashioned varied images of homosexuality. The idea of the homosexual as a distinct sexual and personality type was central. The terms used to describe this identity included *invert*, *uranium*, the *third sex*, and *homosexual*. Although scientific ideas varied about the causes of homosexuality, there was general agreement that the homosexual was deviant and abnormal.

Some scientists believed that the homosexual was a type of gender abnormality, a tragic case of inversion between the sex and gender of the individual. Male homosexuals were viewed as women trapped in male bodies; female homosexuals were understood as men trapped in female bodies. The sexuality of these inverts was viewed as normal or heterosexual, but their gender identity was abnormal.

Other scientists thought that homosexuals were gender-normal individuals (for example, females who were feminine women) who were essentially sexual deviants. From this point of view, the perversity of homosexuality was a sexual drive that deviated from the normal choice, someone of the opposite gender. By World War I, the notion of the homosexual as a distinct abnormal and deviant human type was established. Accordingly, individuals who felt desire for persons of the same sex had to struggle with self-images as sexual and gender deviants.

Although homosexuals were then understood as a deviant social group, there was very little political action advocating their rights. There were few public political battles waged by homosexuals against a society that stigmatized and punished them. There were no national or statewide political organizations dedicated to advancing the rights of homosexuals. This can be partially explained by the fact that homosexuality was often understood as an individual problem. Individuals accepted an abnormal deviant status and tried to conform to society rather than change their status. In an autobiography published in 1939, a woman who called herself Diana Frederics described coming to terms with being a lesbian as a personal struggle. After coming upon a book that discussed homosexuality, she observed: "I was, then, a pervert . . . , 'homosexual.'. . . I was grotesque, alienated, unclean!" She resolved that "no one need know of my emotional inversion. If homosexual love ever came to me I would accept it."[5]

So long as homosexuality was understood as a mental illness or abnormality, individual adjustment, not politics, was the remedy. Of course, the social environment was not friendly to a homosexual movement. Changes in women's status, escalating divorce rates, and growing fears about sexual disease and youthful promiscuity made Americans anxious about marriage, the family, and traditional gender roles; there was little tolerance for those seeking rights and respect for homosexuals.

A national politics by and for homosexuals developed in the 1950s. At this time, the terms *homosexual* and *lesbian* were the preferred self-designations. To be a homosexual or lesbian meant simply to be a person whose sexual preference was for persons of the same sex.

World War II proved crucial in inaugurating this new political activity.[6] The war years were unsettling to Americans in many ways. Men had to leave their families and communities to fight. These men found themselves in all-male environments. For men who had suppressed their homosexual feelings, the military was both scary and potentially exciting. Individuals who were confused about their sexuality or who had never acted on their homosexuality sometimes found homosexually active men in the military. Homosexual liaisons and networks were formed during the war. After the war, many of these soldiers did not return to their hometowns but instead relocated to cities tolerant of homosexuals. These men frequented bars catering to homosexuals; they learned which streets and parks to cruise and which restaurants and clubs to visit; friendships and gay networks were established.

During the war, women too joined the military and found themselves living, eating, working, and sleeping together. Some of these women became aware of their homosexual feelings. Romantic relationships and passionate friendships were formed that often continued after the war.

Moreover, many women who did not go off to the military worked in the factories that produced the weapons, food, and clothing that kept the military machine running. For many of these women, this was perhaps the first time they found themselves on their own and relying on other women for daily companionship. Living without men for often long periods of time made it possible for some women to explore their homosexual feelings. Although the end of the war was accompanied by social pressure for women to return to the roles of wife and mother, many women did not. Some became part of a lesbian culture organized around bars or informal social networks.

As homosexuals were developing into a self-aware group, mainstream America was taking note of this—and not liking it. Remember, this was a time of social anxiety; the war was over, but the cold war was building and the hysteria surrounding communism spurred an intolerance for social and political dissent. Many Americans longed for the peace and quiet of family life. As the growing prosperity of the postwar years allowed many individuals to move to the suburbs and establish families, women were pressured to stop working and to return to being wives and mothers. Mainstream America did not take kindly to the new visibility of homosexuals. This hostility was heightened by homosexuals' role-playing. For example, among working-class, bar-oriented lesbians, it was common for women to assume either the role of a "butch" or a "femme." Although these roles in some ways mimicked men's and women's socially acceptable gender roles, the fact that women were publicly adopting masculine roles threatened both men—whose power was based on their masculinity— and women, who often sought respectability through a feminine self-presentation.[7]

American mainstream society responded to this perceived threat in the 1950s and early 1960s with an unprecedented national campaign to suppress and criminalize homosexuality. Homosexuals had been harassed and subject to discrimination in the previous decades. However, in the postwar period the government pursued a deliberate policy of purging homosexuals from the military, civil service, and federal agencies. Meanwhile, state and local governments enlisted the police to close down gay-friendly businesses, to raid gay bars and baths, and to harass and arrest suspicious individuals for loitering and solicitation; newspapers published the names of those arrested, often resulting in jobs lost and families ruined. While the government spearheaded an antigay crusade, popular culture and mass media promoted a view of the homosexual as a threat to children, families, and national security.

Although many homosexuals took flight into a closeted life of secrecy and shame, others courageously organized to resist this assault. Two new national organizations emerged: the Mattachine Society, which represented men, and the Daughters of Bilitis, which was organized by and for women. These were small organizations, probably numbering no more than ten thousand members at any given time. Most of the members were white and middle class; many had risked their lives fighting in the war and were now confronted with a new enemy—prejudice and intolerance. These organizations were composed of chapters in mostly large cities, such as Los Angeles and Washington, D.C.; small groups of five to fifty individuals would meet secretly in private homes to share stories and to plan responses to discrimination and police harassment.[8]

The Mattachine and the Daughters were cautious, reform-minded organizations. Their goal was to change attitudes and laws so that open homosexuals could become well-adjusted, productive citizens. They held public forums to educate straight society that homosexuals shared with other Americans the wish to be good, patriotic, law-abiding citizens. Their view was that if Americans only understood that homosexuals were just like heterosexuals, with the exception of their sexual partners, they would be tolerant. These organizations wished only that homosexuals be treated like ordinary Americans.

Why did a homosexual politics develop in the 1950s and 1960s? The notion of the homosexual as a distinct identity emerged between 1890 and 1920, but it was only in the 1950s that a sense of community developed. This group feeling was a result of sharing both public spaces (for example, bars, cruising areas) and life experiences of discrimination, harassment, and public disrespect. However, it was only in the late 1960s and 1970s that a strong sense of social injustice, along with an environment favoring social tolerance, helped launch a national gay and lesbian movement.

America was changing. Prosperity followed the lean years of the depression and World War II. Young Americans were entering colleges and universities in record numbers. A sense of possibility, of a good life available to all, was in the air. The election of the young, liberal, and Catholic John Kennedy seemed to symbolize much of the spirit of the times—a nation that felt youthful, energetic, confident, and still idealistic.

Although many Americans had embraced the quiet pleasures of family life, others still had to fight, but this time the battleground was the home front. The postwar years left many Americans feeling left out. Blacks had fought in the war but were asked to return to a segregated nation as second-class citizens; women had run the factories that had kept the war effort afloat but were encouraged to return to the household; a new generation of Americans raised in a post—cold war context were asked to put their lives on the line for a nation—Vietnam—they had never heard of and for a cause—anticommunism—that felt remote. As much as the 1960s and 1970s were a time when many Americans pursued career- and homemaking, it was also a period of widespread protest—against the Vietnam War, against racism, sexism, and heterosexism, and against consumerism and materialism. Although some of those who were discontented sought only a piece of the pie, others thought the promise of America required a social revolution.

This period witnessed a huge change in gay politics. Everything about the movement changed: what had been a small, secretive movement became a public, national movement; a cautious, reform-minded agenda was replaced with a militant, in-your-face agenda; an emphasis on the similarity of the homosexual and heterosexual became a championing of the way gays and lesbians were different. Instead of approaching homosexuality as an individual sexual identity, the movement now viewed it as a social and political identity. Signaling these changes, the terms of sexual identity changed: *homosexual* became *gay*, and *lesbianism* changed from a narrowly sexual term to a political one.

For the first time in America, there was a gay movement that was open and prideful and that commanded national attention.

Commentators spoke of the new homosexual—self-assured, visible, and intolerant toward intolerance.

The Stonewall rebellions in New York City that began on June 28, 1969, are often interpreted as the symbolic beginning of gay liberationism. A dingy bar in Greenwich Village, the Stonewall Inn was frequented by a mixed crowd of street types, hustlers, drag queens, college students, old-style closeted homosexuals, and new-style countercultural types. Like other bars that catered to homosexuals, Stonewall was periodically raided and its clients harassed and sometimes, as was the case on June 28, arrested on trumped-up charges of lewdness and solicitation. However, on this evening the motley crowd rebelled. They resisted arrest and turned against the police. For several days, Stonewall patrons fought the police, ultimately forcing the officers to retreat into the bar for their own protection. This act of rebellion has come to symbolize the spirit of gay liberationism.

Gay liberationism was something new in American culture.[9] Never before had homosexuals openly declared their sexual identity as something good while criticizing American society for its intolerance. Liberationists had a new view of homosexuality: gay was good, by which they meant natural and life affirming. Moreover, gays wanted to build their own community and culture as a way both to affirm themselves and to wage a battle against a hostile society. Liberationists chose to call themselves "gay" in part because they wanted to make the point that homosexuality is not only a sexual but also a social identity. To be gay was to share experiences and community; it was to see homophobia, not homosexuality, as America's problem. Gay liberationism aimed to create a community of proud, visible individuals who would challenge sexual, gender, and social inequalities.

What was the broader political agenda of gay liberationism? Liberationists aimed to change a heterosexist and homophobic society. They argued that heterosexism was not merely a product of individual ignorance or prejudice but that the core institutions and culture of America are organized around privileging heterosexuality and repressing homosexuality. In other words, heterosexual domination was at the heart of America. Gays were not merely targets of prejudice and discrimination; they were oppressed. They were forced into the closet to live inauthentic, shadowy lives in which they had to hide and lie—sometimes marry or change jobs—to avoid condemnation. Liberationism was a revolt against the closet and against a system of heterosexual domination.

Liberationists argued that homophobia was harmful to heterosexuals as well. It forced them to feel uncomfortable, even panicky, toward their own feelings of attraction or even friendliness toward people of the same sex. Men and women were pressured into rigid gender and sexual roles. For example, men had to hide their feelings toward other men; indeed, some men felt that they had to tightly control all emotional expression to avoid being criticized as feminine or gay. The homosexual label was used to force conformity to narrow, mutually exclusive gender identities and roles. The result was that men were unable to express what were considered feminine needs and desires (such as vulnerability or emotional caring), and women could not display so-called masculine behaviors without feeling a sense of risk and the danger of stigma. In short, to the extent that heterosexism and homophobia were harmful to everyone, gay liberationists imagined a movement of human freedom.

For many liberationists, the ideal of a fully humane life and society meant challenging not only heterosexism but also male dominance, white supremacy, corporate greed, and a consumerist culture that was destructive of life-affirming values. Accordingly, liberationists sought to form alliances with the black, Latino, women's, and labor movements around an agenda of social revolution.

Liberationists did not always practice what they preached. Despite liberationists' ideal of respecting all individuals and promoting democratic participation, many nonwhites and women felt like outsiders in white male-dominated groups; moreover, many lesbians were not well received by the women's movement. Gradually, some women broke away from both a male-dominated gay movement and a heterosexist feminist movement to establish their own organizations that promoted both feminist and lesbian goals.

Lesbian feminists shared with liberationists an agenda of social revolution.[10] America was said to be deeply corrupted and far removed from its egalitarian, democratic ideal. In particular, lesbians were doubly oppressed as women and as homosexuals. Accordingly, the fight against male domination became a cornerstone of lesbian politics. In this regard, lesbians made the struggle to change the institutions of marriage and the family central because these were considered seedbeds of a male-dominated, heterosexist society.

Lesbians encouraged one another, as a first act of liberation, to end their dependence on men. To stake out their own identities, they felt it was necessary to create a community apart from men and from male-dominated institutions. Indeed, lesbianism was defined less as a sexual identity than as a political choice to bond with other women against a male supremacist society.

Heterosexual domination was seen as tied to male domination. One way heterosexual men exercised power over women was to force or persuade them to organize their lives around the roles of wife and mother or caretaker to men, which left men free to rule the social and political spheres.

Lesbian feminism gave birth not only to political groups and organizations but also to a women-centered culture that included music festivals, journals and magazines, and women-only spaces. Lesbian feminists aimed to create the beginnings of an alternative society—one in which women would be free to define their own desires and needs as a condition of their freedom.

Though short-lived, the new radical lesbian and gay movements of the early 1970s proved immensely important in shaping gay life and politics. Gay rights bills were passed in some cities, and subcultures developed that provided a sense of self-worth and social belonging; these movements gave a forceful political voice to gays and lesbians. Politics in America would be changed forever.

By 1980, however, political radicalism gave way to a reform-minded movement that focused on winning civil rights and social integration. Gays were likening themselves to an ethnic minority and demanding tolerance and equal rights. Moreover, the AIDS epidemic brought many more gay people into the political process and made basic issues of health care and civil rights urgent. By the early 1990s, partly because of AIDS and partly because of an antigay backlash spearheaded by the Christian right, the gay movement became much more inclusive. Serious efforts were made to bring women, nonwhites, and other marginal segments of the community into its leadership. As the

1990s have stretched into the third millennium, the gay movement has achieved a social and political presence and influence
that its founders could hardly have imagined.

To summarize the current political situation, three developments in the gay and lesbian movement stand out. First, in towns
and cities in virtually every region of the country, gays and lesbians have focused much of their social and political energy on
community building. From small towns such as Utica, New
York, to midsized cities such as Sacramento, California, to urban
centers such as Atlanta and Chicago, gays have created their own
institutions, organizations, clubs, cultural events, and political
groups. Sociologist John Lee comments on the communities that
urban gays have created for themselves:

> A gay . . . can buy a home through a gay real estate agent famil-
> iar with the types of housing and neighborhoods most suitable
> to gay clients. He can close the deal through a gay lawyer, and
> insure with a gay insurance agent. If he is new to the commu-
> nity . . . he can consult the gay Yellow Pages . . . or he can
> consult a local gay newspaper. . . . He will find gay suppliers of
> furniture, houseplants, and interior decorating. He will find gay
> sources of skilled labour or gay cleaning services. Having moved
> in, our gay citizen can clothe himself at gay-oriented clothing
> stores, have his hair cut by a gay stylist, his spectacles made by
> a gay optician. He can buy food at a gay bakery . . . arrange his
> travel plans through gay travel agents. . . . If he wished to re-
> main entirely within the gay culture, he can seek work at many
> of these agencies and businesses. . . . He can . . . participate in
> gay political groups, and enjoy gay-produced programs on cable
> television.[11]

These gay subcultures provide a safe space of comfort and self-affirmation, a feeling of belonging in a society in which integration is still contested, and a social base for politics.

Second, the gay movement no longer aims merely for tolerance or to eliminate discrimination, but it seeks full social equality. At the local, state, and national levels, political organizations are demanding an end to all legal and social obstacles to full equality for gay and lesbian citizens. Beyond equal civil and political rights, gays want equal access to jobs and full participation in institutions from public schools to the military and marriage.

This shift in the political agenda would not have occurred if there had not been the unprecedented mainstreaming of gays in the past decade or so. Gay men and lesbians have become a visible, permanent fixture of American society. They are regularly seen on television and in movies; they are courted by politicians, given grants and awards by foundations, and embraced by many of the nation's political and cultural elites. Gay integration has been accompanied by increasingly vocal demands for real social equality. At the same time, the proliferation of antigay referendums and antigay violence underscores continued opposition to gay rights and equality. As I see it, as gays are becoming part of a multicultural America, there is no turning back to the days of the closet.

Third, as gays have entered the mainstream and gained acceptance, however incompletely, there has surfaced a new political current—so-called queer politics. Less a coherent organized movement than a sensibility and a bubbling of episodic political activity, queer politics champions a return to the radical days of gay liberationism. For example, queers challenge the view that Americans are more accepting of lesbians and gay men today.

They point to the absence of legal protections in many cities and states and at the federal level, to their exclusion from the institution of marriage and to the upsurge of antigay harassment and violence in schools and on the streets.

For some, queer politics is about recognizing and celebrating the differences within the gay movement. Critical of a white, male, middle-class consumerist movement, queers want a movement that speaks to the class and racial diversity of gay people and that pursues alliances with other progressive movements with the aim of changing society.

Still others who think of themselves as queer want a very different kind of sexual politics—something other than identity politics. They argue that even if gays were fully accepted, there would still be a sexual culture that classifies our sexual desires, acts, and relationships as either normal and good or abnormal and bad. Sexualities defined as good are socially approved and privileged—for example, state supported, culturally idealized, and socially valued. By contrast, bad sexualities are stigmatized, repressed, punished, and criminalized.

This sexual system does not merely oppress gay people; it controls all sexualities. For example, straight Americans who like public sex, commercial sex, rough sex, nonmonogamous sex, or fetishistic sex are potentially exposed as outsiders, even criminals. Therefore the fight against homophobia and heterosexism should be part of a broader battle against the tyranny of the normal, which brings to bear the power of the state, medical and therapeutic institutions, the family and schools, and the criminal justice system on all those who violate notions of normal sexuality. The ultimate battle is against this system of sexuality. The goal of a queer movement would be to remove our bodies and sexualities from a network of normalizing social controls and to create a culture friendly to sexual variation.

There is no one reality for gays in America today. For some, their lives are almost indistinguishable from heterosexuals. They have families, live in the suburbs, pursue careers, buy homes, celebrate anniversaries, and have children. Still, even for individuals whose lives are conducted beyond the closet, there are still risks in opennesss, which include harassment, ridicule, disapproval, violence, and discrimination. For others, their lives are built around being gay—their friends are gay, and they live, eat, and work in gay enclaves. For still others, their lives are not all that different from the closeted homosexuals of the 1960s and 1970s: they marry someone of the opposite sex, are silent in the face of homophobic expression, and live in a constant state of fear.

The state of gay youth illustrates the contradictory situation of gays today. On the one hand, many young people are aware and accepting of their homosexuality at a younger age than previous generations. They have been exposed to gay role models; they see healthy, proud gays on television, in movies, and in the news. They may have gay friends and lovers or be part of a gay community. On the other hand, their lives are centered in two of the most homophobic institutions in the United States: the family and the public school. Individual families vary, of course, and the institution of the family has changed and is changing significantly. However, many families are, if not outright hostile, barely tolerant of gays and lesbians. Schools are also notoriously hostile toward gays. Administrators wish to avoid the issue to avoid dealing with parents; teachers wish to avoid conflict with administrators and parents; peers are often aggressively homophobic as they try to establish a respected gender status. Because they are economically dependent on their families and legally compelled to attend school, gay youth have few options. They cannot move and cannot change schools, and few schools have created a positive atmosphere for them. As a result, gay and lesbian youth can experience enormous pain and turmoil. Unable to turn to their families for support and often unable to confide in their peers, they can sadly find themselves feeling isolated, confused, and fatalistic. In the past few years, however, this has begun to change. With the support of some administrators and teachers, gay and lesbian youth have formed support groups in schools, and national organizations such as the Gay, Lesbian, and Straight Education Network are now addressing the homophobia and heterosexism of our public schools.

Gay life in America today is remarkably different and better than it was just a decade ago. Gay men and lesbians are visible, tolerated, and increasingly integrated, if still unequal. The struggle for equality that is being played out in such institutions as marriage, the military, and schools will be at the center of politics for some time to come.

THE POLITICS OF BISEXUALITY

Before the 1970s, there were bi-oriented individuals and informal social networks, but there was no organization in the United States that promoted a positive bisexual identity and political agenda. The absence of a bisexual politics is related to the fact that, aside from some psychologists and physicians, few Americans thought of bisexuality as a distinct sexual identity.

The beginnings of a bisexual politics emerged in the early 1970s.[12] It was not until the 1980s, though, and especially the

1990s, that a bisexual movement gained national attention. Today, bisexual organizations are part of an inclusively defined lesbian, gay, bi, and transgendered movement and exist as a separate movement having its own organizations and social agenda.

Why did bisexuality become an identity and a political movement during this period? First, the rise of a counterculture that rebelled against fixed identity labels and advocated sexual and gender experimentation gave a new cachet to bisexuality. Second, in the 1960s and 1970s such organizations as the Sexual Freedom League and the San Francisco Sex Information advocated a freewheeling, guiltless sexuality; they encouraged individuals to explore their bisexuality. Third, the lesbian and gay movement at times made bisexuality into an ideal. Gay liberationists imagined bisexuality as human's original natural state. People were said to be born bisexual. Moreover, the bisexual was said to be a truly liberated individual, someone who had transcended rigid gender and sexual identities. In the ideal social world, some liberationists argued, there would no longer be heterosexuals or homosexuals; we would all express our feelings and desires for both genders as we wished.

The general public, moreover, seemed to become aware of bisexuality in the 1970s. Reports of "bisexual chic" appeared in *Time* and *Newsweek*; celebrities, such as writer Kate Millet and musician David Bowie, came out as bisexual, and the esteemed scholar Margaret Mead, herself a bisexual, declared bisexuality to be a normal and commonplace expression of human sexuality. However fashionable it might have been to talk about bisexuality, though, being bisexual in the 1970s was difficult. For example, despite celebrating a bisexual utopian ideal, gay liberationists were often ambivalent toward actual bisexuals.

We recall that liberationists were critical of the homophobia of mainstream America and a culture of closeted homosexuals in the 1950s and 1960s. Liberationists emphasized visibility, gay pride, and building a gay community. From this perspective, bisexuals were sometimes criticized for refusing to embrace a proud, open gay life. The bisexual was seen as a gay person who was either too homophobic to come out or too fearful to surrender heterosexual privilege. Many liberationists stigmatized bisexual individuals as closeted, as insufficiently prideful or liberated, or as fence-sitters who were a political liability for the gay movement.

Whereas gay liberationists were ambivalent toward bisexuality, lesbian feminists were often hostile. In fact, many of the bisexual political groups of the 1970s and 1980s were established by women who were unable to find a friendly home among lesbian feminists. Why were lesbian feminists hostile to bisexuals? Recall that lesbian feminists approached lesbianism as a social and political identity; heterosexuality was criticized as the basis of male domination. A heterosexual norm pressured individuals to conform to conventional gender roles that were especially oppressive to women. Lesbian feminists urged women to organize their lives around women as a way to fight male dominance and the norm of heterosexuality. From this perspective, women who claimed to be bisexual were criticized as benefiting from and supporting a male-dominated, heterosexual order. Bisexuals were viewed as unable or unwilling to cut loose from the privileges of being attached to men and to heterosexuality. Some lesbian feminists made the attack personal: bisexuals were accused of being weak, confused women whose dependency on men and heterosexuality betrayed feminists and lesbians.

Bisexuals, in turn, accused lesbian feminists of controlling them and pressuring them to surrender the right to define their own sexuality—precisely what lesbians attacked straight men and women for doing. By drawing a rigid boundary between authentic lesbians and inauthentic bisexuals, lesbian feminists were demonizing bisexuals, stigmatizing them as morally weak, male-identified, and dangerous—exactly the kinds of criticisms bisexuals suffered from straight America. As one bisexual woman remarked:

> While many nonbisexual gays have, as individuals, supported us . . . the lesbian and gay community abounds with negative images of bisexuals as fence-sitters, traitors, cop-outs, closet cases, people whose primary goal in life is to retain 'heterosexual privilege,' power-hungry seducers who use and discard same-sex lovers like so many [K]leenex.[13]

Despite some support from lesbian feminists and gay men, bisexuals could not find a comfortable home within the gay and lesbian movement. Even today, as the lesbian and gay movement emphasizes inclusiveness, many bisexuals continue to feel like outsiders. The lesbian and gay movement remains focused on coming out, gay pride, and gay and lesbian civil rights. And though many lesbians and gay men no longer see bisexuals as closeted homosexuals, the gay movement remains tethered to a type of dualistic thinking in which individuals are either heterosexual or homosexual. This dualistic worldview devalues and marginalizes bisexuals. At the same time, bisexuals are even less tolerated in mainstream America. Their homosexual orientation and their fluid sexuality makes them into deviants. In response to being marginalized by both the straight and gay cultures, a distinctive bisexual movement has developed.

Beginning in the 1970s, bisexuals established their own organizations. Initially, groups formed in major cities such as Chicago, Boston, San Francisco, New York, and Washington, D.C. They adopted names, such as the Chicago Action Bi-Women or the Bisexual Forum of New York. These groups provided social support and functioned as political organizations. They engaged in consciousness-raising efforts with the aim of affirming a bisexual identity. They organized workshops, lectures, and social gatherings and published newsletters; they struggled against being excluded by the gay and straight mainstreams.

By the late 1980s and early 1990s, there were regional and national bisexual groups: for example, BiNet USA, which was committed to "building bridges, breaking stereotypes, bringing equal rights and liberation to all." Many bisexuals, especially bisexual women, began to focus on gaining inclusion into the lesbian and gay community as equal partners. Battles were fought around including bisexuals in pride marches and national events. This pressure, along with AIDS and a well-organized backlash against gays, pushed the gay movement to become more inclusive.

A younger generation that came of age in the 1990s has embraced bisexuality as a primary identity and has pursued an independent so-called *bi politics*. Many bisexuals, like lesbians and gays, have focused on identity affirmation and community building. Bi politics has also become more assertive. At its heart is the fight against monosexism, or the belief that individuals are and should be attracted to only one gender.

Bisexuals are a heterogeneous population. As one activist says:

> When you're dealing with bisexuality you're dealing with such a broad spectrum of people. . . . For instance there are some people who are basically straight and occasionally like same sex contact . . . then there are people . . . who are more lesbian- or gay-identified. And many people who are bi are defensive and hostile toward people who are gay. They've been invalidated and trashed . . . when they've tried to come out and be supportive. So we have enormous diversity.[14]

In fact, bisexuals are divided over the meaning of bisexuality. For some, bisexuality means an attraction to both men and women—thus it involves both heterosexuality and homosexuality. For others, bisexuality refers to an attraction to people regardless of gender. This is a subtle but real difference: the former highlights the importance of gender preference; the latter de-emphasizes gender.

Bisexuals are also divided over the aim of the movement. Some individuals believe its goal should be to legitimate bisexuality as a distinct sexual and social identity. This political agenda does not involve challenging a society that uses the categories of homosexual/heterosexual and man/woman; it wishes only to add bisexuality as a third key category of sexual identity. By contrast, other activists approach bisexuality as a challenge to any effort to label individuals on the basis of their sexual and gender identities. They aim to create a society that would no longer classify individuals in sexual and gender identity terms.

Bisexuals also pursue different political strategies. Some individuals maintain that the key fight for bisexuals is against homophobia and heterosexism. Bisexuals, according to this view, should remain aligned with the lesbian and gay movement. Other individuals argue that because of the gay movement's biphobia and its focus on battling homophobia, not biphobia, they must develop their own movement. Still others wish to be part of a sexual liberation movement that struggles against all rigid sexual and gender identities and roles. From this perspective, bisexuality is politics about creating a society that values sexual differences.

Despite the lack of agreement about the meaning and politics of bisexuality, many bisexuals think of themselves as sharing a common social condition as both part of and apart from the social mainstream. They are part of a heterosexual world and share in its benefits. They also, however, experience the prejudice and discrimination that gays experience. This ambiguous, outsider status is said to be unique to bisexuals. It is the basis of their common agenda: to fight against their social invisibility and marginality, against a culture organized around dualistic thinking, against a biphobic culture that stigmatizes bisexuals as sick, confused, untrustworthy, promiscuous, indecisive, disease carrying, and, most damaging, as not real.

Bisexuals are more or less unified around what they stand for: a view of bisexuality as natural and as central to any notion of sexual and social freedom. Bisexuals often rally around a political vision that champions sexual and social variation. They imagine a world in which individuals are free of rigid identities and roles. Bisexuality is said to stand for an open, tolerant, sex-positive society. As one bisexual activist and writer commented: "I relate bisexuality to openness. . . . I try to be as open as possible toward people of all types—of all sexualities, cultures, races, ages, abilities, lifestyles, and personalities—and look for what is unique in each, so long as they're not oppressive to others."[15]

Chapter Six
THE REVOLT AGAINST
SEXUAL IDENTITY

(co-authored by Suzanne Pennington
and Carey Jean Sojka)

NOT ALL SOCIETIES have a culture of sexual identity. In truth, the notion that individuals define themselves by their sexual desire or behavior is a rather exceptional social occurrence.

Recently, I spent a year in Beirut, Lebanon. I discovered that, despite exposure to American and British culture, very few Lebanese considered their sexuality as a basis for a personal or social identity. For example, while there were individuals who labeled themselves lesbian or gay, they did not think that this label defined them in any significant or core way. Instead they used these terms simply to refer to their sexual preferences or interests. Now, it may be that the absence of a notion of sexual identity is related to the lack of sexual communities. In Beirut, there are informal networks of non-heterosexuals but not elaborate communities of the sort we find in the United States or the United Kingdom. If such communities were to take shape in Beirut, perhaps, so too would sexual identities. Or, it may be that the very idea of separating out or isolating sexuality and imagining it as a basis of identity is simply foreign to Lebanese and Arab culture.

Closer to home, you might be surprised to learn that in Europe too there is nothing quite like the culture of sexual identity found in the United States. It is true that you find pockets of individuals who might claim a sexual identity as an important personal and social identity. But across most of Eastern and Western Europe, we do not find national cultures of sexual identity. For example, in Holland, surely one of the most sexually liberal and tolerant of nations, there developed elements of a culture of sexual identity in the 1970s and 1980s among non-heterosexuals. This was the heyday of gay liberationism and feminism; many individuals across Western Europe were embracing some notion of a gay and lesbian identity, or at least experimenting with sexual identities. However, by the 1990s the Dutch, or at least those in Amsterdam, might have personally accepted the label of gay or lesbian but they were fiercely opposed to the notion that these labels set them apart from the rest of Dutch society, or that claiming to be lesbian or gay revealed their core identity. Throughout the Scandinavian nations, as gays and lesbians acquired full equal rights, including the right to marry, homosexuality has been viewed like heterosexuality—as simply a desire, preference, or behavior, *not* a basis to differentiate types of people.

Curiously, a culture of sexual identities seems to have taken shape primarily in the United Kingdom and her former colonies: the United States, Canada, and Australia. Only in these societies do you see a parade of sexual identities and communities— lesbians and gay men, bisexuals, sadists, fetishists, metrosexuals, and so forth. Whether this social fact is related to British political culture, its free market individualism, or Protestantism, I cannot say. In any event, in these societies sexuality has functioned as a basis for claiming a core sense of self-identity and community. As sexual identity communities have been elaborated, which include myriad associations and organizations, they have become part of the social mainstream. My sense is that a culture of sexual identity will remain a vital part of these nations at least in the near future.

Yet, in the past decade or so, these Anglo-American cultures of sexual identity have been challenged, especially in the United States and the United Kingdom. In this chapter, we examine an emerging ambivalence toward, and at times open revolt against, sexual identity. Today, at least in the United States, we are witnessing something new: heterosexuals, gays, lesbians, bisexuals, and other sexual and gender outsiders, many of whom were until recently fighting for their right to an identity, are now staking out positions against the very idea of sexual identity. Who are these new sexual selves and how are they reimagining the relationship between sexuality, gender, and identity?

THE METROSEXUAL

An inkling that we are in new social territory is suggested by the current tinkering with the meaning of heterosexual and masculinity. To be sure, conventional masculinity and a culture of heterosexual prowess are very much intact. The buzz that began in the 1990s around the idea of the so-called metrosexual, however, points to subtle changes, in particular the prominence of new notions of straight masculinity.

The meaning of metrosexual is admittedly pretty slippery. Generally though, metrosexual refers to men who can claim both masculinity and heterosexuality but also embrace behaviors that have been associated with femininity and with being gay, such as attentiveness to grooming, fashion, and home decoration. Keep in mind that historically conventional ideas of the masculine man have promoted an ideal of a goal-oriented, successful, confident, controlled, and decisive male who would be outwardly indifferent if not hostile toward a stereotypically feminine preoccupation with fashion and style. The metrosexual offers a different model of heterosexual manhood. He is not only career oriented and ambitious but also deliberate and competent in matters of fashion and stylistic choices, and he may be proud of his skills as a cook and home decorator.

The metrosexual is also comfortable with women not only as potential romantic partners but also as friends. Mutual respect between men and women and an ease with being just friends is a signature of the metrosexual. The metrosexual is also not homophobic. Indeed, he may count gay men and lesbians among his wide circle of friends. The metrosexual is at ease in clubs that are sexually mixed. In short, contrary to a model of masculinity that proudly flaunts a certain sexism and homophobia, the metrosexual may not identify as a feminist or gay rights activist but is uncomfortable with public displays of sexism and homophobia.

In the United States, the metrosexual was in no small measure popularized by gay men. One need only think of the popular television show *Queer Eye for the Straight Guy*. The premise of this show is that straight masculine men are motivated and not embarrassed to learn how to be more attractive and to become skilled in fashion and the domestic arts of cooking and decoration. And, they are not afraid to learn from gay men. The queer guys not only educate straight men but also often playfully dress and move them about as virtual playthings. In effect, gay men are rewriting some gender scripts for straight men; the straight male has, literally, undergone a gay makeover on prime-time television. *Queer Eye* encourages straight men to adopt gay male habits, such as grooming techniques, etiquette, and fashion styles, as a way to become more attractive to women and to be more valued by women and by male friends.[1]

Admittedly, the metrosexual phenomenon at times seems like little more than fancy Madison Avenue consumer hype. No doubt the metrosexual helps to sell goods. Yet, there is a subtle cultural shift represented by this figure. This is a man who is friendly to femininity and to gay life, if not exactly to homosexuality. In short, the metrosexual is definitely masculine and heterosexual but is comfortable with loose, somewhat blurry gender and sexual boundaries and hybrid constructions of self. He is also comfortable with being viewed as a sexual object and projecting a deliberately fashioned sense of sex appeal.

THE QUEER GAY AND LESBIAN

Heterosexuality has long relied on a negative view of homosexuality to define itself as normal, healthy, and good. The mainstream of the lesbian and gay movement has aimed less to destroy the hetero-homosexual binary than to renegotiate its meaning. Specifically, this movement has aimed to normalize the status of the lesbian and the gay man. The boundaries between straight and gay would be maintained, but these identities would be understood as normal expressions of a common humanity and acceptable variations of sexual identity. The homosexual would stand alongside the heterosexual as his or her normal counterpart.

In the 1990s, a new queer lesbian and gay emerged. The queer challenged the hetero-homosexual binary and a culture organized around separate, bounded sexual identities. Queers argued that the very notion of separate gender and sexual identities creates unnecessary divisions and inequalities. These identities serve to control us by demanding that we conform to constraining norms of masculinity or femininity or being straight or gay. In this regard, queers challenged the aim of a movement bent on normalizing a homosexual identity. Such a movement, they argued, reinforces a culture of sexual and gender division and regulation.

Queers did not claim to represent a new identity but a "position" of criticism toward the idea that gender and sexuality can or should be thought of as consisting of a set of fixed roles and identities, some of which are normal and others of which are deviant. Queers challenged the very idea of a normal gender and sexual identity. Instead, they championed a social order that valued the blurring of boundaries, hybrid selves and minimal regulation of personal and intimate behavior among consenting adults. To be queer represents a desire to be freed of the thick social regulations centered on gender and sexual identities, especially in a social order that enforces the normative status of heterosexuality and mutually exclusive, antithetical gender identities.

No matter how much identities provide an anchor for us and a basis for group formation, they also control us, tell us how to be, and force us to repudiate aspects of ourselves. For example, straights must disavow same-sex feelings, while claiming a lesbian identity forces women to repudiate any opposite gender desire. Our sexual and gender order has also been organized around a norm of "normality." Some gender and sexual identities and practices are labeled normal while others are stigmatized as abnormal. A world of outsiders (that is, sexual and gender deviants subject to state and medical control) is created that ruins the lives of thousands of individuals. Queers challenge the norm of normality. For every sexual or gender behavior that is accepted as normal, other behaviors are then made into deviant and path-ological. If homosexuality is deemed normal, what happens to bisexuality? And, if bisexuality is normal, what about consensual S/M? Because the concept of normal implies the existence of abnormal, queer is a position that is against the very notion of normal as a regulatory norm for personal and intimate behavior. Of course, regulation is still necessary, but much of our personal and intimate behavior between consenting adults does not need to be regulated by the state. Queer, then, is a revolt against the idea of the normal, and it is a defense of a culture that is comfortable with sexual and gender ambiguity and ambivalence.

Consider the case of queer youth. In the 1970s, 1980s, and early 1990s, young people who became aware of homosexual feelings had two choices: they could repress these feelings and organize a heterosexual life or they could come out as gay or lesbian. Today, there is a third choice: they can accept their homosexual feelings but not claim such feelings as a core sexual identity. Queer youth are finding new ways of understanding and negotiating the meaning of sexuality in their lives.

Some young people are resisting the labels gay or lesbian because they feel that these identities restrict their self-expression and relationships. In response to being asked how she identifies her sexuality, one nineteen-year-old woman said:

> So who's gay? I don't know how you can tell. Am I? Is he? Aren't we all! Shouldn't we be—I mean, if we were really true to ourselves? . . . Who should care? . . . I'm about as much gay as heterosexual, as the next person, or maybe I'm just a metrosexual man posing as a female. . . . [I told my sister that] sex and romance was a big part of my life and [I] didn't want to restrict it. [2]

This young woman tells friends that she is not straight, but she is also not claiming to be bisexual or a lesbian. Once, when she told her sister that she had a crush on a girl, her sister asked if she was gay. This young woman responded that her crush on a woman did not necessarily mean she was a lesbian, nor did it mean anything about her identity. She simply did not want her sexual and romantic choices limited by a sexual identity label.

For queer youth, two questions commonly arise: first, *what does it actually mean to be gay?* In this regard, queer youth resist a definition of their sexuality that does not always suit who they feel they are when they are being "true to themselves." Second, many youth, in response to questions about their sexual identity, ask, *"who should care?"* Many young people, who may not explicitly identify as queer, want more freedom to explore their desires and intimacies free from narrow identity labels.

Some of these youth may understand that their elders have struggled to claim a gay and lesbian or bisexual identity. However, they believe that they should have the freedom to negotiate this sexual terrain for themselves. In particular, queer youth are saying that identity labels constrain sexuality, which they see as more messy and fluid than labels allow for. In an interview between the social psychologist Ritch Savin-Williams and Abie, a college student, the former asks:

> "Is it the romantic, emotional aspect you want and not the sexual part? Does any of this have any relevance for your sexual identity?"
>
> "So you're saying I'm gay?" she responds. "I don't feel gay."
>
> "How do you now identify?"
>
> "I don't. What's the need?"
>
> "But if you had to choose, what would you say?"

Exasperated, she says, "I don't. I don't have to choose. Why do you need to know?"

"I don't."

"All right, how about 'unlabeled'?"[3]

At the time of the interview, Abie was a college sophomore who had mostly dated boys but who had recently become involved with a female college student, Penny. Abie said their relationship was not sexual, but that she and Penny were extremely close and had also "messed around" at a party. Abie felt no need to identify her sexuality in any particular way. For Abie and many other youth, desire, behavior, and identity do not need to neatly coincide. Abie was comfortable being "unlabeled," because in her peer culture she did not feel pressure to adopt a sexual identity.

But is some of this resistance to sexual identity linked to homophobia or the awareness that there are serious negative consequences to identify as gay or lesbian? This would not be surprising given that youth find themselves often facing hostile families and school and peer cultures. We can hear some of this homophobia in the following comments by a young man:

> In junior high I knew that what I was doing with boys might be called homosexual sex, but because I [also] found girls really attractive and was also having sex with them then I knew that I could not be gay because fags didn't have sex with girls, didn't wrestle, didn't like sports, and didn't like guy things, which was all of what I was.[4]

For this young man, it seems clear that part of his resistance to the gay label is homophobic and biphobic, but part is also that he did not want to get trapped in what he thought of as

stereotypes of being gay. A young woman exhibits a similar caution toward sexual identity but less out of homophobia than
from a refusal to be stereotypically defined: "I wouldn't say I'm a
dyke . . . wouldn't even say necessarily lesbian, cause . . . they are
in your face. . . . I used to have a problem with the word dyke,
and . . . queer . . . simply because of those images, and I didn't
want to be a part of that."[5] For this young woman, the words *lesbian* and *dyke* were associated with angry, violent women, which
she was not. However, it is important to notice that it is not
homosexual desire that is being rejected, just the stereotype.

Some queer youth today are rejecting sexual identity labels.
They do not see a reason to connect these aspects of themselves
with an identity label that they feel is often too confining and
inauthentic. For them, being queer does not need to be a key
aspect of their identity. These youth are finding that they do not
need a sexual identity to be comfortable with themselves.

QUEER STRAIGHTS

Not only are queer gays and lesbians challenging rigid sexual
and gender identity categories; as we saw in the case of the metrosexual, straights are also troubled. It seems that gender dynamics are changing in subtle but significant ways in the United
States and elsewhere. Women are staking out clear claims for
self- and social empowerment, and men, or some men, would
like also to be freed of some of the heavy baggage of a constraining masculinity. Some heterosexuals, moreover, are dissatisfied
with the way that sexual labels restrict their intimate choices.
Scholars have begun to capture this ambivalence toward sexual
and gender identities among heterosexuals.

The major gender changes in post–World War II culture were primarily about women, but we may now be witnessing a dramatic renegotiation of straight masculinity among young, college-educated men. Some straight men are modifying gender expectations, refusing to reproduce what they see as outdated patterns that support male dominance and homophobia. The era that has brought the metrosexual is also bringing us the "queer straight."

What does it mean for straights to go queer? Well, it may entail a refusal to support a sexist and homophobic culture, or it may involve forging alliances with LGBT activists. Queering heterosexuality may also mean a new comfort with gender and sexual ambiguity and transgression.

Clyde Smith recounts the development of his sexual identity and a public coming out as a queer heterosexual. Clyde attended college in North Carolina in the 1980s where he studied dance and theater. His dance classes were attended by mostly women and gay men. Clyde grew to accept homosexuality and a broader range of gender possibilities beyond conventional masculinity and femininity. However, Clyde felt that he did not let go of a sexual and gender binary model until he moved to San Francisco in 1989. He was the only straight-identifying man in an all-male dance company, and he received from his fellow dancers an education about the world of queer San Francisco. Sustained exposure to a queer culture brought Clyde to the discovery that "human sexual activities are complex in ways that go beyond labels such as gay and straight and that many if not most of us have unrevealed potentials for experimentation."[6]

Clyde felt that the queer label was too strongly associated with same-sex sexualities to claim it as an identity for himself. After

returning to academia to continue his graduate studies in North
Carolina and then Ohio, he began to think of himself as a queer
heterosexual, or a heterosexual "who is queer without having to
pass for homosexual." For Clyde, queer is an umbrella term that
includes a variety of nonbinary sexual and gender preferences.
Queer is about living on the edge of gender and sexual divisions,
refusing to take comfort in the embrace of any unitary, seamless
identity. Queer is, as he quickly learned, a position of transgression. During a public presentation, he came out as a queer heterosexual; to his surprise, the audience was startled by this identity
claim. Their reaction led Smith to conclude that it was "clear that
this juxtaposition (of the terms 'queer' and 'heterosexual') was a
powerful device to shake up established notions about the boundaries of queerness and of heterosexuality."[7]

Recently, sociologists have paid more attention to queer
straights. One sociologist suggests that "queer-straight males"
disrupt normative masculinity; they challenge what it means to be
straight as well as gay.[8] Heasley provides a typology of queer masculinities, which include *Straight sissy boys, Social justice straight-
queers, Elective straight-queers, and Committed straight-queers.*[9]

Straight sissy boys appear to be the most common type of queer
straight males. These are straight males who cannot perform
straight masculinity. They may appear to others as queer, and
be treated as such, though this is not the sissy boy's intention or
identity. Accordingly, they may experience homophobia because
they appear gay. They are often isolated from straight male culture, or some choose to associate primarily with women.

Straight sissy boys, like other straight men, may be homophobic or exhibit discomfort with homosexualities. Heasley describes his own experience growing up as a sissy boy and being

teased by his family and classmates. He did not play sports; instead he volunteered in the library and took acting classes after school. He describes receiving sexual advances from older men, who mistook him for gay or because he ". . . did not look like the type of young man who would beat them up!"[10] As an adult, he states that he is still mistaken for gay until people learn of his straight marriage. He describes his experiences as a straight sissy as challenging:

> The irony of having to struggle with attacks by straight peers for being a sissy, dismissal by a hegemonically masculine father for not being male enough, and being vulnerable to sexual molestation by adult males because of a sissy presentation, suggests that males in this category can, and do, experience challenges from nearly every angle.[11]

Interestingly, the very same attributes that bring abuse from other men endeared him to women.

Elective straight-queers choose to fashion a queer masculinity as a way to more fully express themselves. They prefer a queer masculinity as a means of liberating themselves from the restrictions of heteronormative masculinity. They flirt with queerness and take on many queer characteristics and ways of interacting within the safe context of queer spaces, such as gay bars. For example, Heasley describes Andy as a thirty-year-old who "identifies as somewhat of a gay spirit" though he is not sexually interested in men.[12] Andy feels that he was a typical straight male. He even engaged in homophobic behavior, until he became friends with a gay co-worker. As this friend became his roommate, Andy's social life began to center around going to dance clubs and hanging out with gay men. Andy recently married a woman who initially assumed he was gay.

THE ERA OF THE BI AND THE TRANS?

The first decade of the twenty-first century in America is an interesting time, especially if we consider sexual and gender trends. On the one hand, there seems to be a longing for an earlier era, where patriarchal families, conventional gender roles, and a strong nationalism prevailed. In many regards, the Bush administration, with its muscular masculine pose and cold war mentality, is a throwback to an earlier prefeminist, pre-queer era. Among many Americans, however, there is a comfort with ambiguity, ambivalence, and fluidity—and with accepting a transitional, in-between status or hybrid identification. This is suggested by the recent surge of queer sexualities and genders. But nowhere is this ease and comfort with ambiguity and border states more clearly in evidence than in the new prominence of the "bisexual" and the "trans."

We know that many individuals who identify as bisexual think of it as an identity, such as straight or lesbian. But there are also, perhaps less visible or vocal, individuals who champion bi precisely because the term resists the pull of identity. These "queer bis" are drawn to bisexuality precisely because of its playful ambiguity and its refusal to stake out a clear, bounded identity.

In general, bisexuality refers to a capacity to be attracted to both men and women. And, most bisexuals would add, not necessarily at the same time. As we mentioned, many individuals embrace bi as an exclusive, well-defined identity. However, there are individuals for whom bisexuality is less about gender preference than about *sexual and gender openness and fluidity*. For example, Sarah is a twenty-five-year-old female in relationships with a woman and two men; one man is her husband in an open marriage. While Sarah thinks of herself as a bisexual, it is the sexual openness of bisexuality that best captures its meaning for her. Sarah tends "to see sexuality as being . . . fluid. . . . Not fixed." And, she adds, "Well I am . . . somebody who's in a relationship with men and with women and . . . am pretty equal about it."[13] At times, people like Sarah, who think of their sexuality in terms of openness and fluidity, prefer such terms as *pansexual*, *panamorous*, *queer*, or, like Bobby described below, they refuse all labels.

Bisexuals provide many reasons for resisting identity labels. Sarah thinks that sexuality is too fluid and multidimensional to reduce to a single trait or behavior, such as gender preference. Bobby, a twenty-year-old college student, has resisted any sexual identity label because he feels that even the term *bisexual* suggests a narrow definition of his sexuality and his sense of self-identity. Bobby says that he and his long-term boyfriend do not label themselves: "We're just two people who happen to be dating. . . . We don't like to think of ourselves as one way or the other . . . we're just humans. That's all that we think of ourselves as." Bobby says that his personal identity does not ". . . revolve around [his] sexuality." This is a common theme among some bisexuals who resist an American culture that tends to reduce people to their sexuality and narrowly reduces sexuality to gender preference.

Bobby also resists identifying as bisexual because he feels that most people confuse bisexuality and homosexuality. He feels that *bisexuality* is "a very misunderstood word" and that many people mistakenly "think it's gay." Bobby may be expressing a residual homophobia, or he may simply not want to be misunderstood and disrespected. Female bisexuals seem to be less concerned with the homosexual connotations of bisexuality. For example, Sarah's main concern is the false stereotype of the sexually voracious bisexual.

One criticism of bisexuality as a sexual identity voiced by many queer bis underscores the point that bisexuality does not capture the multiple possibilities among sexualities and genders. For example, Sarah expressed her frustrations with "the word bi [because] it's just so like, male-female, [whereas] I've had partners who were transgendered and I've had partners who are exploring their gender and I just think, again, there's such a continuum I suppose. And, bi really kind of slices it. You're either here, or you're there, you know. . . . I just have a difficult time reconciling myself to such a binary way of looking at things." Sarah is suggesting that there are and should be more than binary options when it comes to gender and sexuality.

Dana also refuses a bisexual identity on similar grounds. Dana, age fifty-two, is married to a man but has also been involved in several relationships with women. For Dana, sexuality and gender are not divisible into neat categories; instead, she prefers to approach them as "a spectrum" or a continuum. This more fluid gender and sexual ideology is at the root of Dana's rejection of bisexual identity:

> I don't think of myself as bisexual but when I think, well, I've had relationships with both genders . . . if that's a definition of bisexual then I am bisexual, but I have to say I don't exactly think of myself as bisexual. I don't really think of myself as

anything to tell you the truth. It's kind of like, you know, I mean I just think that gender is pretty, it's a spectrum you know and I don't necessarily see that anybody is hetero or bi or lesbian or gay or, you know. I don't see it as being quite that neatly divided.[14]

The championing of ambiguity and the longing for a comfort zone in an in-between space is evident in the recent prominence of the "trans" phenomenon. The concept of the trans can be used as an umbrella term for people who consider themselves to be not normatively gendered in some way. Eli Clare, a transman, writes that "in trans community, we're in the midst of creating a myriad of words: transgender, femmeboy, ftm, transwoman, transsexual, genderqueer, trannyboi, mtf, crossdresser, transman, transie, two spirit, femme queen."[15] While some people claim these words as identities, like straight or gay, many individuals approach these identity terms as starting points to express their rejection of normative understandings of gender.

Consider the term *genderqueer*. Although some people might claim genderqueer as an identity, it serves mostly as a position whose coherence is based exclusively on rejecting normative understandings of male and female identities. Here's how one person frames genderqueer: "If someone doesn't feel male, female, [but] feels both, feels something else, it would be nice if there was some representation of that. Or, alternatively if there was no representation of gender and everyone was just a person. That would be nice."[16] For this person, genderqueer is less an identity than a standpoint defined by the rejection of the idea that people must be classified as either female or male.

Being genderqueer may mean being positioned in the middle or between genders. It can also mean that the person feels he or she can express different aspects of gender at different times or can live outside of a conventional binary gender order. One nontransgender woman, Lisa, said that she felt she was on the border of genderqueer. "Depending on what mood I'll tick whatever. I'll tick female and male sometimes, but there's more female. . . . In terms of where I am in that spectrum I'm not . . . that sort of clear-cut, one pole or the other. I'm very, very sort of borderline sort of genderqueer kind of stuff."[17] Lisa says that people who are not normatively gendered, but who also do not identify as transgender, might consider themselves genderqueer. For Lisa, gender is not something that is fixed. Lisa's gender identity and expression can change depending on the situation and life's circumstances.

Some people who reject normative gender identities speak in terms of being neither or both male and female. Marina, who is genderqueer, embraces an in-between status as her comfort zone. "I now identify as somewhere in between, somewhere . . . just neither female or male, or both. Neither or both is how I identify."[18] Marina's gender identity is neither or both male and/ or female. Marina's understanding of being genderqueer defies a strict binary between male and female, man and woman.

Another gender-variant person, Del La Grace, self-identified as both male and female *simultaneously*. While many people who consider themselves FTM (female to male) also understand themselves as transgender, Del La Grace rejects a transgender identity in lieu of an intersexual identity that signifies something that is more than simply male or female.

I see myself as FTM. "Inter" rather than "trans" sexual. Though this hardly matters in terms of how I am treated. I see myself as BOTH (male and female) rather than NEITHER (male nor female). In my case, the two add up to something non-numerical. I am simply gender-variant.[19]

Del La Grace's chosen identity illustrates a connection between genders instead of a rejection of gender or a transition from one to another. For some people, refusing to identify as either male or female is liberating. Chris expressed this positionality as follows:

> I don't force myself to identify with one or the other but explore both my male and my female sides. It is okay to feel/be male with a feminine side. I think that what makes me/us so special is that we are aware of both sides of our persona and we can express them.[20]

Being able to express different aspects of his gender beyond narrow dualistic understandings of masculinity and femininity allows Chris to feel comfortable with his gender expression.

For a transgender person, claiming a gender identity, such as *man*, *woman*, *male*, or *female*, does not necessarily mean that the person identifies fully with that category. Some transgender people claim one of these identities but also resist that identity. Sometimes this may have to do with how individuals view themselves compared with the ways in which they believe society views them. Louise, a transgender woman, captured something of this seemingly contradictory view:

> Only I need to know that I'm not entirely straight [laughs] and only I need to know that I'm not entirely female, but I don't think anyone is really, I think if anyone says they're entirely one

> or the other they're probably misunderstood, and I think just
> some kind of balance somewhere between. Yeah I think I'm 90%
> female most of the time.[21]

Although Louise is comfortable being read as female, she feels
that this identity is also not entirely who she is. For transgender people like Louise, claiming a particular gender identity
does not limit the ways that they choose to enact their gendered
selves. Louise is comfortable simply being herself, and she does
not feel the need to change her gendered behavior to conform
to expectations. While most people who see her may think that
she is simply a woman, Louise allows herself to exist beyond the
expectations of a female gender identity. Louise is comfortable
being perceived as a straight woman, but she admits that she is
also not entirely straight. Louise might claim certain conventional identities because they express the ways that people inter-
act with her; yet she does not feel the need to let those identities
limit her own gender expression. For Louise, her identities as
transgender, female, and straight are starting points from which
she can begin to express the ways that she transgresses confining
notions of gender and sexual identity.

For some people, being trans can also impact the way they
understand their sexual identity. Marina's genderqueer standpoint also confused any simple categorization of sexuality:

> I've very clearly had straight women attracted to me because they
> thought I was a boy, and conversely I've had gay men attracted
> to me thinking I was a man, and I like that androgyny, definitely
> thrive on that. . . . On . . . a superficial level I actually thrive on
> just letting people be confused and I want them to stay confused.

I don't want them to just only see me one way or the other way. On a deeper level I also, I don't want to be explaining myself all the time, because it's more than just one thing.[22]

The way that people are attracted to Marina depends on how they understand Marina's gender. Being genderqueer thus impacts the way that others understand her sexuality. The ambiguity of Marina's gender led to ambiguity about her sexuality from other people's perspectives. Marina not only avoided choosing a sexual identity, she also "thrived" on other people's inability to define or determine her sexuality. Marina also said that she did not want to have to explain her sexuality all of the time, in part because her understanding of sexuality does not fit neatly into any preconceived notions of sexual orientation.

For many people who are not gender normative, adopting or creating new identities can become a way of resisting the normative gender identities that they feel restrict their ability to express how they understand their own gender. Rejecting the accepted identities of male or female allows people to find new ways of living their own gender expression, whether it involves the creation of flexible identities or a complete rejection of any gender identity.

PART III

INTIMATE LIFE IN AMERICA

Chapter Seven
CHANGING CULTURES OF INTIMACY

MANY AMERICANS navigate an intimate world that is postmarital. It is true that marriage is still promoted by the state as the preferred intimate arrangement; and it is also the case that most Americans want to marry, will marry, and that gaining the right to marry is at the top of the gay/lesbian agenda. And yet, marriage today is no longer compulsory; it is one relational option. Like other intimate relationships, we freely enter and exit marriage; like nonmarital arrangements we enter relationships chiefly to realize intimacy. The latter concept, for the purposes of this chapter, refers to a historically unique kind of emotional and social closeness featuring the depthful sharing of inner lives, negotiating the conditions and dynamics of the social bond, and aspiring to sustain a sense of personal authenticity in an emotionally rich experience of solidarity.

In the past few decades that there has been a dramatic expansion of intimate choice and the federal government has played a key role by constructing the individual as an "intimate citizen." The latter concept asserts that every citizen is recognized by the state as having a right to privacy and considerable control over his or her bodily, erotic, and relational life. At the same time, the government has failed to both fully recognize a reality of intimate diversity (the state "establishment" of marriage), and to provide the resources that would make intimate citizenship a reality for many Americans. Despite an emerging field of expanding erotic-relational choice and variation, intimate life in contemporary America remains heteronormative, marriage centered, and class inflected. Thus, Americans possessing high levels of economic and cultural capital, especially if they are straight and married, can more fully exercise their intimate freedom than citizens with fewer material and cultural resources and opportunities, especially if they are not heterosexual and married. These Americans navigate erotic-relational life as a sphere of insecurity, vulnerable to disrespect, marginalization, and at times criminalization.

In this chapter, I sketch broad changes in American intimate life from roughly the early nineteenth century to the present. I highlight the formative role of the state in shaping a marriage-centered culture and its recent transformation into an intimate culture of relationships. My focus will be erotically oriented intimacies, ignoring a multiplicity of nonsexual, nonromantic intimacies such as friendships; kin relationships; workplace-, cyber-, and object-related intimacies; and so on.

THE VICTORIANS: MARRIAGE AS A STATUS REGIME

Between 1800 and the 1860s, marriage was the only state-recognized, church-sanctioned sexual arrangement, and it was exclusively for opposite-sexed, white couples, and legally free American citizens.

At the heart of Victorian marriage was a specific gender-based status order. Men and women were understood as different but destined by nature and God to form a union. Men were rational, competitive, and sexually driven; they were expected to be the protectors of kin and the rulers of public life. By contrast, women were spiritual, moral, and maternal; they were supposed to organize lives around domestic and religious matters. Women would provide the right moral-spiritual environment for the making of a respectable family and a virtuous citizenry, while men governed inside and outside of the family. Through marriage each sex could realize its gendered nature while also creating a moral foundation for the family and society.

Although Victorians did not necessarily marry for love, love was expected to grow during marriage. But this was less a romantic and passionate love then a sympathetic bond based on both personal affections and shared religious and family values. Sex was expected but chiefly for family making. Sex oriented to carnal pleasure was condemned by the guardians of Victorian America as corrupting the moral-spiritual sanctuary of marriage and the family.

No doubt, a certain intimacy accompanied a life shared over decades. However, intimacy, in the sense of a relationship of ongoing self-revelation and a depthful, enveloping companionship, was not expected and did not serve as a yardstick of a good marriage. To the extent that intimacy was expected, it was during the courting process and as a strategy to determine the moral character and suitability of a potential spouse. Once betrothed, a good marriage was less about intimacy then fulfilling gender and kinship obligations, family making, maintaining civic respectability, and securing domestic and social order.

In the absence of intimacy in marriage, it seems to have flourished among friends of the same sex. Victorians often found a deep moral and psychological affinity with persons of the same sex. For example, men's lives were centered in an exclusively male public world; men worked and socialized together, and often shared sleeping quarters when they traveled. Men's friendships were supported by gender-exclusive clubs. Similarly, friendships among women were emotionally thick, even romantic, and paralleled marriage as long-term committed relationships. Emotionally rich intimacies between members of the same sex, especially among women, were tolerated because they did not threaten heterosexual marriage. Not only were women said to lack sexual passion but marriage was their taken-for-granted destiny.

The intimate culture of Victorians has often been maligned as intolerant. However, looked at from the vantage point of governmental policy and law, the truth is considerably more complicated.

The principle of "coverture" exemplifies marriage as existing simultaneously as a private relationship between two people and as a public institution regulated by the state. Instead of stipulating marriage as an association of two separate and equal persons, this principle held that, despite its contractual origin, marriage transformed the status of two separate individuals into a publicly recognized legal and social unit. Married persons assumed new identities: husband and wife.

Because men were viewed as naturally superior in reason and rulership, they were the sole legal representatives of the family. They were also responsible for financially supporting their wife and children. Coverture was embedded in a patriarchal culture that gave to men the exclusive right to vote, hold office, and possess family property. Wives were obligated to obey and serve their husbands through their domestic labor and sexual accommodation. They could not enter into contracts, own assets, execute legal documents, or enter the labor market without their husband's consent. In short, a wife's legal personality was absorbed or "covered" by her husband.[1]

Despite approaching marriage as a permanent arrangement, Victorians did separate and sometimes divorce. Contrary to contemporary American conventions, separation was not necessarily a step toward divorce but often an occasion to modify the marital arrangement. Without a separation agreement, a wife could not live alone, negotiate a property settlement, use her own funds and earnings, or claim custody of her children. Even after establishing a separate household, she remained married.

States varied as to the conditions of divorce and its consequences, for example, whether the "guilty party" could remarry. Generally, the state alone could grant divorce only if a spouse failed to fulfill gender-based marital duties. Unfit or unsuitable husbands or wives were viewed as threats to the institution of marriage. Divorce then was not about reclaiming a right of intimate choice, but punishing individuals incapable of participating in the institution of marriage. Finally, because states made divorce difficult, many Americans simply abandoned their marriage and some remarried. Despite the Morrill Anti-Bigamy Act of 1862, which made bigamy a federal crime, it was apparently widespread in Victorian America.

Although the government sought to promote and defend marriage as the only respectable intimate arrangement, its power was curtailed by church, local notables, and tradition, thus it had little power to enforce uniform norms of personal-relational life. For example, while restrictive antiabortion statutes passed in many states in the antebellum period, abortion remained a widely practiced birth control method. One historian estimates "that in midcentury there was one abortion for every five or six births."[2]

Often, laws pertaining to personal and family life varied widely among states and were unevenly enforced. A telling illustration is the somewhat unsettled and contested meaning of marriage in antebellum America, as manifest in the ambiguous status of common law or informal marriage ("marriages" lacking a state license). Despite the fact that such marriages occurred outside the law, they flourished well into the postbellum period. Indeed, the division over the legitimacy of informal marriage exposed a basic division: was marriage a private contract based on individual consent and personal well-being or a public status-based institution?[3] Given this cultural divide, it was hardly surprising that the enforcement of state-based marriage varied considerably across states and regions. Referring to the laws and social policies governing personal and familial life in early nineteenth-century America, one historian states: "In many intimate areas—abortion, prostitution, age of consent, and informal marriage—behavior was regulated less by the state than by customary law, family, and community. . . ."[4]

While the state had the authority to construct marriage as a public institution, it did not always have the power to enforce its laws. The result is that this institution coexisted with a diverse world of marital and nonmarital intimacies. There was a fluidity in Victorian intimate matters that belied modern stereotypes. Informal marriages, polygamy, bigamy, slave marriages, even interracial marriages, cohabitation, and same-sex intimacies flourished alongside the rigid scripts of public Victorian culture.

MODERNIZING MARRIAGE: THE MAKING OF AN INCLUSIVE INSTITUTION

Between the 1880s and 1950s, a world of nonurban towns and villages governed by kinship, local customs, and small state governments gave way to an industrial, urban, bureaucratic welfare state. The United States also became a world power.

Many Americans were unsettled by these transformations. In the pre–World War I years, there was a pervasive sense of social crisis. Many Americans believed that at its root was the instability of the institution of marriage.

Critics were alarmed that Americans were choosing to remain single well into adulthood, divorcing with apparent ease, and tolerating the proliferation of pornography, prostitution, and abortion. The rise of same-sex cultures in major cities was unsettling to many Americans.

At the heart of the marriage crisis was a deep anxiety about gender. Women were enrolling in colleges at unprecedented rates, moving into the labor market, mobilizing for the right to vote, and participating in what was an exclusively male public nightlife. At the same time, more and more men were employed in bureaucratic organizations and their work lacked the essential features of Victorian masculinity, for example, self-reliance and physical labor. If the line between women's and men's work and social life was blurring, what would happen to a gender-based heterosexual marital ideal?

In response to this moral and social crisis, some liberal reformers argued that securing marriage required its modernization. These modernizers claimed that marriage needed to be reformed in light of a changing America. They advocated for three big changes. First, marriage should be the only legitimate staging ground for erotic-intimate relations. Modernizers denigrated and sought to criminalize nonmarital intimacies. Second, marriage was conceived as an inclusive institution. Modernizers wished to bundle together sex, love, companionship, and parenthood as defining of marriage. And, third, in a stunning reversal of Victorianism, reformers argued that sexual love should be the cornerstone of marriage.

However, modernizers faced a dilemma: in light of the turmoil of civil society in the early decades of the twentieth century, reformers could not rely on civic or religious associations to establish the new foundations of marriage. They turned to the state to achieve their three goals.

BETWEEN THE 1880S AND 1950S, the state intervened in specific yet far-reaching ways to enforce a specific marital ideal: heterosexual, racial, gender scripted, male dominated but no longer patriarchal, and as the exclusive site of adult sexual intimacy. At times, the state simply formalized what were previously informal, customary laws. For example, outside of the South few states prohibited interracial marriage through the early postbellum period. Yet, by World War I, forty-two states outlawed interracial marriage between whites and blacks and between whites and Asians. Indeed, as late as 1967, sixteen states still prohibited interracial marriage. At other times, state legislation created new illegal sexualities. For example, whereas the Victorians lacked specific laws against same-sex sexualities, in the course of the twentieth century the state began enforcing a narrow heteronormative nationalism while contributing to the making of a culture of homophobia.[5] Finally, the state greatly limited who could gain access to marriage. Although by the twentieth century African Americans could marry within their racial group, an influential eugenics movement helped to create new categories of people excluded from marriage, for example, people who were labeled idiots, feebleminded, or mentally retarded, and those who had epilepsy. Indeed by 1931 the eugenics movement was so successful that twenty-seven states passed mandatory sterilization laws to protect marriage from pollution by inferior and dangerous groups.

In addition to pushing the government to limit which groups could marry, modernizers also sought to restrict sex to marriage. Modernizers successfully lobbied the government to suppress and sometimes criminalize sexual representations, information, and devices that might tempt the young or the morally weak to experiment with sex outside of marriage. For example, reformers succeeded in getting the U.S. Congress to outlaw the advertising and circulation of all birth control materials through the national mail system. By the early twentieth century many states passed laws criminalizing the mere possession of birth control devices.

And yet, contrary to Victorians, liberal reformers recognized that modern marriage could no longer rest on a rigidly patriarchal order. America was changing and these reformers embraced gender changes as a marker of progress. Modernizers aimed to realign marriage with the new spirit of equality and companionship. A modern marriage had to accommodate women's changing status without entirely upending patriarchy. How was this to be accomplished?

Modernizers turned to the state to take the lead in alter-
ing the gender organization of marriage. In court decisions and
legislation, the federal government affirmed the husband's ultimate authority in the family while acknowledging that women
could no longer be denied basic rights and personal autonomy.
In fact, by the early decades of the twentieth century, women
had gained the right to vote, hold office, own property, participate in a wage labor market without a husband's consent, and
freely enter into contracts. The state efforts to modify the gender divide contributed to the making of the new companionate
marital ideal. Yet, the state continued to uphold men's authority
as the chief breadwinner and ruler of domestic and public life.
For example, the GI Bill (which was available only to men) and
other federal legislation such as the Social Security Act (which
did not extend spousal benefits to widowers), affirmed a public world ruled by (white, heterosexual) men, despite women's
enfranchisement.

As the idea of marriage evolved from coverture to a more
equal and inclusive partnership, husbands and wives were to become ideal companions. They were expected to fashion a joint
life based on shared interests, values, friends, and social activities. Passion, reciprocity, and companionship became the signature markers of a modern marriage. The spirit of mutuality and
egalitarianism advocated in sexual love was indicative of this
new marital ideal.

Far from corrupting love and marriage, the sexual instinct
was imagined as at the core of being human and should be at the
heart of romantic love. The giving and receiving of erotic pleasure, which Victorians condemned, often in severe language, was
now promoted as a way to express love. And because sex was

assumed to be natural and primitive, it could truly anchor the marital bond. But for sex to secure love and marriage, men and women had to learn to approach their bodies and sensual desires without shame and guilt; they had to become skilled sexual citizens. In the early decades of the twentieth century, reformers proposed mutual erotic satisfaction as the basis of true love and a likely indicator of a successful marriage.

In the course of the twentieth century, America became a marriage-obsessed nation. Starting in the 1920s and 1930s, Americans married earlier and more than any other European nation, and this held true across social class and ethnicity. By the 1960s almost 95 percent of adults had married at some point in their lives. Historian Stephanie Coontz captures something of the growing power of marriage as an encompassing institution: "Marriage provided the context for just about every piece of most people's lives. It was the institution that moved you through life's stages. And it was where you expected to be when life ended."[6]

INTIMATE LIFE IN A WORLD OF RELATIONSHIPS

The campaign to modernize marriage stigmatized and sometimes criminalized nonmarital, interracial, and nonheterosexual intimate practices. Ironically, this exclusionary dynamic set the stage for a reverse sexual politic. Individuals whose intimate preferences were disrespected appealed to a moral language of normality and a right to personal happiness to press for sexual-intimate rights and dignity. By the first decade of the twenty-first century, a critical identity politic could claim considerable success. In *Loving v. Virginia* (1967), the Supreme Court declared the prohibition against interracial marriage unconstitutional. And while the government continues to privilege heterosexuality, same-sex relationships are gradually gaining public legitimacy. Paralleling a trend toward deregulating intimate partner choice, the state has steadily (if still unevenly) backed women's independence, especially in their personal lives. Since the 1970s, a series of state policies and Supreme Court decisions have recognized a woman's right to freely enter and exit intimacies, to exercise sovereignty over her body and sexuality, including reproductive rights, to be protected from bodily violence, and to participate as equals in decisions regarding intimate matters.

The social status of marriage as an institution has undergone a sea change. For many Americans, the social pressure to marry and the fateful consequences of being single have lessened dramatically. Marriage is today one erotic-intimate arrangement alongside singledom, cohabitation, domestic partnership, civil union, or coupledom without co-residence. Despite its continued state establishment, marriage today is less an institution governed by rigid roles and scripts then an arrangement negotiated by two independent persons. Furthermore, all of the components that were bundled together in marriage—sex, love, companionship, parenthood, and property—are independent arenas of decision making no longer inseparably wedded to marriage. The result has been a dizzying variety of erotic-intimate arrangements, for example, sex without love or marriage, intimacy without sex, parenthood without marriage, coupledom without monogamy, and so on.

I would characterize the change in American intimate culture as twofold. First, marriage has shifted from being a state-enforced legal and moral entity, socially compulsory, and valued for its social role, to a largely private association of two equal persons seeking self-fulfillment and intimate solidarity. Second, a marriage-centered order is giving way to a relationship-centered culture. To be sure, Americans (with the exception of African Americans and the very poor) marry at higher rates than any European nation. Yet, although marriage is still privileged by the state, it is a permanently impermanent arrangement ultimately resting on the private decisions of two independent persons who decide its form, internal organization, and duration. The reality is that, at any given moment, a majority of Americans are today choosing nonmarital intimacies.

In a relationship-centered culture, we feel entitled to freely form and dissolve relationships, but we also assume responsibility for their governance. Furthermore, although erotic relationships are forged and valued for a variety of reasons such as romantic love, economic security, social status, and family making, their ultimate value today, for many Americans, is as sites of intimacy.[7] For many Americans, intimacy is the chief staging ground to realize an authentic path to self-fulfillment along with a secure sense of belonging. Intimacy, however, also carries normative force; it compels selves to share their innermost interior lives and to explore depths of emotional, psychic openness and connection; it demands an empathic, trusting self for whom the sharing of one's inner life is to be treated as a sacred trust.

In contrast with previous regimes of marriage, which relied on fairly rigid gender scripts and roles, relationships rest on bedrock of ongoing communication. Of course gender and other social statuses structure relational dynamics but, in principle, their influence can be made into a topic of deliberation. This condition of interpersonal reflexivity gives to relationships one of their defining features: they are sites of dense talk and ongoing negotiation. Intimate decision making is supposed to be cooperative because relational partners are in principle equal, and the grounds of intimate decision making are no longer taken for granted. For example, an appeal to rigid gender norms no longer suffices to regulate decisions about household tasks, sexual practice, or career priorities.

A world of relationships is accompanied by its own normalizing regulations and expectations. For example, a certain level of competence is assumed in navigating intimacy. Relational partners are expected to be able to access their inner lives; communicate feelings, needs, and desires; listen empathically; and skillfully negotiate the practical demands and disputes of routine intimate life. Likewise, intimate norms compel selves to be socially and emotionally capable of entering and exiting depthful relationships without "falling apart" or suffering a paralyzing rage or remorse. The norms, expectations, and demands placed upon individuals by this culture of intimacy create their own performative tensions and inevitable failures, while producing new forms of anxiety, shame, disrespect, and marginalization.

STATE AND CLASS POLITICS IN THE AGE OF RELATIONSHIPS

In this final section, I comment on the role of the state as a force promoting intimate choice but also imposing social restraints and inequalities.

The decline of marriage as an inclusive institution bundling sex, love, companionship, and parenthood was in part set in motion by state policies that empowered the individual as an intimate citizen. This transformation was made possible by the constitutionalization of privacy. Beginning in the 1960s and 1970s (*Griswold v. Conn.* [1965], *Eisenstadt v. Baird* [1972], *Roe v. Wade* [1973]), the state steadily recognized a personal sphere of decision making and behavior relating to one's body, sexuality, and intimacies that deserved legal protection from arbitrary state or citizen interference.[8] The core juridical unit of the private realm is the individual. From this perspective, erotic-intimate relations between consensual adults are approached as a contractual association between two independent individuals, rather than a marital system of statuses and roles, for example, husband, wife, parent, and child. The government constructed privacy as a safe and secure personal space, which allowed individuals to be psychologically vulnerable and innovative in their intimate choices. A new intimate citizen stepped forward: a woman who felt entitled to fashion her own personal-relational life.

The state protects the individual's intimate decision making from arbitrary citizen and state discrimination and from domestic violence. Simultaneously, the state empowers individuals by granting them rights, such as reproductive rights and basic civil right (including gay men and lesbians), and access to sexual information and resources (for example, birth control). The state also recognizes a plurality of intimate behaviors and arrangements, such as cohabitation, domestic partnership, common law marriage, and many forms of adult consensual nonmarital sex—despite continuing to privilege heterosexual marriage.

PERHAPS EVEN MORE DRAMATIC, the state has steadily withdrawn from wide swatches of personal-relational life, as it has lifted many restrictions on nonmarital sexualities and intimacies. Laws criminalizing a wide range of sexual-intimate practices that were perceived as encouraging nonmarital intimacies have been abolished or greatly weakened. Abortion, birth control, pornography, cohabitation, fornication, adultery, sodomy, and in many respects homosexuality, are today either legal or decriminalized.

The state's retreat from densely regulating personal life has been a powerful force promoting a multiplicity of forms of intimate life. However, this has also meant that the state can argue that it has less of an obligation to provide the kinds of social support, such as family work leave, universal access to inexpensive birth control, universal health care, comprehensive sex education, or the full enfranchisement of nonheterosexual intimacies, that would allow all Americans to fully exercise their intimate rights. For example, since welfare reform during the Clinton years (Personal Responsibility and Work Opportunity Reconciliation Act of 1996), there has been a concerted effort to reduce eligibility and social benefits to the poor, especially mothers. Reduced state support compromises the intimate autonomy of Americans receiving social welfare.

But also, in its effort to reduce access and benefits, the state has at times been intrusive and has restricted some individuals' intimate choices. For example, to qualify for TANF (Temporary Assistance for Needy Families) applicants must identify the biological father *and* cooperate with the state in enforcing his child support. If the alleged father denies paternity, he and the mother may be required to provide sworn testimony detailing their sexual histories to determine the credibility of her accusation. And if this does not resolve the issue, the mother, child, and father must undergo genetic testing as a condition of maintaining eligibility. In effect, the right of privacy and sexual choice is seriously compromised for welfare recipients, the disproportionately young, poor, nonwhite, and mothers. Generally speaking, whereas higher-income, resource-rich citizens can purchase access to family planning, therapists, private physicians and clinics, and legal services, welfare recipients are routinely compelled to expose their intimate lives to scrutiny by the state; their intimate decisions may be shaped by a need to maintain welfare eligibility.

Arguably, welfare reform can also be understood in part as a strategy to enlist the state in securing a hetero-marital regime that is currently being challenged. Thus, TANF provides funds to promote sexual abstinence while unmarried women are encouraged to postpone child bearing, limit family size, and to align sex and parenthood to marriage. Considering the individual components of TANF—family cap, family planning services, paternity identification, teen pregnancy prevention programs, sexual abstinence education, and marriage promotion campaigns—welfare policy today authorizes strategies of state intrusion into the personal lives of its recipients aimed at pressuring disadvantaged Americans to normalize their intimate lives by adopting a heterosexual, marital, monogamous, and nuclear family norm.[9]

Intimate relationships today are then a field of expanded choice but are also subject to state-imposed dependencies, intrusions, and inequalities. This dialectic of intimate freedom and constraint is unevenly distributed across America. Those with economic capital can purchase domestic labor, day care, good schools, private counseling, health care, and legal services;

they can afford to take a family leave or pursue paths to parenthood through expensive alternatives such as surrogacy and adoption. Many lower-income Americans can neither rely on the state, which has been steadily reducing aid, nor draw on private capital to underwrite a support system for their intimate choices. Instead, they are dependent on an already stressed-out informal network of kin, lovers, and friends. And if lower-income citizens do receive government benefits, they are subject to forms of state intrusion into their personal lives that resource-rich citizens are free of. Class dynamics are then at the heart of intimate politics today. Economic inequalities translate into unequal opportunities for exercising intimate choice.

Chapter Eight
THE PROMISE AND PERILS OF CYBER INTIMACIES

IN THIS CHAPTER, I explore various views on cyber intimacies. We consider different theories about the personal and social meaning of cyber intimacies. For example, if digital culture is blurring the line between private and public life, how does that alter the character of intimacy? Is the Internet multiplying our intimacies while at the same time rendering them more shallow and fleeting? What does research tell us about the impact of new modes of communication (cell phones, email, texting, Instagram) on our intimacies? Are online relationships really that different from off-line ones? How, in particular, are young Americans integrating digital life into their off-line intimacies? Many of us, including researchers, have strong feelings about the moral and political significance of the new communicative technologies. My own view is that we are only at the beginning of a new era; asking the right questions may be more useful than staking out hard-and-fast conclusions.

THE END OR TRANSFORMATION OF PRIVATE LIFE AND INTIMACY?

A private sphere distinct from public life has been considered a precondition of intimacy. For many of us, intimacy has been understood to involve personal communication between two or more individuals, which is not shared or potentially accessed by an anonymous public. Recent social developments, not the least of which is the Internet, have challenged this idea of intimacy as the boundaries between the private and public become fuzzy.

In a recent essay, the journalist and author Pamela Haag underscores the blurring of the private and the public realms.[1] Self-disclosures of tragedy or joy, personal and family secrets, and sexual fantasies and behaviors, are now everyday aspects of the public world. What was once considered private feelings and experiences have become the stuff of the media, popular culture, and political culture. The public sphere is becoming more and more filled with emotions and passions that were not too long ago confined to private life. This is alarming to some because a confessional public culture threatens to drown out deliberation and reason, so essential for a democracy, in a sea of irrational emotions. But also, the very core of intimacy, long thought to involve privacy and exclusivity, is threatened by the privatization of public life.

According to Haag, this process began in the 1960s. For example, the feminist slogan "the personal is political" claimed that personal matters from control of women's bodies to their sexuality are political in the sense of being shaped by society and are at the heart of struggles for gender justice. Feminists urged women to think politically about their bodies and to go public with stories of personal suffering and discrimination to reveal gender oppression in a patriarchal society. Similarly, lesbians and gay men, as well as racial minorities and the disabled, made personal issues—from the color and shape of their bodies to their erotic desires—political. By the 1970s and 1980s, a discourse of victimization encouraged a myriad of individuals and groups to bring their private sufferings and discontents into the public, for example, mothers against drunk driving or victims of sexual abuse. Needless to say, the media and popular culture played a key role in this growing privatization of the public. A media that increasingly relies on scandal, spectacles, and confessions dragged people's private lives into the public and kept the public focused on personal matters. These social forces contributed to creating what the author calls a "sentimental culture." This refers to a public life rife with personal confessions, celebrity revelations, political scandal, and victimization narratives. In short, what was once considered private is now increasingly public.

In this regard, the Internet extends and intensifies this process. From social network sites (SNS) such as Facebook to blogs and online dating sites, the Internet is rife with personal stories, private histories, and emotional revelations. Pamela Haag raises a series of compelling questions: Does knowing the minutiae of others' daily lives on MySpace or Facebook make for intimacy? Does the disclosure of personal matters indicate intimacy when they are revealed to an anonymous public? Do the personal confessions on the web create intimacy when they are not exclusive, and not part of an ongoing complex relationship? Has the Internet hastened the diluting and diminishing of real intimacy off-line? Have we, in fact, lost the capacity to distinguish a real, deep sustaining intimacy from a shallow, temporary experience of closeness?

Haag is ambivalent. On the one hand, she argues that SNS do create connections between individuals. Personal stories are shared, and some social bonds may be formed with people we never met or with whom we only have an off-line acquaintance.

These forms of connectedness seem important to many of us, and can evolve into sustaining relationships. On the other hand, she questions whether such connectedness, meaningful as it may be, is accompanied by the kinds of commitments and obligations that many of us associate with intimacy. Will a Facebook friend be the one you call for an emergency or the person you rely on to be empathic in the face of poignant life experiences? Ultimately, she says, "Facebook and the like promote intimacy lite."[2] And the problem with intimacy lite is that it looks a lot like genuine intimacy but it is not. The author worries that these faux intimacies will devalue the significance of real intimacies, and fool people into thinking that these look-alike intimacies are the real thing. In fact, she fears that we may lose the capacity to know what real intimacy is, and worse, the capacity to sustain intimate bonds with their long-term ties of commitment and responsibility. In short, if we let it all hang out with casual friends and anonymous others, will our personal disclosures to intimates really feel special and exclusive?

In a much-debated essay the author Stephen Marche addresses the icon of connectivity: Facebook.[3] In his view, many Americans suffer not from being alone but from loneliness. The social fabric is unraveling, strong social ties are weakening, and families of diverse stripes are overwhelmed by work demands, breakups, and a culture in which relationships seem temporary. Families and communities can no longer provide lasting support for individuals. In fact, many of us live alone and most of us will live alone for extended periods of time. In 2010 almost 30 percent of American households had just one person.[4] Our national celebration of the self and independence has a dark side—a virtual epidemic of lonely Americans.

What is the import of the Internet and especially Facebook in this regard? With almost one billion users, does this site show the connecting promise of Web 2.0? Marche thinks not. We are, he says, both more connected and more alone. Moreover, our web-based connections are shallow, entailing few or minimal obligations, and lack deep knowledge of the other and sustaining obligations and commitments. Ironically, we find ourselves more connected but lonelier. We accumulate Facebook friends and collect personalized messages, updated statuses, and reports of the minutiae of daily life; this may create audiences and networks but not real intimacies.

Worse still, SNS allow us to avoid the messiness of real intimacies and substitute these ersatz shallow connections. We seem to have intimacy, with its confessions, sharing of daily life events and select personal information, and gestures of caring and support, but this is the semblance of intimacy, not the real thing. The performance of spontaneous, authentic connection is belied by the deliberateness and the fake spontaneity of our posts. We are driven to be seen, popular, and appear happy; we desperately wish to be admired and surrounded by friends, but daily postings and "likes" does not create real friends. And, to make matters worse, this ersatz intimacy demands enormous effort—endless checking of SNS, constant updating, and responding to "friends." This cyber-relational work is exhausting and relentless, making us feel connected but empty and alone.

For Marche, the Internet does not generate solid intimacies, but a desperate grab for attention and a pathological avoidance of real intimacies. So, yes, Facebook delivers more connectedness but not intimacy. And underlying our networks of connectedness is an abiding loneliness, a fear of being alone, and a fear of real intimacies. This is the dark side of Internet connectivity.

CONNECTED BUT STILL LONELY

Marche perhaps takes an extreme position as a critic. But even more nuanced, research-grounded critics sound many of the same themes. Consider one the most respected researchers and critics of the web, Sherry Turkle. Author of a series of widely and justly praised books about identity and community on the web, her recent statement, *Alone Together*, betrays a sharply critical edge absent in earlier work.[5] The chief theme of this book is that the heightened connectedness of the web masks an abiding aloneness. True, many of us participate in multiple online communities and networks, but too many of us also feel more alone. When we are physically co-present off-line, many of us are texting, checking email, tweeting, or making calls on our cell phones; we are not fully present and really being together. And when we connect online we often feel misunderstood and do not experience the kind of emotional and social bonding that we associate with intimacy. Our digital lives carry great promise for providing intimacy and a sense of belonging, but all too often the reality is one of social disconnection and loneliness. We invest too much hope in technology, losing sight of the basic human considerations that make intimacies possible—shared emotional and social experiences and interpersonal commitments forged through a history of shared experiences of suffering and joy.

Nowhere is the promise and peril of digital technology more evident and poignant then in the use of robots with older citizens. For several years Turkle and her associates have been researching the impact of introducing robot companions to residents of nursing homes. These robots were developed to address a perceived scarcity of caregivers for the growing elderly population. Traditions in which the elderly live with their children have weakened and institutional homes for older citizens claim to lack the personnel to provide the kinds of personal attention and social bonding that many older folks want and need. In the last decade or so, robot dolls (Paro, My Real Baby, and AIBO) were introduced to address this problem. One looks like a baby seal, with soft surfaces, is huggable, and programmed to have various response capacities. The researchers quickly learned that robots not only provide services like medication reminders and some company but seem to promote intimate social bonding.

Turkle notes that many elderly residents engage robots as if they are humans. They name them, attribute feelings to them, and care for and feel cared about by them. Many of these elderly report that robots really listen, understand, and respond to their specific needs and wants. These machines make them feel less lonely.

For example, Andy, seventy-six, lives in a nursing home and was given My Real Baby. Andy is divorced, his children no longer visit, and he reports being lonely. Andy took to the robot. He first named her Minnie, then Edith, his ex-wife's name. He gave her a baseball cap, introduced her to visitors, held it as if it were a child, and talked directly to her often in intimate ways. "You are so pretty. . . . I love you." And this robot doll, Andy says, seemed to respond. Of course Andy knows it is a machine, but he talks and acts as if it were human; he feels a humanlike intimate connection.

Setting aside whether this human/robot connection is an effective response to a presumed shortage of caretaking personnel, can we describe this type of interaction between humans and robots as intimate?

Some of us might argue that since intimacy with animals is possible, why not with machines? After all, people like Andy insist that robots provide emotional comfort; they seem to listen and respond, and many elderly report feeling attached to these robots. When robots are taken away, these men and women experience a sense of loss and grief. So, if by intimacy we mean feelings of closeness and attachment, and a sense of caring and being cared about, should we then call the human/robot bond an intimate one?

Dissenting from this viewpoint, a strong argument can be made that robots do not actually care, understand, and cannot feel anything, whether sadness, love, attachment, or loss. They are indifferent to what we feel and think; they are programmed to respond as if they feel or think. If intimacy means interacting with another person or entity that can experience its own feelings and thoughts, that can be empathic and capable of spontaneous responses, there cannot be intimacy between humans and robots.

If robots can only respond in programmed and scripted ways, relying on robots for care and compassion is potentially dangerous. We will ask less of other people; we will be less tolerant of human flaws, frustrations, and suffering; and perhaps we will be less motivated to invest in human and humane care for our sick and elderly. If robots seem to serve as companions for the elderly, why not for the sick or children, or for the mentally and physically challenged?

In Turkle's view such bonds between humans and robots cannot be described as intimate. After all, she rightly insists, these are machines that can perform gestures of caring, but they do not actually care, feel compassion, or anything, and therefore cannot know what you feel, need, or long for. Without these distinctively human characteristics it would be misleading to describe these connections as intimate. Of course, this does not mean that such bonds may not promote health and well-being. However, we should not mistake a human/machine interaction with a distinctively human experience of intimacy.

Turkle explores another human/digital interaction that seems to suggest intimacy: a website for confessions called PostSecret. Web participants send postcards to this site with confessions and receive email replies. Why do people participate in this site? For some, its anonymity makes it a safe place to reveal secrets. Also, confessions of potentially shameful feelings or guilt-ridden behaviors, including hateful or transgressive desires, can bring about a lessening of guilt, shame, and loneliness. Participants expect that others will respond with understanding and support. Some web participants hope that kindred spirits will be moved to reach out and new social bonds will form.

Most of us would likely agree that revealing secrets or confessing deeply felt feelings is central to intimacy. But is such confessional sharing the same as intimacy?

One might reasonably argue that confessionals do indeed generate closeness. After all, there is a sharing of something personal and therefore one experiences a sense of personal vulnerability. Social bonds, even intimate ones, may form from such self-disclosures.

Yet, sharing secrets is not the same as intimacy. The latter would seem to involve two or more persons who not only reveal secrets but share a history that allows them to know one another in deep ways, and share expectations that self-disclosures will be met with empathic and caring responses. In intimate relationships, do we assume that confessions are part of a relationship that involves ongoing emotional-social obligations and commitments? Lacking these features, confessions are more like discrete acts of secret telling or episodes of emotional venting that may have personal significance, and may even create a basis for connecting, but are not in themselves acts of intimacy.

Once a celebrant of the web as a meaningful space for self-invention and experimentation, Turkle has become more skeptical. The new forms of connectedness and playful networking made possible on the web has prompted the illusion that it can also, and easily, provide solid intimacies and experiences of belonging. Technology is not the danger; it is our illusions that it can deliver what only messy, unsettling human relations can make possible—genuine sustaining intimacies.

INTIMACIES AND THE CIRCULARITY
OF OFF- AND ONLINE LIFE

Critics have challenged a corporate narrative of technologically driven social progress. Too often the giant tech firms and tech innovators, along with a chorus of media enthusiasts, have blinded us to the downside of the digital revolution. If some critics go too far in damning virtual culture, if some see only loneliness, social fragmentation, and anomie, at least they alert us to potential dangers and provide a much needed corrective to the cheerleaders of tech progress. But, like Turkle, there are critics who do not collapse the digital world into a dystopian future.

Where Turkle sketches a wide-ranging perspective on the web that weaves sociology, philosophy, and psychology, Nancy Baym, a communications professor, is more interested in how intimacies unfold in a social world where trust and authenticity are less taken for granted.[6] What does cyber intimacy look like at a time when conventional notions of erotic and romantic relationships are in the throes of change? How do intimacies take shape on the web and how serious should we take critics' concerns?

To begin at the beginning: how do people meet on the web and what are the unique aspects of mediated meetings? Baym underscores an important point. Web users have access to an expansive pool of potential cyber partners or companions. Potential friends and lovers are not restricted to people you know or encounter where you live or work. From dating sites to SNS, the Internet offers a vast field of possible ways to meet others. This remarkable expansion of the field of potential new social encounters means that web users can meet others across a wide range of social boundaries such as class, race, disability, and sexuality, something that is much less possible in face-to-face realities. Moreover, risking initial social connection is made easier on the web because one can choose to be anonymous, the capacity to control the content and pace of any exchange, and the relatively stress-free exit option at any time.

From Facebook to dating sites to specialized community sites covering every conceivable interest, the web offers an expanded range of ways of meeting others. Individuals choose to participate in specific sites because they share interests, friends, or specific aims and concerns. Often individuals meet simply as participants of a website, just as one might meet in the workplace or classroom. A virtual friendship forms and, if there is chemistry, they might take the connection off-line—perhaps initially through the telephone and then in a face-to-face meeting.

What about trust and the risks of cyber deception? How does one know the other is whom he or she claims? And if trust is always suspect and compromised, how is intimacy possible?

Baym makes two compelling points. First, it is true that many of us play with identity online in ways that have no exact analogue off-line. Yet, many of us recognize that the presentation of ourselves, online or off-line, is not necessarily the same or consistent across situations. We shape ourselves and project identities in part depending on the situation or the people we are with. Online life parallels and perhaps accentuates this protean aspect of our lives. Issues of trust and authenticity (are we who we claim?) are not then unique to online life.

Second, we are not in the dark in ascertaining the sincerity of projected online identities. There are many ways we can gain confidence about another's online identity. For example, in many SNS and certainly in dating sites, participants are required to provide basic demographic and other self-defining information as a condition of membership. On many sites, participants reveal hobbies, interests, friends, and important life events—not to mention photos that are increasingly expected. Finally, the way we use language, including communicating emotional states—emoticons—help clarify identity and secure trust. Baym places considerable importance on the role of language in online relationships. In the online world, we become

sophisticated as readers of the way others use language. We become attentive to their phrasing, cadences, omissions, and use of
emotional accents. Reading language use as a major identity cue
can actually tell us a great deal about the other, at least enough
to make reasonably reliable judgments about whether or to trust
what the other says and who he or she claims to be.

But is lying, plain and simple lying, more of a risk online?
In fact, research suggests that Internet users do exaggerate and
are more likely to present an ideal self, but not a fictitious one.
Contrary to conventional wisdom, Internet users in fact expect
"high rates of honest self disclosure . . . and people seem at least
as likely to be more honest online as . . . offline."[7] For example,
some research suggests that web users trust email more than
the telephone and the latter more than face-to-face interactions
to ascertain the truth.[8] Baym sums up this research: "despite
horror stories about online deception, there's no compelling reason to think that the people one meets online are inherently
less trustworthy than those we meet in embodied contexts. The
identity foundations on which new relationships are built can be
every bit as sturdy online as off."[9]

So, according to Baym and other researchers, what does research tell us about the impact of the new digital media on relationships? Researchers seem convinced that the Internet has
greatly expanded weak ties, though, as we will see, it can also
help weak ties become strong ties. Through the web we come
into contact with many more and varied kinds of people—well
beyond the circles encountered in our off-line experience. But
many of these connections are specialized, with limited disclosure of personal information and restricted obligations and
commitments. Weak ties may involve intimacy but they lack

the depth and staying power of strong ties, which involve frequent contact, ongoing commitments, regular personal disclosure, and mutual understandings that were arrived at through a layered relational history. In short, strong ties signal sustaining intimacies or long-term relationships.

Intimate relationships often evolve on the web through an initial phase of "idealization." Because each party knows little about the other, and the identifying cues are few since we control what is revealed, it is easy for each party to shape his or her message in a highly favorable way and to idealize the other. Our hopes and anticipations may be high in early Internet exchanges. Inevitably, as cues thicken, as personal information expands, and perhaps as photos and complicated histories are exchanged, idealization weakens. We know more about the other, ambivalence enters into the relationship, and differences and disappointments surface. Something else happens: as the relationship thickens and gains traction, we begin to communicate using multiple media. Typically, the relationship is extended from online to off-line. At the same time, we expand the range of media in play—using the telephone, emailing, texting, SNS, and so on—to build the relationship. "Often beginning in public discussion, online partners add private one-on-one interaction via messaging, email, or chat. Without giving up those means of communication, they begin to include the telephone . . . and odds that a pair will meet in person increase."[10] In other words, as relationships develop into intimate bonds the boundaries between media and between online and off-line are blurred and less relevant.

But what about concerns raised that online intimacies either are less substantial or may destabilize off-line relationships? Indeed, some studies indicate that off-line friendships tend to be more solid as friends spend more real time together. Yet, other studies take issue with this conclusion. For example, one researcher concluded that "the differences between online and off-line friendships . . . converged over time. . . . Online friendships are more tentative in early stages, but after six months to a year grow quickly and become more like off-line friendships."[11]

Researchers seem broadly to believe that off-line relationships, especially among young adults, almost always extend online. Furthermore, online connections, typically using multiple digital media, will enrich and solidify the off-line relationship. Broadly speaking, the more couples move fluidly between online and off-line, and the more they use digital media to communicate, the stronger, more reliable, and more committed is the relationship. At the same time, research makes clear that typically, though not always, online relationships turn into off-line ones.[12]

Finally, what do we know about the way specific digital media shape intimacies? Does relying on texting and emails or cell phones signal a thinning out of intimacy? Does disembodied media such as texting and emails speak to a retreat from the anxieties and demands of face-to-face closeness? Do media protect us from being vulnerable and contribute to the transitory character of relationships?

Research raises serious doubts about narrowly critical viewpoints. For example, does reliance on the new media, especially texting and emailing, reduce face-to-face interaction? At least among college students, "the more intimate the American college students relationships I studied the more likely they were to use face-to-face conventions and telephone calls. Their Internet use neither increase nor decrease with relationship closeness . . ."[13] Do these new communicative media thin out connections and relationships? Again, the research suggests otherwise. For example, researchers have argued that many young Americans rely on text messaging and cell phone usage to stay connected and to create a feeling of ongoing routine connectedness. In many respects the content of the communication is less important than just staying connected. These media remain central in romantic relationships. Researchers show that at least among college age students heightened text messaging and cell phone usage enriches romantic ties. Rather than being a substitute for deep intimacy, these media enhance it, allowing romantic partners to stay connected in the course of the day. Young adults report that text messaging and mobile phones allow direct, ongoing communication and reinforce feelings of sustained connectedness and commitment.

Moreover, a key finding, as we noted above, is that as intimacies develop and deepen, partners use more and different media not to avoid closeness but to enhance it. And the more partners use the Internet to sustain relationships, the more likely they are to engage in face-to-face exchanges.

Fears about Facebook in particular seem to ring hollow. Some critics, as we saw, argue that multiplying cyber connectedness and friends on Facebook is also a way to avoid real intimacy, with its demands, obligations, and vulnerabilities. In fact, studies suggest otherwise. By and large SNS are often used to maintain relationships. Individuals go on Facebook as a way to develop and solidify already existing relationships; they are not intended to be the anchors of intimacy. For example, one study of college students found that their friends were mostly established off-line; less than 1 percent reported meeting a new friend on Facebook. For the most part, friends do not rely on Facebook to sustain their relationship. Rather, it is used to post messages, update friends, coordinate activities, make arrangements, and exchange photos.

The key point is that it is not the communicative media that dictate the relationship but the reverse. Solid intimate relationships use multiple media and report high-quality communications regardless of the media used.

Contrary to what many people think, and challenging the at times fevered-pitch alarms about the end of intimacy in the digital world, one researcher concluded: "random sample surveys of Americans have also found that Internet users keep in touch with more people, including family, friends, and professional colleagues, than do non-users."[14] Internet use seems to be positively correlated with more and enhanced social ties; high-level Internet users seem to spend more time participating in conversations and social events. Anxieties of a digital world where social ties will unravel, where isolation, loneliness, and anomie triumph, seem greatly exaggerated and misleading.

FINAL THOUGHTS

So, how is the Internet challenging and perhaps changing the social dynamics of intimacies? I conclude this chapter by making a few general points. First, the Internet has meant that intimacies are much more of a public event then in the past. Through media such as Facebook and Twitter, and through texting or Instagram, the development of intimate relationships are known by many people, including strangers. Indeed, today there are expectations among certain populations that intimacies are to be shared in public websites, and this includes relational updates, often with personal details and photos. Intimacies are public in another sense: other people, and not just family and friends, are actively influencing romantic relationships by responding to relational events posted on the web, by digitally accessing the histories of past partners (including some not so flattering information and photos), and by having the potential to retrieve past web-based communications. Our relational history is no longer just history; it is always potentially part of the present and available to an anonymous public.

Second, the Internet not only expands the pool of potential partners but it also expands the types of intimacies that are possible. For example, compared with off-line relationships, online intimacies can more easily remain shielded from partners, family, and friends. What we might call "secret intimacies," relationships unknown to others, including friends and steady partners, are likely to spread because of the web. The Internet opens up innumerable relational possibilities from exclusively cyber intimacies that are as inclusive and as committed as conventional off-line relationships to specialized cyber intimacies that revolve around specific interests (for example, erotic, intellectual, social, political, sports). Additionally, the web encourages quick and short-term intimacies, experiments in intimacies with limited commitments, but also allows for long-term intimacies enveloped in thick commitments.

Contrary to certain critics, the Internet and new communicative media from texting and cell phones to instant messaging seem to expand a world of connectedness and to mostly enrich and sustain intimacies. As we have seen, researchers seem convinced that many of us use digital media, whether in nonromantic or romantic relationships, to express intimate feelings, stay more connected, and feel more committed; generally speaking, the more we use varied media as part of our relationships the richer and more solid are these connections. To be somewhat reductive, as individuals text and use the cell phone more, they report higher levels of connectedness, relational satisfaction, and relational commitment. Rather than use these media to avoid face-to face interactions, they are more often used to stay connected.

Third, individuals use the new media in purposeful ways. Contrary to some critics who imagine either an unregulated digital universe or one in which digital technology controls individuals, web users regulate their lives on the screen but it is informal and individualized. People regulate whether to use digital media, which media, for what purpose, and the kinds of personal information communicated with each media. We regulate our availability to respond to others—indeed, if we choose to respond, and when and how. In general, we regulate our digital communications in terms of whom we are communicating with, our history with this person, what we intend to communicate, and with which media. For example, there is some evidence that many of us use texting less to convey intimate personal information than to just stay connected or plan a get-together. In romantic relationships, many of us seem to prefer cell phones to convey intimate information. Also, individuals who use texting to communicate intimate information frequently develop their own private codes and languages that feel exclusive and private.

The above comments, if correct, suggest a change in the meaning of privacy. In a world in which the line between online and off-line is getting fuzzy, where our communications more and more move fluidly between real and virtual space, privacy is less a matter of actual physical or social space, or whether we are at home or at work, than a matter of regulating what and how and with what media something is communicated. The conventional view that intimate communications should be confined to the private sphere of one's home or restricted to occasions when the parties are physically co-present is less credible today. Privacy is more about forging codes for regulating information, making decisions about what information is to be disclosed to whom under what conditions, and using which media. Privacy is much more a communicative practice and a matter of degrees of risking its public exposure and as such is more individualized.[15]

Finally, there are new intimate anxieties and insecurities that accompany the web. The demand to be constantly available and responsive can be burdensome and stressful; there are anxieties about the seeming ease of infidelities, fears of intimate communications going public, and dread that past communications cannot be retracted or erased. All web communications, past and present, can be retrieved.

Life on the screen cannot escape feelings of anomie, as the rules governing what to communicate, with whom, and when and with what media, are fuzzy and can bring considerable confusion and potential psychological injury. We are living in a time of rapid and mind-boggling technological change, bringing both high anxiety and sometimes ecstatic hopes.

Chapter Nine
YOUTH STRUGGLES TO NEGOTIATE INDEPENDENCE AND INTIMATE SOLIDARITY

INDIVIDUALS BORN AFTER 1980 came of age in a very different America than their parents and grandparents. There have been several dramatic changes, especially as they relate to intimate life. First, many young Americans have grown up in diverse families—single-parent families, divorced families, combined families, lesbian and gay families, cohabiting families, and single-adult-headed families. One consequence is that today's youth are likely to assume they have options and choices when it comes to deciding on whether to have a family and what form and meaning it will have.

Second, recent generations have experienced significant gender changes. If you were born in the past few decades, you likely grew up with mothers who went to college, struggled to combine work and family, and aimed to forge an independent life as a single mom or in a relationship—and not necessarily marriage. One consequence is that many young women view gender roles as flexible and negotiable. Today, American women have more choices than their parents and grandparents because they are likely to be economically self-sufficient and to feel a sense of being entitled to personal fulfillment.

Third, while most American youth will marry, especially if they are middle class, they will likely marry older, sometime between twenty-seven and twenty-nine. There are a number of reasons for this. But crucial are the following: the time it takes to complete formal schooling and establish careers; the fact that sex, relationships, and even parenthood no longer require marriage; and since the depression of 2007–2008, the U.S. economy has become stingy with well-paying jobs. For the immediate and foreseeable future, young Americans will experience an extended period of sexual and relationship experimentation.

Surveys suggest that Americans who came of age in the 1990s and after are disposed to a libertarian approach to sex and intimacy. They demand and expect more choices and are more accepting of intimate diversity. However, there are some countertrends that complicate this rosy picture. AIDS and sexually transmitted diseases in general, along with a growing public awareness of domestic violence, divorce, and the costs of unwanted pregnancies, infuse caution and anxiety into erotic life. And, for many young Americans, a longing for solid relationships, especially marriage, remains compelling and often taken for granted. Also, let us not forget that some men and women resist libertarianism and long for a fairly traditional America appealing to nostalgic images of gender, marriage, and the family. Finally, it is still unclear how the economic downturn of the last decade will shape intimate decisions as job prospects diminish, pay and benefits are withdrawn, and as high student debt and high cost of living play out—with many young Americans returning to their family home, many are unable to establish solid careers, buy homes, or expect upward mobility. So, while there is more personal freedom for many youth, there are trends and traditions that narrow our personal lifestyle options.

HOOKING UP: THE SEARCH FOR
PLEASURE WITHOUT COSTS

It was not that long ago that youth culture was a dating one. Ideally, at least for middle-class Americans, young people would enter college as virgins; dating and coupling would occur, and sex would then and only then become part of the relationship. If a relationship were serious, engagement, wedding, and marriage—and eventually a family—would be anticipated. This culture of dating was in place through the 1970s and 1980s. This is no longer the case, at least in colleges. A dating culture has been replaced by a college culture of hooking up.

Hooking up is a type of temporary connection, often involving erotic intimacy (for example, kissing, petting, blow jobs, fucking), but minimal obligations and commitments. It may entail a one-night encounter or a periodic get-together for sex. In a hookup culture there is less coupling off than students socializing in groups; they hang out and party together. Individuals may couple off but in a very limited, bounded way—for sex or erotic play. Although hookups are typically short term and with no commitment, they may evolve into a relationship.

Hookups are voluntary. They are not arranged, but are a spontaneous event. They have emerged as a part of a college culture. There is pressure to participate. Typically two individuals will eye each other, signal attraction, and find a way to connect and perhaps hook up. Alcohol and a culture of partying play a key role. Both individuals lower inhibitions, and facilitate a forwardness and frankness that might otherwise be difficult and off-putting. Both men and women can and do take the initiative. Men tend to be drawn to women based on physical attractiveness, while women also value men's popularity, for example, if they are athletes or in fraternities.

We should not exaggerate the prevalence of hookups. Research seems to suggest that about 40 percent of college women have hookups by their senior year, but only three or fewer times. Another 40 percent of women report between four and nine hookup episodes by their senior year. Despite media images of erotic abandon, some 20 percent of all college women surveyed report not having vaginal intercourse.

Furthermore, research suggests that not all students are oriented to hookup culture. Ethnic minorities and very religious students are much less involved. Some researchers estimate that about 25 percent of college students do not participate in hookup culture. Also, juniors and seniors seem to shift to a more couple-oriented conventional relationship, though dating is still exceptional. Research suggests that hookup culture exists alongside a culture of intimate relationships. One study reported that some 75 percent of men and women have had a relationship of at least six months during college years. Also both, men and women in roughly equal number have hopes that hookups might evolve into a relationship. Still, hooking up is an accepted script and an integral part of the culture of straight students.[1]

Although hooking up is voluntary, and is initiated by both men and women, it has different gender implications. For men it confers masculine status and prowess; it validates their masculinity. Also, for men, sex lacks a risk of violence and being stigmatized as loose or immoral. By contrast, hooking up may validate women as desirable and attractive, but it also carries unique risks of violence, unwanted pregnancy, and being labeled as too sexually aggressive and promiscuous. Too much hooking up can lead to a spoiled reputation, which can lessen a woman's respectability and chance of coupling off.

Still, many women choose hooking up as a legitimate alternative to relationships. The latter threatens to take time away from their studies, which are viewed as essential for making a career. Relationships are viewed as risky since women are still expected to be responsible for domestic and caretaking roles and for doing the connecting work that sustains a relationship. So, for somewhat different reasons, both men and women find that hooking up suits their values and goals during the college years. It is sex with minimal demands, while they focus on their studies with the anticipation of building a career, being independent, and eventually getting serious about relationships. Today then for many college students, sex, at least hookup sex, is an arena of play and pleasure, but with some risks.

Hookup culture seems to end or change significantly after college. Young college-educated Americans return to dating. A more or less conventional intimate pattern ensues—dating, coupling off, monogamy, cohabitation, and eventually marriage. Hooking up is then for most straight, college-educated Americans a temporary, life cycle moment. Overwhelmingly, young men and women, like previous generations, want eventually to marry and have families.

Why is hooking-up culture not sustained after college? A central reason is that life outside a college campus is not as safe and secure; individuals meet in anonymous places like bars or clubs where they are mostly strangers. Hooking up presents considerable risk, for example, of violence or disease. Moreover, after college many individuals are oriented to building careers and hooking up outside the safety of the college campus may present considerable risks with potentially great costs. In a context in which individuals are oriented to establishing careers and solid friendships, hooking up has less appeal. Accordingly, some researchers argue that hooking up is made possible by certain unique features of college life—a time of transition, few social obligations, freedom from parental authority, availability of safe partners who look to sex as a site of experiment— ultimately, college itself, for all its seriousness, may be viewed as perhaps the last time to party and let loose.

Still, it seems clear that not all young people fresh out of college abandon hooking up. Among young adults who are part of layered networks that include friends, co-workers, and hang-out buddies, something of college life can be re-created that looks a lot like a hookup culture, that is, partying that involves casual sex with no ties and commitments. Such a hookup culture remains very much a part of young adult life, especially in cities and perhaps especially these days when the economy has delayed settling down.

Hooking up is not unique to straight college students. Indeed, one could argue that hooking up has been part of gay and lesbian life well before it grabbed national attention as a phenomenon among heterosexuals. What was called casual or anonymous sex was and still is fairly common in gay and lesbian life. In particular, surveys and research shows that from Stonewall (1969) through the beginning of the AIDS crisis multiple sex partners were the norm among many circles of gay men, though considerably less so among lesbians. Has this changed, especially among lesbian or queer women?

Consider a recent study of the sexual and intimate lives of queer women at the University of California, Santa Barbara.[2] For these women queer refers to a refusal to identify in terms of the standard sex identity categories. Some of these women have also rejected the word *queer*, preferring *bicurious*, *mostly straight*, *heteroflexible*, *fluid*, or *pansexual*. Most telling about these women is their embrace of a notion of sexual fluidity—as both a way to identify and a description of their practice. They do not want to be stuck in one label or expected to conform to one norm of intimacy.

Hooking up is pervasive among queer students as well. As Lea, a white pansexual student, explains: "To me hookup means going home with somebody and having sex with them and leaving in the morning. I mean that's definitely big in the queer community." What counts as sexual behavior is up in the air in queer hookup culture. For example, hooking up, says Lea, can mean having gone to "second base," which she defines as "above the waist" with a woman but not having lost "the second virginity . . . not yet." She finds it easier to hook up with men because of her lack of experience in making the first move. Her use of the "second-base" metaphor prompts a discussion with her interviewer, echoed by other students, of what counts as sex between two women. Although there is no agreement about whether hooking up requires sex, Lea thinks that "fingering" and oral sex count as sex between two women but not between a woman and a man. Morgan, a white student who identifies as pansexual and who, at the time of her interview, had recently broken up with a boyfriend and began her first relationship with a woman, says: "Now that I'm in a relationship with a woman, sex is, I mean, there's no penis, so obviously my definition of it changed a little bit. . . . Everything . . . counts as sex."

A second theme among these women is their preference for a language of fluidity and pansexuality to describe their identities and attractions. Gabriella, an African American student who identifies as genderqueer and protested the lack of a gender-neutral restroom in her residence hall, says: "Sometimes I'm lesbian. And I used to be bisexual . . . then after that I guess I was like, I was like fluid. I still am fluid, kind of. And then it's lesbian—it was lesbian, and then I was fluid again. And now I'm just queer." For some of these women, the language of pansexuality is embraced to avoid rigid identity categories. Jessica's definition of pansexual includes an attraction to "any genders that fall outside" male and female. A multiracial student, Missy, defines "pansexual" as acknowledging "the possibility of, you know, being attracted to someone that doesn't fall into those two like male or female categories." Liliana, who does not like using labels "because I just don't like limiting myself to just one thing" thinks even "bisexual" specifies just women or men "but I feel like if you say sexually fluid, that includes transgender, literally anything."

As we have seen, middle-class straight-identified youth are questioning their parents' scripts for sex and intimacy, not so much rejecting as reconsidering the range of legitimate options in aligning sex, intimacy, and family. Queer youth inherited a lesbian and gay culture that had already challenged a heteronormative culture, even if aspects of it have been embraced. Some of these youth are today also deconstructing the beliefs of their queer predecessors; they are critical of the now conventional identity labels of lesbian and gay culture. Some youth are experimenting with sexual desire and intimacies in ways that aim to go beyond both heteronormativity and gay/lesbian cultural normativities.

Intimacies after College: Managing Work and Family

College is not a social framework that is sustained in adult life. It is a temporary and transitional time that allows for sexual and intimate experimentation. While this experimentation does not come to an end after college, the overwhelming majority of young Americans desire a more settled and largely conventional intimate arrangement. As they reach their late twenties and thirties, whether they live alone, cohabit, or marry, most young American adults will forge intimate romantic relationships. There is one telling way the generations coming of age in the first or second decade of the twenty-first century are different from previous ones: with the massive entry of middle-class women into the workforce, the balancing of work and family is no longer a challenge only for blue-collar or lower-income Americans but is today experienced across social classes. The shape and emotional and social texture of intimacies will in no small measure reflect the way individuals manage the conflicting demands of work and family.

In *The Unfinished Revolution*, Kathleen Gerson speaks to this issue in compelling ways.[3] Based on interviews with 120 men and women of varied races and classes (5 percent being gay and lesbian identified), she offers a snapshot of these struggles. To begin with, virtually all of her interviewees, men and women, blue or white collar, want to work, be self-supporting, and have a rich personal life that includes a romantic relationship, often with the anticipation of children. Most want at some point to marry but they are comfortable in delaying this until economically and psychologically ready. Most also recognize that marriage is a loose institution today. People enter and exit as a matter of choice and it is considered acceptable to forge an intimate life outside of marriage. Similarly, most men and women want children but understand this as a personal choice rather than a social obligation; being in an intimate relationship and deciding not to have a child is a legitimate option. And most dramatically, there is considerable tolerance for single women to have children outside of marriage or a relationship. Despite these more or less shared beliefs and values, men and women (Gerson does not consider transgendered or transsexual individuals) differ in important ways in terms of how they negotiate work and family and in terms of balancing autonomy and intimacy.

Today's young women understand that it is unlikely that they can have it all—personal freedom, career, motherhood, and a committed egalitarian, companionate relationship. Something has to give; compromise is the sobering reality most women come to expect. The question is, what is to be compromised?

Gerson divides the women she interviewed into roughly two groups: women who prioritized family ("traditionalists") and those who would not compromise on economic autonomy ("self-reliant women"). Speaking in broad terms, she found that the clear majority of women, across race and class, preferred self-reliance as they negotiate work and family. These women understood that relationships, including marriage, despite one's best intentions and hopes, are often impermanent. And because of the experience of their mothers and/or other older women, these women believe that many women have suffered because they were not prepared for breakups or divorces. They do not want to find themselves alone and without a solid job and a network of close friends. They understand that failed relationships render women vulnerable to hardships and a level of insecurity and loneliness they wish to avoid.

Self-reliant women have made economic independence, along with forging networks of supportive friends and family, into a condition of personal fulfillment. For them, work is part of their desire to achieve personal fulfillment and a full sense of being adult. They also believe that the array of rights and freedoms women have gained in the past few decades can only truly be maintained if they are economically independent. They are all too aware, though, that self-reliance may have its costs, such as forgoing marriage or motherhood, or single parenthood, or living alone for long stretches of adulthood. But they have learned through their parents and friends, and their own relational breakups, that ultimately they have to be able to support themselves.

Not so unlike their parents and grandparents, both traditional and self-reliant women want personally satisfying intimacies, preferably at some point marriage. Unlike previous generations, their standards are somewhat different. They expect to work and expect their partners to accept and support their careers. Their ideal partner would be flexible and accommodate their work and broader aspirations for self-fulfillment. She does not expect to give up her own friends and social activities, but to selectively meld them with her partner's. Not least, she expects her partner to share in the demands and responsibilities of the household. In short she aspires to an intimate, companionate, egalitarian relationship where each partner finds self-fulfillment but also shares responsibility for creating a mutually satisfying common life.

There is one area of heightened tension in their approach to intimacy, namely parenthood. Today's young women want to be parents. Yet, many women, including those aspiring to self-reliance, want to be independent as much as they want to be mothers. This is a conflict that men do not experience in the same way; when push comes to shove, men prioritize work and personal independence. Moreover, many women in heterosexual relationships feel they are better prepared, and more motivated, than men to be parents. Accordingly, women may devote much more time to parenting than their male partners, thus undermining an equalitarian gender ideal. Moreover, to the extent that most men concur that women are better parents, along with their prioritizing of work, they too end up reluctantly embracing a gender division and inequity in their relationships. And, to the extent that men do not assume equal domestic and parenting responsibilities, women will experience levels of stress and perhaps discontent that will be lacking for men. The reality then is that continued gender inequality remains a defining part of the personal lives of many women, and a major stress point in balancing work and family.

Even traditionalists are rethinking the old model of being a woman. True, like their predecessors, they define themselves primarily through their roles as wife and mother. However, they are all too aware of the potential costs of divorces and separations to themselves and their children. And they too look to work as an avenue of personal satisfaction and growth, not just a source of income. So, for many new traditionalists, they will make motherhood primary during a child's early years while entering the workforce as the child gets older, often with the support of a male partner.

Young men want what women want: satisfying work, successful careers, and an intimate and egalitarian romantic relationship, including marriage and eventually children. They face similar struggles as they deal with negotiating being independent and forging solid relationships as they balance the demands and attractions of work and family life. However, whereas this has been a long-standing issue for many women, for many men it has not since it has long been assumed that they would be breadwinners and their wives would be the primary parent. Today that is no longer the case for many young Americans. Women are firmly in the workplace and want economic and social independence. They also want men to be engaged parents. So, men too must find a compromise they can live with.

Men today face unique challenges. Coming of age in the first decade of the twenty-first century, they face a reality of pervasive job insecurity, stagnant incomes, fierce competition, often extraordinary time demands at work, high costs of day care, and women's new expectations for men to share domestic responsibilities. How to combine being a breadwinner with being an equal family member when the demands of work escalate, when men are still often the primary earner, and when families seem to require higher incomes? At the root of men's response to this dilemma is the fact that most men continue to want to be, and are expected to be, the primary earner. Yet, not only is this traditional role threatened by the economy and women's

advancement but it conflicts with their strong desire and expectation to be equal intimate partners at home.

Faced with these cross-pressures, something has to give. For
most blue- and white-collar men, their default position is to focus on the breadwinner role. It is not just that men continue to
make more money than women, but men continue to place economic success and a breadwinner role as central to their identity.
While we hear a lot about some men abandoning their work role
for a domestic-centered life, "almost every young man rejected
the idea of staying at home, even if it were possible." The bot-
tom line is that most men "equate responsible manhood with
earning a 'good enough' living."[4]

At the same time, most men actively support the work aspirations of their female partners. They do not want a permanent
stay-at-home wife or partner. They also recognize and accept
that women want to work and desire a satisfying work life for
their sense of self-worth and personal satisfaction. Yet, the reality is that these young men feel they must establish a career and
support themselves and their family. As a result, their caregiving role often takes a backseat. Moreover, "neotraditional men"
believe that child care, especially for young children, is best provided by mothers, not farmed out to day care centers or paid
workers. Of course, this means opting for a more traditional version of gender relations, despite their egalitarian ideals. Men rationalize this as a necessity given the economy, and by believing
that in the end their female partners choose this role out of their
own desire and in the interests of the family. As Gerson says,
"they profess support for the ideal of equal parenting, but they
fall back on the practical advantages of devoted mothering."[5]

In her research, Gerson found that a significant percent of men (30 percent) rejected the primary breadwinning role. They did not want to support a partner, whether as part of a couple or as a family with children. They want and expect their partners to be self-supporting. In the absence of this, they prefer to be single and avoid family obligations. In part these men are responding to an economy that can no longer promise them security and well-paying jobs. In part, reflecting their parents' experience, they wish to avoid getting trapped in jobs that consume all their time to sustain a relationship and family, which often results in diminishing satisfaction at work and at home. These "autonomous men" want satisfying work and equal fulfilling and egalitarian relationships; they also hope to maintain their independence, a combination that is not easy to achieve.

INTIMACY AND PARENTHOOD AMONG THE POOR

Despite more intimate choices for many working- and middle-class Americans, the reality is that there remains a dominant and still normative model. It stipulates the following intimate trajectory: establish a career or job security, date, get engaged, and wed; ideally, parenthood follows after the couple has achieved relational and economic security. Of course there are lots of variations—single parenthood, cohabitation, living apart together, coupledom without children, singledom, and so on. Still, education followed by job security followed by cohabitation and typically marriage and eventually a family is the prevailing and preferred intimate ideal for most working- and middle-class Americans.

But this is not the model for many poor women and men, regardless of race. Interestingly, these Americans want the same things as Middle America—economic security, solid relationships, marriage, and a family of their own. However, they approach these aspirations differently.

Most dramatically, for many poor women, motherhood does not need to be coupled to marriage or a serious relationship. True, they would like to marry or have a long-term relationship but this is typically a far-off, often unrealized, ideal. Indeed, many of these women idealize marriage but, because it is unlikely to happen, they prioritize motherhood; parenthood is an acceptable status both before establishing a solid relationship and before securing a steady job. Furthermore, as in the working and middle classes, they would like to parent with a male partner (assuming a heterosexual context), but only if he accepts her independence, is self-supporting, and treats her and her children respectfully. The reality, then, is that marriage is a separate decision from becoming a mother (among the poor, some 40 percent of women have children outside marriage). And, while single motherhood is acceptable within their communities, bad marriages or ones that quickly end in divorces are considered signs of immaturity and bad judgment.

What does it mean to be a mother for these women? To address this question, I drew heavily on *Promises I Can Keep: Why Poor Women Put Motherhood before Marriage* by Kathryn Edin and Maria Kefalas.[6] These researchers spent six years living in poor neighborhoods in New Jersey and Philadelphia. They interviewed 162 women—white, black, and Hispanic—all being poor or earning annual incomes less than sixteen thousand dollars. Their average age was twenty-five. Seventy-five percent had a child as a teen; about 50 percent collected welfare at some point in the past two years, while roughly half worked in low-paying service jobs. They all identified as heterosexual.

The reality faced by these women is stark: they have few opportunities for well-paying careers, economic mobility, high social status, and marriage. These statuses are typically structurally unavailable. By contrast, motherhood can be chosen and it is a chance to excel at something while also gaining a respected status in their communities. Motherhood gives moral and social coherence to their lives. Many women talked about how motherhood straightened them out; it made it possible for them to shift from a troubled street life to a stable, purposeful, and responsible life. Contrary to middle-class patterns, motherhood often led to steady work and a return to school, as well as a life without drugs, alcohol, and crime. As they became mothers, these women report great satisfaction in having created a family of their own and having someone who will always be there to love and be loved by. Finally, among kin and peers, becoming a mother was taken as a sign of maturity or of choosing a respectable, responsible life. As an aside, contrary to popular stereotypes, the average number of children in these poor families is just over two.

Poor women aspire to be good mothers. A good mother means always being there for the child—sacrificing as well as providing and protecting the child. A good mother keeps the child out of trouble—in particular, away from the temptations of the street. She keeps the child clean, well dressed, and well behaved. For many of these women, a woman is judged a good mother by surviving day to day, and keeping alive a hope that the child will do better than she in the future.

Contrary to what we might expect, the decision to become a mother does not seem to lessen poor women's social and economic prospects. Whether or not they have children, their prospects for a well-paying, upwardly mobile job and for marriage remain slim. The reality is that many of these women, whether or not they are mothers, will drop out of school and likely face a life of low wages and live most of their adulthood as single parents.

How to explain this retreat from marriage among poorer women? Access to welfare support does not seem to hold as an explanation. In fact, single motherhood among the poor has continued to increase even as state support has significantly diminished after President Clinton's welfare reform legislation of 1996. Moreover, almost half the women in this study are not on welfare, but work. Some researchers have argued that the decision not to marry is related to the lack of available men who can be steady providers and fathers. In this regard, the flight of manufacturing from inner cities is said to have had a devastating impact on men. Add to this that many men in poor neighborhoods have sporadic work histories, survive by living off the street, and many will spend considerable time in prison.

But Edin and Kefalas offer an alternative explanation. In the past several decades, there has been a broad societal redefinition and retreat from marriage. Once an enveloping institution that bundled together sex, love, companionship, and parenthood, this is no longer the case. Today, these dimensions of marriage can be pursued outside marriage. Americans can have sex and love without marriage; the same is true for companionship, intimacy, and parenthood. Marriages today is optional, impermanent, and is less a solid institution that grounds and defines one's life than a symbolic marker of adulthood. It may still be the preferred end point of a relationship but it is no longer a necessary framework for intimacy and parenthood. Accordingly, the retreat from marriage among poor Americans should be viewed as consistent with an evolving social mainstream.

If many poor women are choosing motherhood outside of marriage, even as they continue to hope to marry in the future, what of the men who father these children? What meaning does fathering have and what intimate ideal motivates them?

We know the stereotype. Lacking other ways to establish and validate their manhood, fathering children becomes a marker of manliness. Unfortunately, this choice proves to be a social disaster, producing a world of poor, angry, fatherless children many of whom will repeat this pattern. But is this stereotype true?

Much research suggests that it is not. In a recent book, *Doing the Best I Can: Fatherhood in the Inner City*, Kathryn Edin and Timothy Nelson provide a compelling critique of this stereotype.[7] Living in poor, inner-city neighborhoods of Philadelphia where they interviewed black and white young fathers, the authors provide an alternative perspective on why these men become fathers. These men do not take fatherhood lightly and they struggle to sustain a meaningful bond with their children. In fact, these men anguish over their children, consider their erratic parental engagement as a serious failure, and do not abandon the ideal of being good fathers. They know, all too well, the troubling consequences of growing up fatherless.

Still, many of these men father children with multiple partners and their parenting is often marked by periods of neglect, broken promises, and not infrequently abandonment. So, why do they become serial fathers?

Inner-city men have few prospects for a good job, economic mobility, high-status roles, and marriage. Their lives are often rough and unstable as they try to navigate a street culture of crime, violence, drugs, and alcohol. Fatherhood is one of the few statuses they can choose, gain respect in their neighborhoods, and serve as a way to redeem their lives. To be sure, they are aware of their failures as parents, but they sustain hope that in their current or future relationships they will prove a worthy partner and parent. Practically speaking, there is little to lose. It is well understood that women have ultimate responsibility for children in these communities. They are expected to provide, protect, and care for their children, while men come and go. With few socially imposed expectations to maintain steady fathering, the end of their relationships often means that men move on to new relationships with renewed opportunities to once again prove themselves as good fathers.

Unlike in the middle class, pregnancies are often not planned. Typically, if a man hangs out with a woman, they will view each other as "together." Being together is somewhere between hooking up and being in a committed relationship; it does not assume a history of dating or extended time spent together. Pregnancy and birth will often motivate a good-will effort to transform being together into a "real relationship." In the back of their minds, each partner may hope for eventual marriage, but this is a far-off aspiration. To prove his worth as a partner and father, he must settle down, contribute to the income of the family, and be present for the child and any other children in the household. The reality is often sobering: very few of these relationships turn into marriage and cohabitation is often a temporary status before men leave or are asked to leave. The reasons for this instability are all too obvious—erratic, low-wage jobs, the lure of the streets with its promise of fast and big money, domestic violence, or incarceration.

But there is another telling point to be made: in contrast with relationships among blue- and white-collar Americans, these men enter into "real relationships," not so much for love and companionship, but for the sake of their child. It is the child, not the relationship, that is the real glue of the family. If the latter dissolves, most fathers intend to sustain contact with the child. However, in the absence of living together, his presence in the child's life may become irregular and may gradually thin out. At times, mothers will bar men's access or a new boyfriend will take over the father role. In these cases, many fathers will drift into another relationship, often fathering another child with hopes of redeeming his role as a parent and partner. Still, these young men try, as best they can, to stay connected to all their children. In fact, many fathers do maintain weekly or monthly contact with their children.

You might think that after several failed relationships and disappointing experiences of parenting, these men would choose to stop being fathers. But this is often not the case. Why? One reason is that inner-city men want to be fathers. They "find children immensely attractive, and . . . eagerly many embrace new opportunities to father . . ."[8] These men want to prove that they can be good fathers. A good father is self-supporting, contributes to the economy of the household, and may serve as a negative example of what the child ought not to do, a life path to be avoided.

It may come as a surprise to some readers to learn that these men embrace a unique version of the new father model. For the past few decades, a new model of fathering has taken form in the working and middle classes that combines the traditional role of a breadwinner with the expectation of being an engaged, loving father. The new father is expected to spend quality time with his children and to form solid emotional and social bonds that display nurturing and tender behavior. Inner-city men have embraced the new father idea, with one significant twist: they minimize the breadwinner role while emphasizing the "softer" or more "feminine" side of fathering. Marginalizing the breadwinner role is understandable given the high levels of unemployment among poor young men, the low-wage jobs that are available, and the high rates of incarceration. They simply cannot fulfill this role. However, they can be good fathers by contributing what they can financially, but mostly by their emotionally supportive and loving role. This is a remarkable gender reversal that is perhaps unexpected and often goes unnoticed by researchers and public commentators. Women are expected to take on the breadwinner role—to be the providers and protectors of their children; men are embracing something of the more traditional roles of women, taking on the "softer relational aspects" of parenting. Being a good father means showing love, spending quality time with his children, and sustaining and deepening the father/child bond with the aim of becoming friends.

If the dreams of the poor for economic independence, companionate intimacies, marriage, and children are not very different from the working and middle classes, the realities suggest a divided society. For the inner-city poor, living in a world where work and social status opportunities are few, where marriage is less and less a practical reality, parenthood often holds out a realistic dream-filled possibility of achieving a respectable status and an intimacy otherwise out of reach. Parenthood at once provides a rich, potentially stable and deeply fulfilling loving bond, respectable identity, and not least promises a life of moral coherence in an otherwise chaotic and hard-edged environment.

Intimate life in contemporary America is perhaps best captured by underscoring a vital tension. There is no denying the ongoing power of traditions that link romance to heterosexual marriage, monogamy, and family; these traditions continue to be enforced, above all, by the state and the church. But, there is equally no denying that there is looseness to this intimate norm that has allowed a staggering pluralization of American intimate life. Americans today, especially the young, have real intimate choices—to remain single, to live apart together, to cohabit or marry, to parent in or outside of an intimate relationship, to have sex in or outside of love and a committed relationship, to have exclusively online intimacies, and so on. For better or worse, we are making and participating in a new world of relational life.

PART IV

THE CULTURAL POLITICS OF SEX

Chapter Ten
INTO OUR BEDROOMS:
THE STATE TAKES CHARGE

MANY OF US like to think of sex as very personal. And it is personal, in the sense that desire, fantasy, sensual excitation, and most of our sexual behaviors are personal—and very private. But, as soon as we consider the meaning of these desires and fantasies, and the way we express and organize them, we quickly recognize that sex is squarely a social fact. Perhaps even more unsettling for Americans, the reality is that the state routinely interferes with and regulates these very personal desires and behaviors. The state criminalizes certain desires, acts, and identities; it disenfranchises specific practices and the individuals who engage in them; it regulates which sexual selves gain entry into the nation and which are refused; it monitors media representations through authorizing federal agencies to set standards for public talk and images; and with the force of law the state has sanctioned the exclusively heterosexual character of marriage. In short, the state is a powerful social force that constructs and controls our sexual lives.

As a social institution, the state also changes over time. As a nation that lacks the tradition of a powerful central state (by contrast, think of France or Russia), the U.S. government has been reluctant to intervene into private matters. In fact, from the early years of the republic through the later part of the nineteenth century, the state, especially the federal government, played a minimal role in affairs of the body and heart. This changed dramatically in the first half of the twentieth century. A wave of social reformers made the case that developments in the intimate sphere could bring social ruin to the nation. Moral panic led to stepped-up state control over the bodies and sexual lives of its citizens. World War II interrupted the busy work of the vice squads and moral crusaders. After the war, the crusading energy seemed almost spent, but not quite. There was, after all, the campaign against homosexuality, with its new laws, criminal prosecutions, censorship, and job firings. America, however, was changing, and the public was growing weary of moral crusaders. The emergence of new social movements for social justice driven by blacks, women, and gays and lesbians—accompanied by a spirit of sexual liberalization associated with a dynamic youth culture—demanded more personal freedom and tolerance of intimate choices. The state bent to these forces. Sexual desires and behaviors previously criminalized were decriminalized; a wider spectrum of intimate choices were protected or enfranchised; the state stepped back from intimate life, thus giving the individual more latitude to organize his or her own intimate affairs, while also protecting these choices from interference by other citizens. In short, since the 1970s, America has witnessed, broadly speaking, a liberalization of intimate life. The expansion of intimate choice has had one sharp boundary—it was not to threaten the norm and ideal of heterosexual marriage. Moreover, tolerance may have been expanded, but not all choices were tolerated nor were they equally valued. This battle over sexual choice and variation is one of the chief themes of the story of the state and sexuality in the United States.

A RIGHT TO BE SEXUAL?

During the founding years of America, sex laws were aimed at protecting marriage.[1] The state criminalized a wide range of nonmarital forms of sexuality, from rape to adultery and fornication. Moreover, by appealing to the elastic legal category of "lewd and lascivious" behavior, the state aimed to promote a culture of sexual respectability that sought to confine sex to adult behavior of a married couple in the private sphere.

Restricting sex to a private, procreative marital act was a social ideal. In fact, in the first century of the new republic, the state was not especially active in enforcing sex laws. Prostitution and pornography flourished throughout the nineteenth century. Similarly, abortion was reportedly widespread and barely regulated by the state. For example, abortionists advertised and conducted business openly. Even more threatening to a marriage-centered culture was the dramatic rise in divorce toward the close of the nineteenth century. Scholars estimate that by the 1920s one in six marriages ended in divorce. In short, a world of sex outside marriage and a reality of public and commercial sex contradicted the Victorian cultural ideal.

Sensing a crisis in American sexual culture, social reformers turned to the state to enforce a strict Victorian morality. Between 1860 and 1890, forty states enacted antiabortion statutes.[2] Among the various purity groups and moral crusaders seeking to end abortion were medical doctors. A fledgling American Medical Association sought to enhance its power in relation to other medical practitioners by supporting the criminalization of abortion:

> By the end of the century, the physician's campaign to criminalize abortion had succeeded. . . . Congress had outlawed the dissemination of birth control information through the mails; many states restricted the sale or advertising of contraceptive devices. . . . Comstock [a moral crusader for sexual purity] was waging a ceaseless battle to enforce these laws. . . . Large sectors of the medical profession were declaring against artificial methods to limit fertilization. Birth control information had virtually been driven underground.[3]

Similarly, between the 1870s and World War I, antiprostitution legislation was backed by suffragists, purity reformers, and the surging medical community. For example, the American Social Hygiene Association proposed sweeping antiprostitution legislation that would give individual states wide latitude in regulating commercial sex. Such provisions as the "Red Light Abatement Act" gave the government the authority to regulate saloons, dance halls, and bars, as well as the people who owned and managed them. Such laws permitted ordinary citizens to close places suspected of harboring prostitutes. Aggressive, far-reaching antiprostitution laws were promoted in state after state so that "by 1920, ten states had passed laws that enacted these provisions . . . and thirty-two states had laws that enacted at least some of these provisions."[4]

Movements aimed at enforcing a culture organized around marriage and women's moral purity also spearheaded an attack on public sex. For example, the courts and the legislature sought to suppress sexual representations in public life by expanding the category of obscenity: "The American courts heard very few obscenity cases between 1821 and 1870. . . . Only four state legislatures enacted obscenity laws prior to the civil war." However, in 1873 the Congress passed "an act for the suppression of trade in, and circulation of obscene literature and articles of immoral use."[5] By the early twentieth century, virtually every state regulated the public character of sexual material, and this extended to commercial publishers and writers on sex education and birth control. Furthermore, a eugenics movement enlisted the state to promote an aggressive policy of sterilization:

> By 1930 half of the states had enacted compulsory sterilization laws. These laws covered convicted criminals, but also persons considered "feebleminded" or suspected of "sexual immorality." In the first third of the century, approximately 20,000 involuntary sterilizations were performed by order of state law.[6]

By the early twentieth century, birth control, abortion, interracial marriage, prostitution, commercial sex, forced sterilization, and public sexual representations had become the business of the state. The result was *the unprecedented expansion of governmental control over sexuality*.

In the years between the two world wars, the tide slowly began to turn against repressive state control, at least with regard to consensual heterosexual adult behavior. For example, a flourishing birth control movement challenged state repression. In the 1930s and 1940s, birth control clinics cropped up in cities and towns across the country. Restrictive birth control legislation, such as laws prohibiting the shipping and advertising of birth control devices, were repealed. Similarly, by the 1940s sexually provocative images and ideas began to regularly appear in the public realm. Big business had discovered that sex sells, and artists and writers found in sex a powerful theme to explore the character of personal and social life in America. This new sexual openness was, to be sure, met with resolute opposition by a revitalized purity movement championing Victorian ideals of sexual respectability. By the 1950s, a trend toward the retreat of the state from the repressive control of consensual adult heterosexual conduct was evident. Developments in the judicial sphere are both indicative and crucial to these liberalizing trends.

The Model Penal Code of 1962 became the chief guide to legal reform through the 1970s and 1980s. A product of the American Law Institute, sex law was thoroughly recast. At the core of the code was the decriminalization of adult consensual behavior. Its guiding idea was that sex is *a fundamental individual right*. Sex was thought to be so integral to the well-being of the individual that it needed protection from government interference and citizen harassment.

The code became the model for criminal legal reform and, in particular, guided a series of key U.S. Supreme Court decisions. For example, in *Skinner v. Oklahoma* (1942) the Court struck down the practice of sterilizing individuals convicted of a wide range of nonsexual crimes. Subsequent Court decisions decriminalized fornication and declared unconstitutional laws that banned or limited birth control practices, such as the use of contraceptives. In *Griswold v. Connecticut* (1965), the Supreme Court declared unconstitutional a state law that criminalized the use of contraceptives by married couples—thereby implicitly recognizing the legitimacy of nonprocreative sex. The Court appealed to a zone of privacy in marriage that was said to be established in the U.S. Constitution. In *Eisenstadt v. Baird* (1972), the Court extended this protection to unmarried couples. Nowhere has the retreat of the state from intimate life been more apparent than in the sphere of the heterosexual family. One scholar has argued that "over the past twenty-five years, family law has become increasingly privatized. In virtually all doctrinal areas, private norm creation and private decision making have supplanted state-imposed rules and structures for governing family-related behavior."[7] In short, a clear trend in court rulings has defined sex as a sphere of personal expression or a zone of individual choice, which, like religion or occupation, merits state protection.

The legal safeguarding of consensual adult heterosexual behavior in private was paralleled by the liberalization of laws regulating public sex speech. In *Roth v. United States* (1957), the Supreme Court ruled that only sex speech that appeals to prurient interests is obscene. Subsequent cases further weakened obscenity laws. In *Memoirs of Women of Pleasure v. Massachusetts* (1966), the Court narrowed obscenity to material "utterly without redeeming social importance." In *Miller v. California* (1973), the Court further liberalized public sex speech by appealing to "community standards" as the criteria to determine obscenity. By the mid-1970s there were few legal restrictions placed on sexual representations in public.

By strengthening a zone of privacy that included sex, and by expanding protections for public sex speech, the postwar state enlarged the sphere of sexual autonomy for heterosexual adults. This change was, at least in the immediate postwar period, less a response to pressures from social movements (excepting laws around birth control) than a return to long-standing American traditions championing minimal state regulation of consensual adult intimate behavior.

To illustrate these shifts in state regulation of sexuality in the United States, let us consider three areas: women's sexuality, homosexuality, and interracial sex.

WOMEN'S SEXUALITY

In mid-nineteenth-century America, it was common, at least among the white middle class, to view women as not especially bothered by sexual desire. Women were viewed as emotional, maternal, and nurturing, whereas carnal desire was thought to be more characteristic of men. Women were expected to be sexual but mostly it was a marital duty and ultimately a necessary condition for creating a family. Curiously, though, by actively embracing this view of women as moral-spiritual beings, women could actually enhance their power. It gave them a basis to refuse sex, and at a time lacking modern birth control, this could be literally lifesaving; it also allowed women to exercise moral authority in the family and beyond.

As more white middle-class women moved out of the household into the workplace in the twentieth century, following many nonwhite, immigrant, and blue-collar women, they began to feel more independent. Women were now claiming to have their own sexual needs and desires. The big change occurred after World War II. During the war, women had learned to live on their own and were not about to surrender their newfound sense of individual autonomy. By the 1960s, popular books like *Sex and the Single Woman*, magazines like *Cosmopolitan*, and feminists like Betty Friedan were championing women's social and sexual autonomy, sending shock waves through masculinist culture.

These women fueled the women's movement; at its core was the belief in women's entitlement to self-fulfillment in both personal and public matters. Women were no longer going to surrender their own desires and ambitions for the sake of their fathers, brothers, boyfriends, or husbands. Almost immediately, they pressured the state to extend first-class civil and political rights to all adult women; they also pressed the general public to recognize women as sexual beings aspiring to the same sexual rights as men. The state gradually and reluctantly accommodated with a wave of laws that enhanced women's (hetero) sexual autonomy, however unevenly and incompletely.

On the one hand, legislation and court decisions gave women more control over their own bodies. Consider, for example, the issue of abortion. Abortion was illegal through the middle decades of the twentieth century. Specifically, prior to *Roe v. Wade* (1973), abortion was illegal in two-thirds of the states, except in cases where it was necessary to save the life of the mother. Still, women had abortions. They sought illegal, back-alley abortions, often at great personal risk. It is estimated that in the years immediately preceding 1973, more than one million women had illegal abortions each year! Between one thousand and five thousand women may have died from illegal abortions.

By denying women the right to an abortion, the state was assuming control over their sexuality. In effect, every act of coitus risked pregnancy and the fateful choice of becoming a mother (perhaps out of wedlock) or breaking the law to have a life-risking abortion. For many women, their growing social and economic independence was contradicted by their lack of control over their sexuality. Clearly, many women felt that this condition was unfair and dangerous. In this context, the women's movement advocated the legalization of abortion as part of an agenda promoting women's sexual rights. While the government distanced itself from a broader feminist agenda, in *Roe v. Wade* (1973) women's right to privacy was recognized as encompassing "a woman's decision whether or not to terminate her pregnancy."

On the other hand, the women's movement pressured the state to enact new laws or strengthen existing laws to protect them from men's harassment and worse. For adult men, sexual autonomy meant reducing state regulation: for example, making divorce easier or permitting the public circulation of sexual images. For women, however, the meaning of sexual autonomy was a little different. For women who chose to be wives, a world of easy divorce was an economic threat. If women were expected to sacrifice careers for the sake of their family, they needed assurance that the state would protect them if their marriage ended. Similarly, it is mostly women, not men, who live with the danger of sexual violence. According to the National Crime Victimization Surveys, women are ten times more likely than men to be victims of sexual assault. Roughly one in five college-age women report being forced to have sexual intercourse. In 2000, the FBI reports recorded more than ninety-five thousand rapes in the United States. Clearly, sex carries greater risks of bodily danger for women than for men. The women's movement responded to a reality of sexual violence by advocating state legislation that would protect them.

Throughout most of the past two centuries the state did not adequately protect women from sexual assault and violence. Through the early twentieth century, rape laws were designed to limit criminalization and prosecution. For example, most states required that a woman had to demonstrate physical resistance to prosecute rape. Moreover, low age of consent laws (typically ten to twelve years of age in most states) and laws that did not include marital rape limited criminalization. The women's movement challenged and changed this legal situation. It raised awareness of the pervasive reality of rape and sexual violence and put pressure on the state and the criminal justice system to prosecute rape. In 1975, marital rape was recognized as a crime and by 1993 it was the law of the land; in the 1980s, date or "acquaintance" rape was written into law. In short, from the 1970s on, there was an unprecedented expansion of law and social policies criminalizing sexual violence and workplace harassment.

To be sure, these legal reforms were often inadequate as vehicles to create gender equality. For example, while the state expanded reproductive rights through the courts and support of family planning services, legislation such as the Hyde Amendment (1977), which cut off federal funds for abortion and required parental notification, restricted the actual exercise of this newly won right. Indeed, the state effectively annexed abortion rights to an agenda of population control and public health, which gave to governmental agencies and the medical establishment enhanced power over women. Nevertheless, the effect of these laws was to transfer considerable control over women's sexuality from the state to the individual. As the scholar Rosiland Petchesky observed, despite state opposition to a far-reaching feminist agenda of expanding women's sexual autonomy, *Roe v. Wade* "established the legality and legitimacy of abortion, and it did so within a normative framework that emphasized women's health . . . rather than abstract moralism or 'fetal rights.' In this sense, it was progressive, and its immediate impact was to expand women's access to abortion significantly."[8]

HOMOSEXUALITY: THE BATTLE FOR RIGHTS

The chief focus of the women's movement was initially to enact laws and legislation to protect women's bodily and sexual autonomy. By contrast, the early focus of the gay and lesbian movement was on removing the layers of repressive law and governmental policy that accumulated in the twentieth century.

Prior to the 1950s, few laws and scarcely any legislation directly addressed homosexuality. The very term *homosexual* or terms like *invert* and *Urning* that circulated in Europe to refer to homosexuality were absent from American sex law through the nineteenth century. From the founding years of America through the nineteenth century, homosexual behavior was legally classified under the category of sodomy, a criminal offense that included a wide spectrum of nonprocreative, nonmarital sexual acts.

The legal regulation of homosexuality changed in the twentieth century. As the public came to think of the "homosexual" as a deviant, abnormal type of person, the state responded with an aggressive strategy of suppression. From roughly the 1930s through the mid-1960s, the government sought to control the homosexual by using laws that did not directly address homosexuality: for example, statutes that pertained to loitering, child molestation, sex offender law, prostitution, public lewdness, disorderly conduct, indecent exposure, cross-dressing, and obscenity. Moreover, until the 1970s, laws at the local, state, and federal levels provided no protection to homosexuals or lesbians from citizen, state, and institutional discrimination. As a consequence, homosexuals were routinely arrested; their names, home addresses, and places of employment were printed in newspapers; they were discharged from the military and civil service, denied immigration or citizenship, and harassed in bars and the streets; and their businesses were closed and publications censored.

The legal scholar William Eskridge summarizes the legal status of the homosexual in 1961:

> The homosexual in 1961 was smothered by law. She or he risked arrest . . . for dancing with someone of the same sex, cross dressing, propositioning another adult homosexual, possessing a homophile publication, writing about homosexuality without disapproval, displaying pictures of two people of the same sex in intimate positions, operating a lesbian or gay bar, or actually having oral or anal sex with another adult homosexual. . . . Misdemeanor arrests for sex related vagrancy or disorderly conduct offences meant that the homosexual might have her or his name published in the local newspaper, would probably lose her or his job. . . . If the homosexual were not a citizen, she or he would likely be deported. If the homosexual were a professional . . . she or he would lose the certification needed to practice that profession. If the charged homosexual were a member of the armed forces, she or he might be court-martialed and would likely be dishonorably discharged and lose all veterans benefits. . . . [Eskridge concludes:] This new legal regime represented society's coercive effort to normalize human relationships around "heterosexuality."[9]

The postwar years witnessed the rise of a gay and lesbian movement that challenged state discrimination. From the Mattachine Society and the Daughters of Bilitis in the 1950s to gay liberationism and lesbian feminism in the early 1970s, the gay and lesbian movement challenged the government's repression of homosexuality. In a context moreover of general social and legal liberalization, the state gradually, if incompletely, retreated from its antigay politics. In the course of the past three decades, broadly framed laws that were used to suppress gays and lesbians were either considerably narrowed or repealed. Furthermore, new legislation decriminalized homosexuality and extended positive rights to gays and lesbians, thereby acknowledging their status as citizens. Most of this change was brought about because of the national mobilization of a gay and lesbian movement.

From the late 1950s through the early 1970s, the gay and lesbian movement successfully challenged the constitutionality of using vagrancy, loitering, and cross-dressing laws to criminalize homosexuals. Appealing to constitutional principles, such as due process or the freedom of speech and association, municipalities were taken to court to halt bar raids and unnecessary search and seizure and to bring an end to government actions that shut down businesses catering to gays. For example, in the course of the 1970s, the state supreme court and legislature in California deregulated consensual same-sex adult behavior by considerably narrowing its laws applying to public decency, lewdness, vagrancy, and cross-dressing. Similarly, obscenity laws that were used to censor gay public speech were successfully restricted to a degree that for all practical purposes ended censorship of the gay press.

By the mid-1970s, an assertive gay and lesbian movement challenged laws that explicitly criminalized homosexuality. In the aftermath of the *Griswold*, *Eisenstadt*, and *Stanley* U.S. Supreme Court decisions, gay and lesbian activists argued that acknowledging the fundamental role of sexuality for personal well-being, which was at the heart of cases that extended privacy rights to adult private consensual sex, should include homosexuality. Such arguments underpinned the repeal of state sodomy laws. By 1983, twenty-five states had decriminalized consensual sodomy, while eleven states reduced sodomy to a misdemeanor. In the 1990s, many states and cities banned anti-gay discrimination in state employment. While Congress has continued to block federal civil rights legislation that would include sexual orientation, the Civil Service Commission and ultimately an Executive Order by President Clinton ended legal job discrimination in all federal agencies.

Simultaneously, the gay movement has sought positive liberties. The aim of so-called gay and lesbian rights ordinances is to get the state to recognize lesbians and gay men as deserving state protection from job and housing discrimination. This legislation acknowledges the right of lesbians and gay men to pursue job and housing opportunities free of acts of prejudice. While only forty communities passed such laws through the 1970s, by 2000 the number swelled to more than three hundred. Moreover, gay rights law is no longer confined to urban centers but has been enacted in small towns and suburban communities—not only in the Northeast and West but also in the South, Midwest, and Northwest. The wave of domestic partnership law beginning in the mid-1990s is indicative of successful efforts at legal normalization. By the late 1990s, 421 cities and states and more than 3,500 businesses or institutions of higher education offered some form of domestic partner benefit.

Eskridge nicely summarizes this period of legal liberalization as follows:

The gay rights movement had won many successes by 1981—
judicial nullification or legislative repeal of laws criminalizing
consensual sodomy in most jurisdictions, of almost all state
criminal laws targeting same-sex intimacy, and municipal cross-
dressing ordinances, of the immigration and citizenship exclusions,
of all censorship laws targeting same-sex eroticism, of almost all
laws or regulations prohibiting bars from becoming congregating
places for gay people, and of exclusions of gay people from public
employment in most jurisdictions. . . . Since 1981 an increasing
number of states and cities have adopted laws affirmatively protecting gay people against private discrimination and violence,
recognizing gay families as domestic partnerships, and allowing
second-parent adoptions by a party of a same sex partner.[10]

This wave of legal reform has made possible a "post-closeted
regime where openly gay people could participate in the public
culture."[11]

The legal integration of lesbian and gay Americans has not
been an unqualified story of success, to say the least. Many cities, counties, and states lack laws that protect gay people from
housing and job discrimination. Federal civil rights statutes still
do not include sexual orientation. Moreover, antigay actions and
movements continue to threaten, sometimes successfully, to repeal affirmative gay law. Governmental policies such as "Don't
Ask, Don't Tell" (1994) and the Defense of Marriage Act (1996)
and judicial decisions like *Bowers v. Hartwick* (1986) and *The Boy
Scouts of America and Monmouth Council, et al. v. James Dale* (2000)
underscore America's continued resistance to gay integration. In
general, the gay and lesbian movement has been successful in re-
pealing laws that discriminate and criminalize homosexuality, but
when it comes to full gay equality, state opposition has stiffened.

Consider the issue of gay marriage. The institution of marriage in the United States is invested with national significance. Whether it is the legal restriction of marriage to heterosexuals, the state privileging of heterosexual marriage over all other forms of intimate solidarity, or the idealization of marriage in popular culture and commerce, the ideal national citizen is married. America may be more tolerant today of nonmarital choices, such as being single or cohabiting, but these choices occupy a lesser status than marriage. For this reason, the struggle to extend marital rights to gay men and lesbians is as much about symbolic struggles to be recognized as first-class citizens as about the politics of legal equality.

The issue of the state recognition of gay and lesbian relationships has bounced around the courts for some time. However, in the past decade or so as lesbians and gay men were forming stable, long-term families, and as AIDS made "intimate rights" an urgent health-care issue, the gay movement made state recognition of gay and lesbian relationships a political priority. While some individuals in the gay and lesbian community defend domestic partnership legislation as part of an agenda that aims to end the norm of marriage, for perhaps most lesbians and gay men it is a compromise of their aspiration to achieve equal rights. Gay marriage became a national issue after the Hawaii state supreme court ruled in *Baehr v. Lewin* (1993) that precluding gays and lesbians from marriage was a form of gender discrimination. However, even before the courts could resolve the issue, the Hawaiian legislature in 1994 restricted marriage to heterosexuality. Other states quickly followed suit and in 1996 the U.S. Congress passed, with the overwhelming support of the Democrats and the president, the Defense of Marriage

Act, which reaffirmed a national ideal that restricts marriage to heterosexuality. The recent recognition of the right of gay and lesbian marriage in Minnesota, New Jersey, Hawaii, Illinois, and New Mexico suggests that this issue will be at the center of American sexual politics for some time.

INTERRACIAL MARRIAGE:
THE POLITICS OF APARTHEID

From colonial times through the mid-twentieth century, there were laws in most states against interracial marriage. Interracial sex was a crime punishable by public whipping, fines, or imprisonment. The aim of laws against interracial sex and marriage was clear: to maintain racial separation and white supremacy.

The first antimiscegenation law was passed in Maryland in 1661. In the course of the 1700s, as black slaves replaced indentured white laborers, these laws rapidly spread in the South. They were a response to the growing closeness between blacks and poor whites who often worked side by side. For whites, the relative scarcity of white women drove cross-racial intimacies. For blacks, marrying across the color line opened the door to white privilege. However, if whites were allowed to marry blacks and raise a family, how could blacks be treated as subhuman, as mere chattel? Cross-racial marriage was seen as a threat to white privilege, which rested on white purity and racial separation. Antimiscegenation laws were the response.[12]

By the early 1700s, southern whites were forced to address the problem of the status of mixed-race offspring: mulattos. Were they to be treated as white or black, or should such children assume a new hybrid status? To the extent that some mulattos could pass as white, mixed-race children were seen as even more of a threat to the racial order than interracial marriage. These mixed-race children threatened to blur the boundaries between the races, thereby undermining a hierarchical racial order. States responded to this danger by adopting the "one drop rule," which classified as "black" anyone who had any black or African ancestry. To be legally classified as black meant being denied citizenship, which was reserved exclusively for whites through the eighteenth century.

In the course of the nineteenth century, antimiscegenation laws spread quickly from the South to the West and from targeting blacks to including other racial groups, in particular Asians. By the end of the century, some thirty-eight states prohibited Chinese, Japanese, Filipinos, Hawaiians, Hindus, and Native Americans from marrying whites. This racial politics was a response to the massive immigration of Asians to the American West beginning in the mid-1800s. Asian immigrants were classified as nonwhite and therefore excluded from citizenship. Despite the gradual inclusion of blacks into the circle of American citizenship after the Civil War, Asians, especially Chinese, were explicitly excluded. The Chinese Exclusion Act of 1882 outright banned all Chinese immigration. In popular culture, Chinese immigrants were seen as promiscuous, immoral, inferior, and a danger to young and vulnerable white women. This law remained in effect until 1952, when racial restrictions were removed from immigration law.

Despite some civil rights gains by blacks at the turn of the century, their status as the inferior other to whites was maintained by antimiscegenation laws through the early decades of the twentieth century. In fact, it seemed that every step toward equality was accompanied by a new aggressiveness in enforcing racial separation and inequality. During the twentieth century, however, the North had also become a major battleground of racial politics. As part of Reconstruction, many blacks migrated from the South to northeastern cities looking for work and expanded freedom. The intermingling of the races, intensified by unprecedented immigration, was an inevitable part of city life.

This period witnessed two odious strategies of race politics. First, a eugenics movement sought to maintain racial white purity and supremacy by prohibiting interracial sex and, ominously, by preventing the reproduction of "inferior" races through sterilization. Between 1907 and 1931, twenty-seven states passed laws requiring sterilization, most of which were subsequently ruled to be unconstitutional. Second, the race threat saw the rise of white vigilante groups, such as the Ku Klux Klan, and a wave of racially motivated lynchings.

The first half of the twentieth century was indeed a time of heightened anxiety about America's future. World War I brought a new world threat: Russian communism. The rapid urbanization of the American social landscape created exaggerated concerns about the vulnerability of single women. Without kin and neighbors to supervise and protect young single women, and in an urban milieu of strangers and predators, an almost hysterical fear of the spread of sexual immorality and looseness instigated a sense of public panic. The race fear was part of this moral panic. The response, predictably, were the vice squads and expanded state and municipal efforts to control sexuality through new laws and the enforcement of old laws, sterilization, the enforcement of antimiscegenation, and racial violence in the service of sexual and racial purity.

In the aftermath of two world wars America was changing—in some ways, dramatically. After fighting and losing their sons, fathers, and brothers in the war, blacks were in no mood to go along with their inferior social status. During the 1950s and 1960s, a national civil rights movement took shape that aimed at establishing the full legal and social equality of black Americans. In 1967, after the state mandated the desegregation of public schools, and after the Civil Rights Act of 1964, the Supreme Court in *Loving v. Virginia* ruled that antimiscegenation laws were unconstitutional. In effect, the Court recognized an adult person's right of sexual choice, including the right to marry regardless of the race of the partner.

The end of a state-enforced system of racial separation did not, in fact, mean the end of racial segregation in intimate life. The individual right to sexual and marital choice did not translate into a reality of interracial intimacy. Black-white intimacy remains restricted to a very small segment of Americans. The vast majority of black men and women are marrying within their race.

According to a 2010 Pew Research Center report, 15.1 percent of all marriages are interracial. Interestingly, whites (9.4 percent) are the least likely to intermarry, then blacks (17.1 percent); Hispanics (25.7 percent) and Asians (27.7 percent) are by far the most open to interracial marriage, but tellingly they are by and large marrying white Americans. This pattern is repeated among newlyweds. In 2008, just 9 percent of whites and 16 percent of blacks, compared with 26 percent of Hispanics and 31 percent of Asians married someone of a different race or ethnicity. If we look further at the data, we find that among blacks it is primarily black men (27 percent), not black women (9 percent), who are marrying outside their race.

The 2012 U.S. Census Bureau figures indicate that while roughly 10 percent of black men are in interracial marriages, the number for black women is just over 4 percent. So, despite overwhelming evidence that in the past few decades the rates of interracial marriage are steadily rising, blacks, especially black women, give truth to the claim that in American intimate life the reality of racial segregation and division remains all too alive.

Chapter Eleven
POPULAR CULTURE INTRODUCES THE NEW NORMAL CITIZEN: THE GAY AMERICAN

WE HAVE BECOME accustomed to thinking of the 1960s and 1970s in the United States and in parts of Europe as a period that experienced a sexual revolution. Without doubt, it was a time of turbulence and change. Just consider the following: birth control pills, rock 'n' roll, *Playboy*, feminism, gay liberation, *The Joy of Sex*, hippies, "make love, not war." For many of you reading this book, these changes happened to your parents, and it may seem a stretch to think of them as sexual rebels! After all, they are more than likely married, have raised a family, and have a sex life that seems unremarkably private. More than likely, you will follow a somewhat similar path. True, you might have more premarital sex and romances, and experiment more with oral and perhaps anal sex, and you may cohabit longer or get married later than your parents did, but on the whole it is the continuity between your parents and you that is perhaps striking. So, has there really been a sexual revolution in America? Here we arrive at a paradox. There have been some dramatic changes but *for most of us the core of American sexual culture, heterosexual romance and marriage and the ideal of monogamy and family making, have remained remarkably stable.*

What, then, has changed in the past few decades? I would say that there have been at least two significant changes in American sexual-intimate life.

First, although Americans continue to marry, the culture of heterosexual intimacy has changed considerably in the course of the twentieth century. The form of intimacy may not have changed much (coupledom, romantic love, marriage, nuclear families), but the inner dynamics (which are not necessarily visible) of heterosexual intimacy have changed. I will address changes in the meaning and practice *inside heterosexuality* in the following chapter.

In this chapter, I focus on a second major change in American intimate life: the emergence of a popular, mass-mediated culture as a core feature of American life. Of course, there was popular music, dance, movies, and magazines prior to the 1950s. However, the scale and impact of popular culture has changed dramatically since the end of World War II. Among the key developments have been television, especially cable television in recent years, the world of DVDs, cinema complexes, the rise and omnipresence of the Internet and the cyber world, and the formation of youth cultures that both produce and consume popular culture. In a way that was not true for your parents, and most definitely not true for your grandparents, Americans today live in a world saturated by pop culture. For many of us today, it is pop culture 24/7, something unimaginable just fifty years ago.

If religion formed a central cultural background and setting of individual and social life in the nineteenth and early twentieth centuries, today it is popular culture. Pop stars and celebrities, pop art and design, and a pop vernacular have become the very grammar of art, advertising, and the source of models of self, family, and lifestyle. Pop culture is the one product on the global market that continues to be stamped "made in America."

Pop culture is among the most important social forces that shape and organize our sexual-intimate lives. Unlike government or churches, pop culture is not remote from our daily lives, is not something we are exposed to only on specific days or hours or occasions; it is an integral part of our daily life, everyday and throughout our lives. Whether we are watching TV or a DVD in the evening, reading a magazine as we wait in a doctor's office, or listening to music in a car or on our iPod as we shop or jog, we live and breathe pop culture in such a close, intimate way that we are hardly aware of its pervasiveness. Pop culture constructs a world of sexual meanings, furnishes sexual norms, projects gendered sexual ideals, and subtly and not so subtly instructs us about with whom to have sex, at what point in our lives, and what it is supposed to mean. There is no understanding American intimate culture without placing popular culture at its center. In this chapter, we will consider the way homo- and heterosexualities and men's and women's sexualities have been constructed in American pop culture.

HOMOS AND HETEROS IN HOLLYWOOD

By the 1970s, Hollywood, like the rest of America, had no choice but to respond to the new visibility and assertiveness of gays and lesbians.[1] After World War II, and after having served the country, some Americans decided they were no longer going to keep quiet about their homosexuality. In the major cities of America, these individuals began to meet in bars, clubs, and private homes; they gradually resolved to challenge the prejudices, laws, and institutions that had forced them into lives of quiet desperation or great risk. By the 1970s, a noisy, in-your-face army of militant lesbians and gay men were publicly announcing that they were queer and proud and no longer resigned to living in the shadows.

Mainstream films of the 1970s and 1980s greeted gay and lesbian liberationists with a resounding and unambiguous declaration of war. The so-called new homosexual, self-styled as "gay" and "lesbian," was met with an unending stream of polluting, demeaning, and pathologizing images. The homosexual was represented as a serious threat to America's children, families, moral values, and indeed its national security. If the homosexual could no longer be silenced or confined to a shadowy, closeted world, this figure could at least be portrayed as the *polluted other to the pure heterosexual*.

Consider some of the films in the 1970s and 1980s that featured gay characters. In *Sudden Impact* (1983), the fourth of the "Dirty Harry" films, Harry (Clint Eastwood) is a police detective who wages war against a corrupt world. Harry believes that crime, civic rudeness, and immorality are ruining America. He dedicates himself to purifying America—by any means necessary.

Harry is investigating a series of murders. The perpetrator is Jennifer (Sandra Locke), whose killing spree is revenge for her and her sister's rape. One of the rapists is Ray—a white lesbian in her twenties.

Reflecting the new social reality of gay and lesbian visibility in the late 1970s, Ray is part of the public world but, as we will see, she is the antithesis of the respectable heterosexual American.

We first meet Ray in a bar. She is the only woman. Flagging the lesbian's suspect moral character, the bar is crowded with marginal and deviant social types and has the feel of a space of danger and criminality. Ray has short hair, wears blue jeans and a jean jacket with the sleeves cut off. She smokes, curses, and talks in a hyperaggressive masculine style. Ray is the stereotypical gender-inverted, mannish woman who, it turns out, is sociopathic and violent. As an accomplice to the rape, Ray plans to kill Jennifer. However, Ray is killed first. The presentation of the lesbian as a psychopathic killer who is murdered by her intended victim perhaps expressed America's unconscious fear of the homosexual's new public assertiveness and a desire to expel her from civic life.

Looking for Mr. Goodbar (1977) depicts a world shaped by the sexual and gender liberationist ideas of the 1960s. Theresa (Diane Keaton) grew up in a repressed Irish Catholic family in Brooklyn. She moves to Manhattan to find herself. Theresa's journey of self-exploration involves sexual adventurism.

In the course of her sexual coming-of-age story, we encounter homosexuals. In one scene, Theresa finds herself in a gay bar. Men are dancing and laughing. The bar scene focuses on two men. Gary (Tom Berenger), a muscular, handsome man in his twenties, dressed in 1970s clone-style jean pants, T-shirt, and jean jacket, approaches a much older, wealthy-looking man. They kiss in a way suggesting intimacy.

The two men reappear in a New Year's Eve scene. They are celebrating in Times Square. The older man is dressed as a clown, and Gary is in drag. A fight breaks out and the two men run to escape the violence and exchange the following dialogue:

OLDER MAN: Did they hurt you?

GARY: No, don't ever ask me to wear this crap again. I'm no nellie. You ought to know that. Christ, look at us. We're a couple of freaks.

OLDER MAN [crying hysterically]: I'm sorry.

GARY: I've had it with you . . . fancy shirts, shoes. . . .

OLDER MAN [desperately holding Gary]: Please don't go. [Gary hits him.]

OLDER MAN: Please don't go. . . . I'll wait for you at the apartment. You need some money?

GARY: You're the nellie, not me. I'm a pitcher not a catcher, and don't you ever forget that.

In this scene, the homosexual relationship is portrayed in highly stigmatizing ways. In contrast to an assumed heterosexual ideal of a love-based companionate intimacy, the homosexual relationship is presented as an exploitative and corrupt exchange of youthful beauty for material comfort. The older man is wealthy, closeted, and effeminate; Gary is an ex-con who trades on his masculine sexual attractiveness for material comfort. Gary's true sexual identity, however, is unclear.

Gary's status is clarified in the final scene. Theresa and Gary meet for the first time in a bar. They go to her apartment. Gary is unable to fuck. He is upset. "In my neighborhood if you didn't fight you were a fruit. In prison if you didn't fight you spread ass." Gary again tries to fuck but cannot. Theresa asks: "What are you trying to prove?" Gary says: "You think I'm some kind of flaming faggot." He then rapes her, but he can only fuck her in the ass. Humiliated by the implicit acknowledgment of his homosexuality, Gary stabs Theresa repeatedly.

If the older man is a pathetic and pathological figure who must purchase the affections of young, handsome men, Gary is a psychopath. Filled with rage and self-hatred, he murders to cleanse himself of his homosexuality. Both figures represent social threats to the American public. The older homosexual has the power to seduce and corrupt innocent vulnerable youth; the younger man presents a mortal danger.

In films such as these, and there were dozens at the time, the nation is imagined as divided into a heterosexual majority and a homosexual minority. This is a moral division: the heterosexual signifies a pure and good human status in contrast to the impure and dangerous homosexual. The link between homosexual pollution and social repression is established through the notion of moral contagion. Heterosexual exposure to homosexuals threatens seduction and corruption. Accordingly, homosexuals must be excluded from the public world of visible, open communication by means of repressive strategies, such as censorship, civic disenfranchisement, and sequestration. In short, these films project a social world in which heterosexual privilege is reinforced by purifying the heterosexual while vilifying and symbolically positioning the homosexual outside of normal, respectable American civic life.

Beginning in the early 1990s, the status of gays and lesbians changed dramatically. Despite antigay mobilization by a Christian Right, enhanced visibility seemed to promise a more tolerant America. Hollywood both reflected and promoted this change. It fashioned a new representation: the normal gay as the counterpart to the normal heterosexual. The normal gay and lesbian are presented as fully human or the psychological and moral equal of the heterosexual. Hollywood seems to be saying that the homosexual figure should be tolerated as a visible, legitimate part of the institutions of the public world. She and he can—or should—be permitted to work, form relationships, hold office, and mix freely with heterosexuals.

However, Hollywood was careful to limit the scope of tolerance. Lesbian and gay citizens are to be tolerated but only if they are "normal." The normal lesbian or gay man is gender conventional, links sex to intimacy and love, defends family and Protestant work values, and displays national pride. Hollywood has created a division between the good and bad gay citizen. Only the former was to be tolerated; importantly, *the normal gay leaves in place the normative ideal of heterosexual marriage.*

The big hit comedy, *In and Out* (1997) tells the story of the coming out of Howard (Kevin Kline). As he is unintentionally "outed" by a former student turned actor, Cameron Drake (Matt Dillon), Howard's family and friends and the small mid-American community in which he lives are forced to deal with the issue of homosexuality. Initially in denial, Howard gradually acknowledges and accepts that he is gay.

Coming out is not, however, the chief story of the film. Howard's coming out is almost painless. For example, after Cameron's outing of Howard, his parents are immediately comforting. "Howard, we want you to know that we love you—gay [or] straight. It's not a bad thing." Another coming-out scene similarly conveys its anticlimactic character. As the outing of Howard becomes national news, a TV reporter, Peter Malloy (Tom Selleck), is assigned to cover the story. Peter matter of factly tells Howard that he, too, is gay. Howard asks Peter how others have reacted to his coming out.

PETER: I came out to everyone, my folks, my boss, my dog. One day I snapped. I couldn't take lying to the people I love.

HOWARD: What happened?

PETER: My mom cried for exactly ten seconds. My boss said, who cares? My dad said, "But you're so tall."

By portraying the social response to both Howard's and Peter's coming out as accepting and quite ordinary, the film is saying that it is not only gay people who have normalized a gay identity (for example, Peter) but also much of straight America.

In this regard, it is not coincidental that the movie takes place in a small town in the Midwest (Greenleaf, Indiana). If the film is, indeed, announcing America's growing acceptance of the normal status of being gay, where else should it take place than in the nation's heartland? Greenleaf is pure Americana—white-picket-fenced homes, a gemeinschaft-like community, marriages that are permanent, men who work as farmers (Howard's father), and women who are housewives and mothers (Howard's mother). If Greenleaf citizens can accept the gay citizen, the film seems to be saying, all Americans can and should.

Howard comes out on the day of his wedding, but it is anticlimactic because his new sexual identity has already been accepted by himself and his parents. The most dramatic scene is graduation day at the high school. Howard has been fired by the principal and was not expected to attend. Encouraged by his father, Howard shows up just in time to hear Cameron Drake—who returns to his hometown to set things right—ridiculing the homophobia of the school administration. Drake asks the principal why Howard is no longer a teacher.

PRINCIPAL: The community felt that it was a question of influence. It's all right to be this way at home, but Mr. Brackett is a teacher.

DRAKE: So you're thinking about the students. What you're saying is that because Mr. Brackett is gay he's going to send out some kind of gay microwaves to make everyone else gay. Well, kids, you've had Mr. Brackett, is that the way it worked?

Mocking the belief in the contagious polluted status of homosexuality, a student says: "I had Mr. Brackett and I must be gay." After other students similarly ridicule this homophobic logic, the principal declares that the community has made its decision. At that point, Howard's father declares: "I'm his father and I'm gay." Howard's mother says: "I'm his mother and I'm a lesbian." Soon the entire community joins in what I would describe as a public ritual of gay normalization. Greenleaf citizens are not only ridiculing the notion of homosexual contamination, they are signaling the end of the polluted status of the homosexual. By publicly identifying with Howard, they are declaring that the gay individual is a normal human being, one of their own.

The film's message of tolerance of the normal gay citizen does not, however, challenge the norm of heterosexuality. The social world of Greenleaf is overwhelmingly heterosexual. Aside from Howard, all Greenleaf citizens are assumed to be heterosexual, and most are coupled or married. Furthermore, the film celebrates the institutions of heterosexual marriage and family. Howard's parents' marriage is portrayed in ideal and nostalgic terms. They are small-town folks who grew up and still live in Greenleaf; the father works as a farmer, and the mother is a housewife; they are unconditionally loving and supportive of Howard; and they are so happily married that they celebrate their fiftieth wedding anniversary with renewed wedding vows. In short, although the film champions the homosexual as normal, America—as symbolized by Greenleaf—is a nation where almost all of its citizens are heterosexual, and the institutions that sustain heterosexual dominance such as binary gender roles, weddings, marriage, and the nuclear family remain unchallenged.

Since the 1990s, Hollywood films have revealed a cultural shift: the polluted homosexual is gradually being replaced by images of the normal gay and lesbian citizen. The status of "normality" makes possible an open, integrated life, but it also restricts tolerance to individuals who display the traits or behaviors that are associated with normality. Only gays who are gender conventional and connect sex to romantic, monogamous, marital, and family values are considered "normal." Individuals who do not conform to this norm of sexual normality are considered deviant. Moreover, the very traits and behaviors that have the status of "normal" (for example, gender binary) reinforce a *narrow ideal of heterosexuality*: gender conventional, married, and family oriented. The normal gay helps create a social division not only between the good and bad gay but also between the good and bad heterosexual American.

To the extent that the homosexual acquires the status of normality, social control shifts its focus somewhat from homosexuality per se to the normal, good sexual citizen. *In other words, in films that legitimate the normal gay and lesbian American, the bad sexual citizen becomes the focus of pollution and social control.* Who are the bad sexual citizens? Any individual, whether homo- or heterosexual, who is gender different, does not always link sex to intimacy or a long-term relationship, and enjoys sex for different reasons and with multiple sex partners.

Ironically, then, in films that promote gay normalization, there is a tightening of heterosexual regulation or a lessening of tolerance for heterosexuals. Heterosexual practices that deviate from a narrow romantic-companionate-marital-family norm are now viewed as somewhat deviant, inferior, dangerous, and less acceptable. Ironically, the cultural normalization of homosexuality in Hollywood is accompanied by a sexual ethic that legitimates sex—for both heterosexuals and homosexuals—exclusively in intimate, preferably love-based, committed, preferably marital or quasi-marital relationships. Socially integrating gays and lesbians apparently creates an anxiety that other proscribed sexualities (for example, sex workers, sadomasochists, pedophiles, polygamists) will make similar claims for normality and social inclusion. Hence, bringing homosexuality into the heart of America raises fears of unleashing an unbridled eroticism that will bring chaos and decline.

The narrowing of tolerance for heterosexuals is dramatized in the character of Cameron Drake (Matt Dillon) in the film *In and Out*. In one scene, Cameron, the movie star, is portrayed as living a "Hollywood lifestyle"—surrounded by beautiful women and suggesting a life oriented to pleasure and play and conspicuous consumption. Cameron returns to Greenleaf, where he grew up, to help Howard. Unexpectedly, he falls in love with Howard's ex-fiancée who, in contrast to his beautiful, bimbo-type girlfriend, is a plain-looking, overweight, clumsy, small-town high school teacher. The film creates a good/bad moral division between the hedonistic, narcissistic sexual values associated with Hollywood and the romantic, marital, and family values of Greenleaf.

Despite endorsing gay normalization, *In and Out* was a huge commercial success in part because it evoked a nostalgic ideal of America. This film champions an America where individuals marry as virgins for love and life, where marriage inevitably leads to family, and where conventional gender roles are sustained. The real threat to this America is not the normal gay citizen who is a variation of the ideal national citizen, but hedonistic, narcissistic, and consumerist sexual and social values that are dramatically symbolized by Hollywood.

PROMS, WEDDINGS, AND THE MAKING OF A CULTURE OF HETEROSEXUAL ROMANCE

The change in the status of gays and lesbians in the past two decades in the United States and across much of Western Europe has been dramatic. While the legal recognition of gay and lesbian relationships, even gay marriage, has become routine across Europe, the level of visibility and social integration in daily life in the United States is unprecedented. Only in the United States are there lesbian and gay employee associations in almost every Fortune 500 corporation, community center, and social and political organization of every possible kind in almost all midsized and large cities across the country.

But, as we have seen, the cultural normalization and mainstreaming of lesbians and gay men in popular culture has not meant the questioning of the normative and superior status of heterosexuality. In the end, Howard was embraced by his community, but the movie ended with a *renewal of his parents' wedding vows after fifty years of marriage*. The idealization of marriage serves not only to reinforce the norm of heterosexuality but also to enforce a particular heterosexual norm: lifetime marriage based on love and family obligations and conventional gender roles.

There is a similar message in the Oscar-winning film *As Good as It Gets* (1997). The story revolves around Melvin (Jack Nicholson), an obsessive-compulsive misanthrope who falls in love with Carol (Helen Hunt), a waitress and single parent whose life is stressed by a sickly son. Melvin's neighbor is Simon (Greg Kinnear), a gay artist. The lives of these three characters get intertwined, though the drama centers on the heterosexual relationship between Melvin and Carol.

The film presents Simon's gay identity in a matter-of-fact way. Only Melvin exhibits homophobia. However, Melvin dislikes everyone, especially people who are different from him because of their racial, ethnic, or sexual identity. In other words, Melvin's homophobia—not Simon's homosexuality—is defined as a social problem. Gradually, Melvin learns to accept Simon, signaling the film's message: the acceptance of the normal and good homosexual.

Tellingly, though, as Melvin learns to accept Simon, the heterosexual romantic relationship between Melvin and Carol heats up. What is really interesting is the way this romantic plotline unfolds, as if right out of the sitcoms of the 1950s. Neither Melvin nor Carol have sex with each other or anyone else before they declare their love for each other. This romantic comedy depicts a virginal courtship based on love and ending, we are led to believe, in marriage and a family. The audience sits comfortably with the one normal gay character in part because this movie recalls a nostalgic idea of a love-based, virginal marriage with a breadwinner husband and, if not a domestic wife, then a motherly wife.

The American audience for these movies is not expected to question the normality and rightness of heterosexuality. The reason, in part, is that by the time Americans attend such movies they have already absorbed a culture of heterosexual intimacy that naturalizes and normalizes romance, marriage, and family making. But, how does this happen? More specifically, what role does pop culture play in making this happen almost seamlessly, as if confirming something we already knew? How does pop culture create the sentiments, beliefs, and ideals of romantic heterosexual intimacy so that this norm feels like second nature?

To simplify matters, let us imagine a young girl as she slowly becomes an adult. She will likely grow up watching Disney movies. Think of those classics of animation that continue to be viewed by children: *Snow White*, *Cinderella*, *Sleeping Beauty*, *The Little Mermaid*, and *Aladdin*. Such films convey a range of beliefs and values, such as the beauty of nature, the value of showing kindness to animals, the magic of hope and faith, and so on. But Disney tells one tale over and over: the story of heterosexual romantic love that ends in marriage. More specifically, Disney films speak directly and powerfully to young girls by suggesting that the true dream of all young girls is to fall in love and marry a prince of a man. Whether the plotline involves the forbidden love between a Native American and a white man (*Pocahontas*) or the fairy-tale story of a downtrodden, abused princess whose inner beauty is recognized by the handsome prince (*Cinderella*), these films construct a world of heterosexual fantasy addressed primarily to young girls. One researcher sums up a study of Disney films as follows:

> Much of the magic that is produced by Disney is entangled with notions of romance, true love, and the white wedding. While promoted as stories of adventure, of youthful rebellion, and of coming of age, the majority of Disney animated films center on the theme of the marriage plot: finding true love and, inevitably,

marriage. By examining these films, we are able to uncover . . . the ways in which heterosexuality is institutionalized in the United States.[2]

At some point, the young girl becomes an adolescent. The school and her peer group move to the center of her life, and so does pop culture. She will likely be immersed in a world of TV, teen magazines, movies, clothes, advertising, and popular music. She will absorb its culture of heterosexual romance. This is a two-sided process. On the one hand, there is the absence, or near absence, in teen pop culture of alternatives to heterosexuality. The young teenager will likely not be exposed to positive images of nonheterosexuals on TV, in the movies, magazines, or music videos. "Heterosexuality . . . almost entirely comprise[s] the plots of . . . [TV] shows. There is little room for gay and lesbian identity or desire in most of this adolescent pop culture."[3] On the other hand, pop culture actively promotes heterosexuality. Heterosexual romance is at the center of young girls' lives; it infuses their dreams of womanhood and daily regime of dress, grooming, peer group chatter, and social life.

A teen culture of heterosexual romance is reinforced as the young girl enters high school. A sociologist studying adolescent girls in two high schools, one predominantly black and working class, the other white and middle class, found virtually no significant differences in the role of pop culture and its aggressive promotion of heterosexual romance. She summarized her chief conclusion:

The pervasiveness of popular culture at both schools was tied very closely to the single most important theme that emerged from the data: the dominance of the sociocultural norm of heterosexuality in the girls' lives. . . . Compulsory heterosexuality functioned as the core ideology underpinning the girls' interpersonal and intragroup transactions.[4]

For many girls, the high point of their school years and adolescence is the high school prom. This event is fantasized and planned for months in advance, involving the entire family and considerable sums of money to be spent on clothing, hairstyling, cosmetics, and the partying after the prom. It is talked about among peers for the entire senior year. In the course of the year, girls are exposed to a steady unrelenting stream of prom images in magazines, TV, movies, music, and school culture. The prom, as both image and event, aggressively promotes a conventional gender ideology (feminine women and masculine men) and the taken-for-granted status of heterosexuality. In many schools, only heterosexual couples are permitted to attend the prom, dress codes often mimic 1950's gender norms, and, yes, hard to believe, but the crowning of the king and queen is still the prom climax. Many women experience a full-blown Cinderella fantasy, as this one high school student did:

> As a little girl, I always fantasized about this famous night where I would resemble Cinderella in my gown. . . . My Romeo-type boyfriend that showers me with flowers and compliments me the whole night through. Nothing would go wrong on prom night and 'perfect' would be the only word to describe it.[5]

Needless to say, it is not always so perfect. Indeed, it is a time of considerable anxiety—as young women worry about their sexual desirability, about whether they will be asked and by whom, and what will be expected of them after the prom!

As the young woman steps into the world of college or work, there is no break in the culture of heterosexual romance. The couple-centered, marriage-oriented culture that was a fantasy in her teen years is now a real possibility, and it is no less infused with dreamy hopes. Boyfriends become potential spouses; long-term dating raises thoughts about marriage. It is true that today cohabitation is a legitimate option for couples, but this accounts for a very small percentage of American households; most of these relationships end in marriage.

As the young adult's thoughts turn to marriage, a rich fantasy world is incited by two of the most anticipated life-shaping events: the engagement and the wedding. The engagement marks a turning point in a heterosexual relationship; it signals a public commitment to the relationship and, most important, the intent to marry. Although the engagement centers on the couple, it also involves friends, family, co-workers, and parties, rings, and dinners; in short, engagements are complex social and commercial events.

However, the engagement is just the warm-up act to the climactic romantic event: the wedding. The sociologist Chrys Ingraham estimates that more than two million American couples have a wedding each year at an average cost of twenty-eight thousand dollars.[6] The actual wedding event is but one aspect of the "wedding-industrial complex," which includes magazines oriented to weddings (brides magazines), wedding planners, the factories (many of which are in Third World nations) that produce and market wedding-related items from gowns to flowers and invitations, the hairdressers and stylists, the jewelers, photographers, musicians, and the honeymoon travel agents and destinations. The wedding-industrial complex amounts to a global industry producing the tidy sum of some $80 billion!

Curiously, though, it turns out that while spending on weddings has increased, Americans, like Europeans, are getting married or remarried less. Between 1996 and 2006, the marriage rate dipped from 8.8 to 7.8 per 1,000 American adults. But you would never know this from a glance at the culture of weddings, which seem to be in a bull market. Bridal magazines by the dozens (*New York Weddings*, *Weddingbells*, *World Class Weddings & Destinations*); television shows with such titles as "The Real Wedding Crashers," "For Better or Worse," "Perfect Proposal"; Hollywood blockbuster wedding movies, such as *Father of the Bride*, *American Wedding*, *Runaway Bride*, *The Wedding Planner*, and *The Wedding Singer*; and books and websites on every aspect of weddings imaginable, all speak to the power of the wedding-industrial complex to shape a culture of heterosexual romance that is so embedded in our lives that we do not recognize it as socially produced. But the wedding phenomenon is not only social but also political, as it reinforces a sexual and gender order that privileges men and heterosexuality.

My general point is *not* that heterosexual romance or marriage is evil or undesirable. Clearly, it infuses deep meaning and purpose into our lives and brings psychological and social benefits, such as providing a sense of belonging, intimate solidarity, household stability, economic well-being, and so on. I want to leave you, though, with three points to consider. First, to the extent that heterosexual marriage is the model or ideal of intimacy, it devalues, sometimes stigmatizes, a wide range of intimate choices: for example, all nonheterosexual intimacies and all heterosexual intimacies that are not about love or marriage. It turns out that the decoupling of sex and love, romance, and marriage is disproportionately the choice of the young, the poor, and racial minorities. Second, privileging heterosexuality means enforcing a gender order that sustains dichotomous gender roles that constrain men (for example, the burden of always having to perform, compete, succeed) while systematically disadvantaging women (the expectation of always having to be in caregiving, nurturing roles). Part of the way gay men and lesbians challenge the norm of heterosexuality is by imagining intimacies, and by implication personal and social lives, that are beyond gender. Third, the taken-for-granted status of heterosexuality and marriage, the sense of its facticity, of it being an arrangement that has always been and will always be, easily allows us to lose awareness of its socially produced character. Neither our bodies nor our psyches, nor any social imperative or law, requires that selves be gendered, that heterosexuality be anything more than one sexual-intimate choice among many, and that intimate solidarity be secured by the state-enforced institution of marriage. These are matters of social and political convention with considerable personal and social consequences that should be deliberately decided upon by the community, or at least publicly examined from time to time.

Chapter Twelve

HETEROSEXUALITY IN PANIC:
DOCTORS TO THE RESCUE

RELIGION HAS OFTEN been understood by Americans as an enemy of sexual choice and pleasure. Think of the way the word *Puritan* has come to stand for sexual repression and intolerance. In fact, the real Puritans, those people who settled in the American colonies, understood sex as a positive aspect of heterosexual marriage. A good marriage, they thought, would necessarily involve mutual sexual pleasure. Likewise, it is often assumed that Christian fundamentalists are antisex. In fact, as we will see, many Evangelicals defend a passionate notion of sexuality in the context of heterosexual marriage. In short, religion, like many other institutions, has become a battleground where Americans struggle over the meaning and regulation of sexuality. Social and moral division is as much the rule in our churches as it is in our schools, families, and workplace.

If religion is (misleadingly) imagined as a bastion of sexual repression, science and medicine is often assumed to be the path to sexual enlightenment. But this view is also misleading. The Judeo-Christian religion may label homosexuality sinful, but it was science and medicine that classified homosexuality as a disease and as a symptom of an abnormal sick personality. While the church may exile the sinner from the religious community, scientific medicine exiles the homosexual from the respectable circles of society. Or, to take another example, religious reformers in the nineteenth century crusaded against masturbation as lustful and sinful, but it was scientific and medical reformers who declared masturbation a serious threat to the physical and mental health of every American. These experts advocated purging children and young adults of this dangerous desire, and they encouraged, as a matter of good parenting, enhanced surveillance and control of young people's bodily conduct.

My point is not that science and medicine are more sexually repressive than religion; rather, these institutions and their ideas have complex and sometimes contradictory implications for the regulation of sexualities. There is an additional sociological point I want to make: alongside the state and popular culture, science and medicine have become in the past century or two key social and political forces constructing and controlling our sexualities. In this chapter, we will consider the sociological role of science and medicine in fashioning the *inner dynamics* of heterosexuality and their role in shaping successful heterosexual selves and marriages.

SEXUALIZING LOVE AND MARRIAGE

If we were able to return to the America of the 1850s, we would find a world at once familiar and strange. Familiar in the sense that sexuality was understood as something natural. The Victorians spoke of a sexual instinct. This instinct was understood as heterosexual. Nature programs, so to speak, individuals to be attracted to the opposite sex or gender. As one medical writer put it: "Mutual attraction is a species of real Animal Magnetism, the male being positive and the female negative. . . . [And] they are drawn irresistibly together."[1] In the Victorian world, and still in many respects in our world, the naturalness of heterosexuality was thought to be self-evident, imprinted in the physical and psychological differences and complementarity between men and women. Men were intellectual and phallic while women were imagined to be emotional and receptive; men and women need each other so that each can be complete and fulfilled. Females and males have evolved or have been created to form a natural unity, at least that was what our Victorian predecessors believed.

The Victorians also held that marriage, and only marriage, is the appropriate social arrangement for our sexual-intimate lives. Why did they believe this? Marriage had the capacity, they thought, to lift humanity from an animal-like level to a spiritual plane. As a union based on spiritual love and mutual respect, marriage brings out the best of what it means to be human. In these beliefs, the Victorians were not much different from people today. They had a view of marriage, however, that is likely not shared by many Americans today. The Victorian men and women of science held that only marriage can control our sexual instinct. Our nineteenth-century ancestors were convinced that the sexual instinct would bring personal and social ruin if it was not tightly controlled. If we surrendered to our sexual cravings, the pursuit of sensual pleasures would bring about self-destruction. So powerful, so seductive is the sexual instinct that unless we exercise considerable self-control, aided by society (for example, parents, church, schools), it will drive us into a life of indulgence and will visit upon us a host of horrible physical and mental ailments. Summarizing what many men and women of medicine believed at the time, one medical popularizer listed some of the ill effects of sexual excess as follows:

Languor, lassitude . . . general debility and heaviness, depression of spirits, loss of appetite, indigestion, feebleness of circulation, chilliness, headache, melancholy, hypochondria, hysteria, feebleness of all senses, impaired vision, loss of sight, . . . disorders of the liver and kidneys . . . the genital organs, weakness of the brain, loss of memory, epilepsy, insanity, . . . and early death of offspring—are among the common evils which are caused by sexual excesses.

Only marriage could contain and control the power of the sexual instinct.

Since they viewed the sex instinct as potentially overwhelming and harmful, the Victorians allowed it only a very small place in marital life. Sex had primarily one purpose: procreation or family making. Sex for the purpose of erotic pleasure had no place in marriage. As one physician confidently declared: "All sexuality is in the idea of creation and . . . serves high and holy purposes. *It was never intended to be mere carnal pleasure.*" But, how to control carnal desire in marriage? Victorian men and women of science had little doubt: it was ultimately *the responsibility of women to control men's sexuality.* This was because men were thought to be carnally driven and less capable of self-control, and because women were said to be driven less by carnal desire than by a maternal nurturing instinct. As one woman medical writer wrote, "women are not like men in sexual matters. They . . . do not love lust for lust's sake. Passion must come to them accompanied . . . with the tender graces of kindness." It was then women's role in marriage to domesticate men's sensual impulsiveness. With these beliefs we are most assuredly encountering a world very different from our own.

Between roughly 1900 and the 1950s, America and its sexual intimate culture changed dramatically. America emerged as an urban industrial world power. The small farmer or businessperson was being replaced by the blue-collar laborer and the white-collar corporate employee. Gender patterns and roles were also changing. Working in large factories or bureaucracies, men were valued as part of a team and rewarded for their ability to communicate and cooperate. Women were stepping out of the household and the domestic sphere into universities and the workplace. With their growing social and economic independence, women were also claiming their sexual independence. Both men and women were presented with options that were unavailable to their parents and grandparents. They could marry or remain single; they could marry but choose not to make a family; and they could, and indeed did, choose to separate and divorce if their marriage was no longer fulfilling.

These social changes were unsettling for many Americans. What values and rules would now govern and organize American sexual intimate life? It was a time of great uncertainty, and many Americans wanted answers. Various groups and organizations, from churches to the YMCA, had an opinion about sexual matters. However, while religion remained a powerful spiritual and social force in America, it was the scientists and medical doctors who could now persuasively claim the title of experts. If religion claimed authority in matters of the soul, science spoke with an unprecedented social authority in the affairs of the body and mind, and that included sexuality. An army of psychologists, sexologists, psychiatrists, psychoanalysts, social scientists, and medical doctors stepped forward to write the new rules governing sexual life.

Certain fundamentals from the Victorian era were not to be challenged. Above all, *heterosexual marriage was taken for granted as the norm and ideal*. Indeed, for the first time in the United States, a scientific-medical discourse defined same-sex sexuality, now labeled "homosexuality," as a sickness or pathology. A new personage was invented: the homosexual as an abnormal, perverse, and deviant human type. By stigmatizing homosexuality, indeed by interpreting same-sex desire as a sign of a pathological and perverse personality, the scientific and medical reformers were establishing heterosexuality as the only normal, healthy, and acceptable sexuality. By normalizing heterosexuality they were also declaring the naturalness and normality of a gender order that linked being male with masculinity and with men's roles as rulers while connecting being female with femininity and roles centered on caregiving.

These new experts addressed the question, What were to be the new rules organizing heterosexual marriage? Against the conventional wisdom of their Victorian predecessors, the new doctors declared the naturalness and normality of sexual expression and pleasure. Indeed, excessive sexual repression was now said to be unhealthy and abnormal. In a radical break from the Victorians, these new scientific-medical reformers argued that sexual pleasure and satisfaction should be the cornerstone of a good and successful marriage. In a statement that could not have been written just fifty years previous, a popular marriage manual declared:

> The basic marriage bond is sex attraction, the sex urge; and this being an inborn drive, its normal satisfaction becomes . . . a condition for sustained harmony and mutual satisfaction in all the other areas of the marital relationship. . . . Harmony and mutual

satisfaction in the sexual sphere is likely to be the sustaining vital health of the marriage as a whole.

Too often, the new experts argued, marriages fail due to sexual dissatisfaction, frequently caused by sexual ignorance and inhibitions. According to this argument, modern Americans must change their sexual attitudes and practices to succeed in their marriages.

The belief that sexuality was a necessary and positive basis of marriage was connected to other ideas that challenged the Victorians. For example, women were considered men's sexual equal. Drs. Hannah and Abraham Stone voiced the new orthodoxy: "Women's erotic desires are just as strong as those of the male." However, women's sexuality was not exactly the same as men's. In a stunning reversal of Victorianism, these experts claimed that "the clitoris is perhaps the main seat of the woman's sensuous feelings." It follows that mutual sexual satisfaction requires that men and women accommodate to their respective sexual capacities and needs. "The joy of sex is increased for both when it is mutual." These ideas indicated a huge shift in American intimate culture. Whereas women's "spiritual" nature served as the basis of a good marriage in the Victorian era, in the new modern order it was women's carnal or erotic fulfillment that was to make possible a solid and satisfying marital bond.

Marriage in the twentieth century was to be based on mutual sexual satisfaction. This required a sexually enlightened citizenry. The popularization of the new science of sexuality was to be the major vehicle for a social process of sexual enlightenment. In this regard, the early decades of the twentieth century saw the proliferation of a popular medical literature directed toward married couples. Volumes such as *Sexual Responsibilities in Marriage, Sex Technique in Marriage, Love without Fear,* and *Ideal Marriage* filled the bookstores and libraries, spreading the word that the age of sexual enlightenment had arrived.

But, was there not a danger that sexual pleasure and satisfaction could prove an unstable and unreliable foundation for marriage? The new scientific reformers were aware of this potential problem and addressed it head-on. If the giving and receiving of sexual pleasure is a way to express love, mutual sexual satisfaction can become the glue cementing the marital bond. In other words, if love is sexualized, the pursuit of mutual sexual pleasure becomes an expression of intimate solidarity. In *Woman, Her Sex and Love Life,* a book that went through seventeen editions in a little over ten years, the author opined, "The foundation of, the basis of all love, is sexual attraction." Another medical popularizer wrote, "In marital sex relations . . . the [sex] act is the most intimate expression of . . . love. . . . Aside from any procreative purpose that is its meaning and its justification in marriage."

If mutual sexual satisfaction is understood as an expression of love and a primary source of the marital bond, the erotic or sensual aspects of sex acquire a new legitimacy and importance. Spouses were expected to be knowledgeable and skilled in the carnal arts. Once again, the new doctors of sexuality stepped forward to educate the public in the erotic secrets of sexuality. Men and women, the doctors declared, must be taught to become comfortable with their bodies and with the practices of carnal pleasure. They must become skilled in sexual techniques, positions, and acts; they must learn to approach the body as a site of erotic experimentation and expression.

A new sexual norm within heterosexual marriage took shape: the norm of *good sex*. Good sex involves an ethic of mutuality; each spouse must work to bring sexual satisfaction to the other. This requires that each partner be knowledgeable and attentive to the sexual needs and pleasures of the other; each must abandon or overcome sexual fears and inhibitions. No matter how sexually motivated a husband and wife may be, without proper knowledge and skills sexual fulfillment will elude them. Knowledge of sexual technique and practices is crucial; beyond that, however, the new sexual citizen must understand the complexities and sequential logic of good sex.

In one of the most popular marital advice texts of the time, *Ideal Marriage*, the author describes a series of phases that served as a guideline for achieving good sex, or mutual sexual fulfillment. In stage one, "the prelude," erotic desire is awakened. Sexual interest is displayed in words and smell but not in touch or taste. In the second phase, "love-play," there is mouth-to-mouth kissing, which gradually extends to body kissing and the "genital kiss." In love-play, the hands and the mouth are essential instruments bringing sensual joy. As sexual excitement builds, the marital couple reaches the climax: coitus. This is "the culmination of sexual satisfaction which . . . concludes with the ejaculation . . . of semen into the vagina." Orgasm initiates the final phase, "afterglow," where "their souls meet and merge."

Faced with a time of uncertainty, with anxieties raised by the rise of divorce and abortions, and with single men and single women stepping out together in the evening, the new sex doctors prescribed a new cure: reinvigorating the marital bond based on mutual sexual satisfaction. But, we should be clear on one point: eroticism or the pursuit of sensual pleasure was considered legitimate *only* in heterosexual marriage. Sex before marriage or outside of marriage was unacceptable, a potential sign of a personality disorder and a potential social danger.

The idea that sexual satisfaction was fundamental to love and marriage became the conventional wisdom after World War II. Men and women incapable of experiencing erotic pleasure or uncomfortable with eroticism were labeled prudes or, in medical scientific language, "frigid" or "impotent" or suffering from a neurosis or personality disorder. From the 1950s onward, Americans have looked to sexual fulfillment as essential for self-fulfillment and intimate happiness.

AMERICA'S CRISIS OF SEXUALITY

The world of eroticism that the new experts of sexuality help create has become a major battleground. For several decades now, the linking of eroticism to love and marriage—and the very norm of heterosexual marriage—has been challenged. The appearance of such mass-circulation magazines as *Playboy*, *Hustler*, or *Cosmopolitan*; popular sex-advice literature, such as *The Joy of Sex*, *The Sensuous Woman*, and *The Pleasure Bond*; and a billion-dollar porn industry promotes the idea that sexuality has varied meanings and purposes, from procreation and love to pleasure, self-expression, and communication; moreover, eroticism, some argue, is legitimate outside of marriage. Surveys from the 1960s through today reveal that American youth overwhelmingly see no reason to confine sex exclusively to marriage. If sex can be a valued source of pleasure or communicative bonding in the context of love and marriage, why can it not be similarly valued in exchanges between consenting adults without the higher purpose of love or marriage?

Then, there were the women's and gay movements, which directly challenged the norm of heterosexual marriage. The former raised serious doubts about the institution of marriage. Is it based on the subordination of women to men? Does marriage require that women sacrifice their career ambitions for motherhood while requiring no such compromise for men? The latter movement threatened to expose heterosexuality as a social convention, and one that no longer should claim exclusive legitimacy. Why make heterosexuality into an institution rather than just a desire or lifestyle? If love and intimacy are equally possible for nonheterosexuals, why should heterosexuality be the exclusive norm? Similarly, lesbians advanced a powerful challenge: if women's sexuality revolves as much around clitoral as vaginal pleasures, and this is what the doctors of sexuality were saying, does their sexuality open equally to women and men? The notion that sex was legitimate only if tied to the higher purpose of love or family making, and only if it was part of a marital bond, could no longer be taken for granted. By the 1980s and 1990s, it seemed as if the floodgates of sexual desire were blasted wide open and there was no way to shut them.

It did not take long before some Americans grew alarmed and anxious. The Christian Right and the right wing of the Republican Party have tried to rally the nation around a defense of heterosexual marriage. Initially they blamed the current ills of America—AIDS, sexual disease, high divorce rates, abortion, teen pregnancies, single-parent households—on women's new freedom of sexual choice and on the gay/lesbian movement. Opposition to abortion is still a cornerstone of the Christian

Right, but there is little popular support for women's return to the household. Women's place in the public world of work and government is here to stay. The Christian Right has not relented, however, in its struggle against the gay and lesbian movement, but at least since the mid-1990s the attempt to blame the problems of marriage on gays and lesbians has lost credibility. The unmistakable trend in the United States has been toward gay and lesbian normalization and social integration. Once again, the doctors and experts of sexuality step forward to defend heterosexuality and heterosexual marriage.

DEFENDING THE NORM OF HETEROSEXUALITY

Let us keep in mind that the legitimacy of heterosexuality was never seriously challenged. Rather, it was the *normative and socially privileged status* of heterosexuality or its "institutional" or compulsory status that was questioned. If all sorts of rights, responsibilities, and privileges are to be accorded to heterosexuality, a society must be able to give compelling reasons that heterosexuality deserves state and social support. If heterosexuality can no longer be defended by simply pathologizing and stigmatizing homosexuality (because the doctors have declared homosexuality to be normal), how is it to be justified and secured as normative?

One justification for heterosexuality as the norm is to defend a gender order (m/f, men/women, and masculine/feminine) that secures heterosexuality as natural and "normal." There can be no norm of heterosexuality, indeed no notion of heterosexuality, without assuming two genders that are coherent as a relationship of opposition and unity. If there were no fixed categories of gender, if there were no "men" and "women," there could be no concept of heterosexuality! So, heterosexuality is anchored by maintaining a gender order through either celebrating and idealizing gender or by stigmatizing and polluting gender nonconformity. This is where the doctors come to the rescue, once again.

In the past decade or so, scientists (from medical doctors to sexologists, biologists, and neuroscientists) have appealed to genes, hormones, neuro pathways, and evolutionary adaptations to make the point that the social differences between men and women have a basis in biological differences between males and females; being gendered is, as it were, wired into our nature.

One version of this science of gender is the recent emergence of a new medical diagnostic category, "Gender Identity Disorder" or GID. This category initially appeared in 1980 and over the past two decades has evolved into a diagnosis of a disorder based exclusively on the assumed misalignment between sex (f/m) and gender identity (woman/man). In other words, individuals who are assigned the status of male or female at birth, but whose sense of gender identity and/or behavior indicates a contrary gender, are said to be suffering from a medical condition: GID. No matter that such individuals may not be suffering or that they may not wish to cross over to the opposite sex/gender status, or that they may have lifestyle or political reasons for their nonconforming gender presentation; despite those realities, the cultural dissonance between sex and gender is labeled a pathology, an abnormal medical condition.

As much as this diagnostic category makes it possible for some individuals to undergo sex reassignment surgery, something some prefer, the diagnosis of GID presents gender nonconforming individuals with a stark set of choices: pass if you can, cross over through sex reassignment surgery, or occupy a medically stigmatized status. GID makes it harder for individuals to occupy ambiguous gender positions or to challenge the gender underpinnings of compulsory heterosexuality. As the sociologist P. J. McGann says,

> Gender identity disorders reflect and reinforce . . . essentialist understandings of the 'natural' relationship between sex category (m/f), gender identity (man/woman) and gender embodiment (masculine/feminine), by pathologizing alternative configurations of sex and gender. Non-normative ways of doing gender—a feminine man . . . [or a] female-bodied person who identifies as male—[become] examples of clinical 'gender dysphoria.'[2]

In short, the biomedical diagnosis of GID has the social effect of enforcing a gender order that renders heterosexuality a normal expression of what is generally known as human nature.

EXPERTS DEFEND HETEROSEXUAL MARRIAGE

In truth, the normative, institutionalized status of heterosexuality has never been seriously threatened in contemporary America. Aside from a very small minority of lesbians and gay men who have challenged its normative status or sexual rebels who champion a fluid sexuality, the real challenge has been to the tight link between heterosexuality and marriage. Even in this regard, however, Americans are not abandoning marriage; they may be delaying marriage, having sex prior to marriage, cohabitating, and divorcing, but they are still getting married and remarried. Still, intimate life in America today is messy in a way that was not true just fifty years ago. More Americans are living as single persons for longer periods of time, some are choosing parenthood without marriage, and few doubt the legitimacy of divorce and sex outside of marriage. These developments have *raised serious doubts about the obligatory social status of marriage*. The moral and social pressure to organize intimate life around marriage, the belief that only marriage confers legitimacy on intimate relationships, is today in doubt.

Once again, the doctors are in the thick of battle. In the main, they have sided with the promarriage camp. They have proposed a mix of Victorianism and modernism. While urging Americans to rediscover the moral-spiritual core of the marital bond, they have also extolled the importance of the sexual side of marriage.

Citing the AIDS and herpes epidemics, along with an "epidemic" of teen pregnancies, abortions, single parents, sexual violence, and divorce, sex doctors take aim at the very sexual revolution they helped to launch. Americans, they say, are confusing love and eroticism. In *Rediscovering Love*, the psychiatrist and popular author Dr. Willard Gaylin advises Americans to rededicate themselves to the spiritual essence of love. "Love beyond pleasure, is a dedication of the self through trust and commitment to an expanded experience. . . . It is a willing and conscious utilization of all our capacities for generosity, altruism, empathy, service, self-sacrifice, and devotion." A culture that champions erotic pleasure and choice has gone too far; the results, say the medical experts, have been devastating. In a best-selling volume, *Lifemates: The Love Fitness Program for a Lasting Relationship*, Dr. Harold Bloomfield and Sirah Vettese provide just the kind of clear diagnosis and prescription that many Americans apparently want. "Liberated sex has bred sexual exploitation, performance fears . . . unwanted pregnancies, boredom . . . spiritual malaise [and] AIDS." The prescription, say the authors, is lifetime heterosexual love in which "intimate sex is a spiritual joining to discover how open, sensitive, caring and loving you and your lifemate can be." The renewal of love and marriage as an institution requires, say the new sex doctors, that Americans devote themselves to the morally uplifting virtues of restraint, obligation, self-sacrifice, and altruism—and to a culture of courtship and spiritual romance, which has been weakened and downgraded in the contemporary era of sexual permissiveness.

At the same time that sex doctors are spreading the gospel of the spiritual renewal of marriage, they are by no means calling for abandoning eroticism. Despite the sexualization of American culture, they seem to believe that there is widespread sexual dissatisfaction. Newspapers, magazines, and talk shows alert the public to our apparent waning of sexual desire, especially in marriage. Even Dr. Phil declared that "sexless marriages are an undeniable epidemic." There is, then, no turning back to Victorianism. A good, successful marriage, declare our experts, requires a healthy, vigorous sex life. On this score, Evangelicals are no less modern than their secular counterparts. The former may repudiate homosexuality and abortion, sex education and feminism, but the Christian Right is equally certain that good sex in marriage is a way of doing God's work. "Open any Christian sex advice book published within the last several years and you will read comments like this: 'some people have the mistaken notion that God is anti-sex. . . . In fact, he's outspokenly pro-sex. He invented it. . . . Passionate sex was God's idea.' And, there is this: 'Orgasm is an integral part of God's design for sex.'"[3] Sex doctors and their popularizers worry as much about the sexual as the spiritual malaise that has descended upon heterosexual marriage.

Whereas prior to the 1990s the sex doctors sought to enhance Americans' sexual knowledge and skills, the new experts rely on biomedical intervention. The appearance of Viagra in 1998 changed the sexual terrain. To promote Viagra, Pfizer Inc. had to convince Americans that (1) they had a sexual problem, (2) it was not psychological but a physiological "medical" problem, and (3) this drug would deliver on its promise of sexual performance. Viagra was initially marketed as the solution to the medical problem of "erectile dysfunction" (ED) but quickly was advertised as a way to enhance the sex lives of men and women in general. Let us be clear: Viagra has been chiefly marketed as a way to enhance heterosex, especially coital sex in marriage. In a study of the images and ideas that accompany the marketing of Viagra, two researchers observe: "The focus is very much on the couple . . . and promotes normative assumptions of male sexuality, heteronormativity, monogamy. . . . The advertisements . . . feature older, married . . . heterosexual couples."[4]

Viagra has been a monumental marketing success, as the well over nine million American users suggest. However, trouble remains in the new pharmaceutically induced sexual paradise. Women, it seems, are not all that happy about their spouse's renewed sexual vigor. Women do not necessarily look to coitus for their erotic pleasures, and many women, especially older women, do not necessarily value the erotic aspects of sex as much as they appreciate its emotional aspects. The problem is that Viagra, both the drug and its sexual imagery, seems to encourage a narrow penis-and-coital-centered approach to sex. Viagra seems also to have the effect of reducing women's control over when to have sex. After all, once the man consumes the "blue pill" the performance begins, ready or not.

It did not take long for the pharmaceutical giants to figure out a solution to women's sexual "problem." It came with the name "female sexual dysfunction" (FSD). Women diagnosed with FSD are said to have a low level of desire, interest, or arousal, or they experience difficulties in achieving orgasm or are in discomfort during coitus. FSD, like ED, declare the doctors and their popularizers, threatens to sink an otherwise good marriage in a swamp of sexual dissatisfaction. Needless to say, Pfizer and other pharmaceutical companies are busy trying to find the female counterpart to Viagra. To date, there is no pink pill to "energize" women's sexual equipment. And Viagra has just not worked. This has not stopped the sex doctors from blaming women and urging them to "turn on" to their husbands, even when they might not be in the mood. Two sisters, Laura (sex therapist) and Jennifer (urologist) Berman have become perhaps the public face of the biomedicalization of women's sexual problems and liberation. This dynamic duo have made the rounds of popular talk shows and magazines geared to women; they have established treatment centers for women's sexual problems and published two best sellers, *For Women Only: A Revolutionary Guide in Overcoming Sexual Dysfunction and Reclaiming Your Sex Life* (2001) and *Secrets of the Sexually Satisfied Woman: Ten Keys to Unlocking Ultimate Pleasures* (2005).[5] Their message is that women must take responsibility for the sexual side of marriage by doing whatever it takes to re-energize their own sexuality. This may mean having sex even if they lack motivation. Commenting on America's so-called sexual crisis, Dagmar Herzog observes:

A remarkable amount of effort is also now going into telling women to have sex even if they feel no desire. *Self* magazine advises that women should give sex with their partners a whirl even if they don't think they want it. . . . *Redbook* makes the same point: 'Have sex—even when you don't want to! . . . Once you get going, you'll probably find yourself enjoying it.' *Family Circle*, too, advises wives to stop saying no and to surrender in the bedroom even when they are not in the mood themselves.[6]

Whether or not women want sex less than men is unclear. However, it is clear that for many straight women sexual satisfaction is connected to clitoral along with vaginal sex, and to the emotional bonding that can occur during sex. This is not a pharmaceutical problem but a question of the gender dynamics between men and women.

PART V

SEXUAL ETHICS IN A
TIME OF UNCERTAINTY

Chapter Thirteen
PORN WARS

As we saw in Part II, a chief focus of sexual policies is identity. In societies such as the United States or Australia, certain desires are understood as signaling a person's sexual identity. For example, a person attracted to the opposite sex is said to have a heterosexual identity; adults attracted to children are labeled pedophiles. Some identities are classified as normal, healthy, and good. These identities are protected and supported by the state and other institutions; they are celebrated on television, in movies, and in popular music. There are also sexual identities that are labeled abnormal, unhealthy, immoral, and bad. These identities may be the target of ridicule, harassment, criminal prosecution, and cultural stereotyping. The politics of homosexuality and bisexuality are examples of the politics of sexual identity.

Conflicts over sexuality are not only about identities. Citizens often disagree about which sexual behaviors are appropriate—and when, where, and in what kinds of relationships. Citizens dispute what place sex should have in society. Should sex be part of public life? Are the sexual lives of public figures something media and the public have a right to know about? I call such conflicts "boundary disputes." Every society establishes boundaries between good and bad sexual acts and identities; these boundaries are often contested.

Boundary disputes are conflicts over the meaning and morality of sex. What is sex? What counts as a sex act? When is sex appropriate and with whom? These disputes are also conflicts over the meaning society assigns to marriage, the family, work, and the private and public spheres.

Boundary disputes often become the focus of considerable public attention and social conflict. They are always political. Marking out which sexual desires, acts, identities, and intimacies are good and should be institutionally supported and which are bad and should be punished creates social hierarchies between good and bad sexual practices and sometimes between good and bad sexual *citizens.* For example, if we view prostitution as immoral or beyond the pale of tolerable sexual expressions, we might label sex workers "bad citizens"—dangerous, disreputable disease carriers.

In Part V, I consider some key boundary disputes in the United States. These disputes speak to deep divisions among Americans over the meaning and morality of sexuality. We begin with the conflict over pornography.

Pornography refers to graphic sexual images that are meant to be sexually arousing. Porn is distinguished from sexual representations that are valued for artistic or other nonerotic purposes. Obviously, the line between porn and non-porn is blurry; the Supreme Court has ruled that ultimately each community must decide what counts as porn.

The conflict over porn is a legal and moral dispute. The moral issue, which is the concern of this section of the book, revolves around the social and political meaning of porn. Does porn teach citizens to approach their bodies and sexual feelings in a guiltless, playful way? Does it teach skills that help people become knowledgeable, skillful, and responsible sexual citizens? Or, does porn promote violence, especially toward women? Is its celebration of sensual pleasure apart from intimacy demeaning and socially harmful?

The debate over pornography is not new. Historians have documented the prevalence of "obscene" materials in the nineteenth century, especially in the form of picture books and pulp novels.[1] Still, the rapid commercialization of sex in the twentieth century has pushed the issue of porn into the center of American culture and politics. Whereas entrepreneurs approach porn as a potentially profitable business, moral crusaders and guardians of a culture of sexual respectability view porn as morally offensive; they have pursued legal action to censor or criminalize it.

In the late nineteenth century, moral crusader Anthony Comstock inaugurated a government-backed campaign against vice and obscenity. Old laws were reinforced and new legislation was passed to address the perceived spread of this "moral cancer." The intent of this campaign was to keep sex and sexual images exclusively private. Comstock and many reformers of the time championed an idea of social respectability that confined sexuality to marriage and to the private sphere.[2]

Social trends, however, worked against these Victorian crusaders. In the last decades of the nineteenth century, America was becoming a more open, diverse society; its traditions of individualism, free speech, and free enterprise provided a favorable social environment for porn to flourish. In addition, the Victorian norm that restricted sex to marriage for the purpose of reproduction came under assault in a culture that looked to sexual pleasure as a cornerstone of love and marriage.

By the early decades of the twentieth century, sex was becoming part of the public world; it was in magazines, books, art, and movies, and it was evident in the new dance halls and taverns, which even respectable women were now frequenting. Entrepreneurs seized on sex to market whatever it was they were selling. This liberalizing trend extended to the courts. By the early 1960s, the censorship of public sexual representations in effect came to an end. As historians John D'Emilio and Estelle Freedman write:

> From the 1930s onward, the courts in the United States steadily narrowed the definition of obscenity until by the mid-60s they had virtually removed the barriers against the forthright representation of sexual matters in literature and other media. The veil of nineteenth century reticence was torn away, as sex was put on display.[3]

As the 1960s gave way to the 1970s and 1980s, there was no stopping the spread of porn into the American heartland. The Supreme Court cast a wide net protecting public speech, which made efforts to remove porn from the social mainstream difficult. As the sexual and social revolutions of the time buried whatever was left of Victorian norms of sexual respectability, entrepreneurs were free to make porn into a huge and profitable business. Magazines such as *Playboy*, *Penthouse*, and *Hustler* sold in the millions; the paperback revolution made dime-store novels with romantic and often steamy sexual scenes available to all Americans; corporations from car manufacturers to the new multi-billion-dollar cosmetic industry filled the public world with sexually provocative imagery. Critics and crusaders challenged the new porn industry. The spread of porn, they said, indicated a dangerous moral laxity and permissiveness in America; they raised fears of youth and adults out of control. Nevertheless, the porn industry flourished.

By the 1980s and 1990s, adult theaters, triple-X movies, and mass circulation sex-oriented magazines had become a fixture of American society. The porn industry was generating between four and seven billion dollars in U.S. sales alone. As videos, cable television, and the Internet became a part of the daily lives of ordinary individuals, porn found its way into the living rooms and bedrooms of virtually every American.[4]

In the 1980s, a new voice emerged in the battle over porn: feminism. Some feminists were already organizing against violence toward women; they sought to include porn as part of their agenda. Porn was seen as promoting a culture that devalued women. Feminists targeted porn as another example of the pervasive sexism of American culture. This misogynist culture, they said, encouraged violence toward women. Feminist critics organized marches, protests, and even tours of porn shops. They sought to expose the deep hatred of women that they believed to be the essential meaning of porn. Two prominent feminists, Catherine MacKinnon and Andrea Dworkin, drafted legislation aimed at allowing civil suits to be brought against porn manufacturers on the grounds of gender discrimination.[5] Their proposed law would allow women to file a civil complaint for compensatory damages; porn that was clearly demeaning or violent toward women would be removed. As porn moved into the center of feminist politics, other feminists defended porn not only as a free-speech right but also as a tool for promoting a culture of erotic choice and variation. A debate ensued among feminists about the meaning and politics of porn.

Porn is today a highly charged focus of public debate. On the one side, advocates of sexual liberalization defend porn as a form of free speech that encourages a guiltless eroticism and sexual variation. On the other side, a curious alliance of conservatives and feminists condemn porn for being primarily about violence, moral degradation, and male dominance. Although the conflict over porn has been fought in the courts, it is fundamentally a moral conflict.

DEFENDERS OF PORN span the political spectrum from liberal free-speech advocates to sex-radical defenders of sexual variation. But virtually all defenders of porn at some level rely on the notion that watching or purchasing porn should be an individual choice. Accordingly, I group the arguments defending porn under the rubric of "libertarian."[6]

Libertarians aim first of all to protect porn as free speech. Some may not like porn, but they oppose censorship because of its potential to put a chill on a wide range of unpopular public expressions. They ask if porn is outlawed, which representations and which groups will be censored next? It is better for a society to suffer some moral excess than to risk widespread censorship. However, tolerating porn does not mean defending all public sexual images in all places. Violent porn, such as images depicting dismemberment or murder, should be strongly criticized.

Libertarians hold that individuals have a right to view pornography. At one level, it is a matter of the kind of society we want. Do we want a society that tells us what images we can and cannot view? At another level, libertarians underscore a reality of conflict around the meaning of sex. The fact that porn is mass consumed suggests that many Americans value sex for its expressive and pleasurable qualities. Sex carries multiple meanings today. Most Americans value sex primarily as a way to build intimacy, but many also value sex as a form of pleasure. Individuals should be able to choose their own pleasures, provided they are consensual and between adults. As with any other marketed products, the decision to purchase porn should be up to individual consumers.

Some feminists have also made the libertarian case for pornography. In general, they have argued that a good deal of porn promotes the values of sensual self-expression, sexual experimentation, and sexual choice and variation. Moreover, porn can teach sexual skills and impart knowledge about different sexual acts and techniques. Porn also can be defended on the grounds of promoting women's empowerment. Porn often presents women as erotically aggressive, as lusty individuals who can and should pursue their own sexual fantasies. Porn actors are not afraid to touch themselves or to explore sex for fun and pleasure. Often in porn, women step forward as sexually provocative and naughty in ways that mock the prudish norm of the "good girl."

Critics of porn are not of one stripe. Conservatives are offended by porn's graphic sexuality, its freewheeling eroticism, and its public nature. Sex, they say, should be a private matter and should always be about human caring. Conservative critics argue that porn is a form of moral violence. They say that sex for pleasure, apart from intimacy or love, is demeaning to individuals. If sex is at the core of the self, then separating sex from intimacy means treating the self instrumentally, as a mere physical vehicle of pleasure. Porn demeans the sexual act by lowering it to an animalistic level, to a mere physical sensation.[7]

Feminist critics are less focused on moral than on physical violence. They argue that most porn is about violence toward women. Porn depicts women's sexuality in dehumanizing and demeaning ways. Women are seen as sex objects who take plea-sure in servicing and pleasing men, or as masochists who desire and enjoy punishment and pain. Porn depicts women as little more than sexual playthings and conveys a view of women as inferior. Moreover, the image of women's sexuality in porn ex-presses men's fantasies, not women's actual desires. Finally, inso-far as porn eroticizes sexual violence and aggressiveness toward women, porn encourages actual violence toward women. Hence the saying "Porn is the theory and rape is the practice." Porn, then, is fundamentally about gender; its sexual images reinforce men's social dominance.[8]

Conservative critics make a serious point: a society that values sex primarily for pleasure or self-expression runs a risk of pro-moting a narrowly body-centered, technique- and performance-oriented type of sexuality that is potentially demeaning, ir-responsible, unhealthy, and undermining of sexual-intimate bonds. But there is no reason why valuing sexual pleasure can-not be coupled with an ethic of responsible and respectable be-havior. We can both value erotic pleasure and champion stable, romantic, intimate bonds. On this score, I side with the liber-tarian position. However, porn makers need to be held morally accountable; they must be mindful of the messages porn con-veys about sexual health and responsibility.

Feminist critics make a point that strikes me as especially com-pelling: porn may not be the main cause of women being treated badly, but if its images are consistently demeaning, it surely rein-forces male dominance and violence. Degrading images of women should not be censored by the state, but they should be criticized. Moreover, it is not just porn images that are hurtful to women;

the industry is male dominated. Men own and run the production and distribution of porn. Women have little say in the business and are typically badly paid and have few benefits; their bodies are at times surgically refashioned to conform to male fantasies; their work is sometimes dangerous. In addition, critics rightly insist, many of these women did not choose to be in this industry but were forced into it by circumstance—by a history of abuse, racism, or unemployment; by false promises of glamour and wealth; even by kidnapping and coercion. Many women who become part of the porn industry are teenage runaways dependent on drugs or alcohol.[9]

Defenders of porn cannot simply claim that individuals choose to purchase porn or to be porn actors. This is a weak argument in the face of industrywide sexism and women's limited options for better-paying jobs. Acknowledging and criticizing the sexism and racism that is at the heart of the porn industry does not necessarily mean supporting censorship.

The root problem of porn, as I see it, is not its erotic images, nor even its sexual objectification, but that it is a part of a system of gender inequality. Let us be frank: most porn is made by and for straight men. Porn needs to be criticized as part of a system of male domination. Women work in porn because they have fewer options for well-paying jobs than men; they have fewer options because the culture often evaluates them by their physical attractiveness and sexual availability, and this view of women as sexual beings feeds into a view of them as not as smart, decisive, and thoughtful as men. Men consume porn at least in part because it reinforces their sense of control over women, something they perhaps feel is otherwise diminishing in their

. So, at the root of many of the problems of porn is a society that continues to treat women as inferior to men. I would, then, defend the right of people to make and consume porn on the grounds of promoting a culture that values erotic choice and variation, but I would critique porn's sexism, violence, and ethical failure to address issues of health and responsibility.

Chapter Fourteen
SADOMASOCHISM, OR, THE PLEASURES OF PAIN

SADOMASOCHISM (S/M) involves the use of power or roles of dominance and submission for the purpose of sexual arousal. Sexual pleasure is based on exercising (sadism) or submitting to (masochism) power. S/M may involve physical acts (for example, bondage, slapping, whipping) and verbal acts (for example, orders, commands, submissive statements).

S/M raises the question of what sorts of behaviors should be considered legitimate sexual expressions. Is S/M simply one sexual expression among many? Or is it a psychological and social pathology? Some feminists have also challenged the legitimacy of S/M as a sexual practice. They argue that S/M role-playing reinforces a male-dominant gender order. So: is S/M between consenting adults just a sex act to be valued for its erotic inventiveness? Or is it a symptom of an individual or social problem?

Until recently, S/M barely registered on indicators of public opinion. But in the past few decades, movies such as *Blue Velvet*, *Exit to Eden* (based on Anne Rice's popular novel), and *Pulp Fiction*; the popularization of Robert Mapplethorpe's art; the best-selling novels by Stieg Larson (*The Girl with the Dragon Tattoo*) and E.L. James (*Fifty Shades of Grey*); and researches estimate that between 5 and 10 percent of Americans have engaged in S/M practices.[1] Indicative of the new visibility of S/M, organizations have cropped up in virtually every major city and in many midsized cities. At the State University of New York, Albany, where I teach, a group called Power, which is openly supportive of S/M, was established in 2000 with the support of the Student Council and the university president.

Why has S/M emerged as a potentially legitimate sexual act and identity, as the basis of a subculture, and as part of popular culture?

S/M can be seen as part of a broader set of changes in American sexual culture. To characterize this change in a nutshell: sex is no longer exclusively tied to reproduction, love, or intimacy. Today, many Americans value sex as a form of pleasure and self-expression, and as a mode of communication apart from love or a committed relationship. Americans may still prefer sex in an intimate, loving relationship, but sex for pleasure between adults who are not in love or married is now considered a legitimate lifestyle choice by many citizens. From this perspective, S/M can be understood as part of a culture that tolerates separating sexual pleasure from love, marriage, and procreation. Once sex is valued as a source of pleasure or as a form of self-expression, heightened attention is paid to the erotic potential of specific sexual practices. Individuals may organize their erotic lives around specific sex acts, such as anal sex, oral sex, or S/M.

Sexual pleasure has not always been celebrated or even tolerated. In Victorian America, sex was supposed to be about procreation. Individuals were expected to confine sex to marriage for the chief purpose of having children. Pleasure was at best a side effect of sex, not its aim. In fact, our Victorian ancestors believed that sensual pleasure had the potential to corrupt young people and to cause serious physical and mental illness. Sex for pleasure was seen as threatening to love and marriage; it reduced the spiritual essence of intimacy to an animalistic instinct.

Victorian culture was in crisis by the early 1900s. The world of prostitution and obscenity that flourished underground in the nineteenth century went public. Brothels, pornography, and public advertisements for abortions shocked respectable Americans. Marriage was in crisis. Not only were more people choosing to be single for longer periods of time, but more people were getting divorced. In this context, some reformers began to reassess the place of sex in American life. Against Victorian culture, they promoted mutual sexual satisfaction as an essential part of a good marriage. Of course, marriage was to be based on love, but now giving and receiving sexual pleasure was understood as a way to express love. Sexual satisfaction between spouses was a sign of a successful marriage. As a result, the erotic or pleasurable aspects of sex were understood and valued as a vehicle to express love and strengthen marriage.

The birth of a culture of eroticism in the early decades of the twentieth century meant a new focus on the body as a source of pleasure. Husbands and wives felt a marital duty to explore a variety of ways to experience mutual sexual pleasure. A new language of sexual technique, act, and position, of orgasm and erotic zone, was born. In the first decades of the twentieth century, the pursuit of pleasure was acceptable, but only in marriage and only if erotic pleasure was expressed in tender, caring acts. Sexual pleasure was tightly wedded to a culture of romantic love.

The so-called sexual revolution in the 1960s and 1970s loosened the connection between eroticism and romantic love. Sexual pleasure no longer had to be linked to intimacy, love, or marriage to be tolerated. Sex was now valued as a source of pleasure and self-expression apart from any connection to love or marriage. In principle, an individual could choose to have sex for pleasure, for love, or for the purpose of creating a relationship or children. An individual could choose to have sex in an intimate setting, as part of a marriage, or in a casual, consensual encounter. From this libertarian perspective, an individual could choose whatever acts were pleasurable so long as they were between adults and were consensual. An individual might prefer tender, gentle romantic acts or acts that involve social roles and power; all consensual erotic acts were legitimate.[2]

As the link between eroticism and romanticism was weakened, individuals could be more openly imaginative and inventive in their sexual preferences. Every part of the body could be freely explored, even such hitherto forbidden erotic zones as the anus; power and sex toys could be used to find new ways to generate sensual pleasure. This culture of eroticism made it possible to approach S/M as just another sex act.

S/M might not have gained social visibility without changes in the status of women. As long as women were viewed as interested in sex only as a means to establish intimacy or to create families, S/M could not be considered a legitimate sex act. It would be difficult for women to approach their bodies as vehicles of sensual pleasure if they still imagined themselves as "pure" or if the norm of the "good girl" still required an exclusively romantic approach to sex. Women had to be seen as pleasure-oriented before S/M could be considered a legitimate sexual expression.

Finally, it is hard to imagine the mainstreaming of S/M without the growing prominence of gay politics. The gay movement made a nonconventional sexuality into a positive basis of identity, community, and politics. Gays and lesbians challenged laws, stereotypes, and social policies; they demanded respect, rights, and justice. The gay movement served as a kind of model for other sexual outsiders, such as bisexuals, transsexuals, fetishists, and sadomasochists. Indeed, a well-organized, politically assertive S/M movement took shape initially within lesbian and gay communities. Queer S/M groups cropped up across the country; they created organizations, published newsletters, held lectures, and ventured into the public world. They claimed that S/M was a legitimate sexual identity deserving of respect. Today, there are hundreds of S/M organizations, clubs, bars, publications, and social networks. In short, S/M is an organized community in both the straight and gay worlds. As individuals "come out" as sadists, masochists, or members of an S/M culture, the debate over the meaning and morality of S/M has intensified.

It may seem odd that some feminists defend S/M. After all, at the heart of S/M are roles of dominance and submission, the very dichotomy that the women's movement has fought against. But, in the early 1980s, a group of lesbian feminists publicly came out as sadomasochists and formed a group called Samois. Challenging stereotypes, they argued that although S/M involves the use of humiliation and physical force, it is not about violence, punishment for its own sake, nor degrading people, especially women. It is about using power to create pleasure in what is often an intensely trusting relationship.[3]

But how can this be, when S/M entails physical punishment and real pain? Advocates make two points. First, acts such as slapping or bondage are voluntary, not forced; both parties agree to these practices and both agree on a "safe word" that is intended to immediately bring an end to the S/M scene. Second, what one person may experience as physical pain, another might view as pleasure. The meaning of physical sensations depends on the emotional and social context of the act. Being slapped or burned may be painful and violent in one context, but in an S/M scene these same acts might be welcomed as sources of pleasure and sensual excitement. Moreover, advocates say, S/M is less about actual pain and punishment than about exploring the fantasy of submission and domination. S/M is closer to theater than to actual acts of pain and humiliation.

Some critics respond by arguing that S/M attracts psychologically imbalanced or troubled individuals. Why would someone experience pleasure from dominating or being dominated? Advocates argue that aggressivity and passivity, or a wish to dominate or be submissive, are part of all relationships. Some of us experience erotic pleasure from taking charge and directing our partners. Others of us are aroused by submitting to a partner's will. We want to feel the partner's hands and voice directing us; we want them to take erotic charge; we get pleasure from trusting that our partners will be beneficent in their sexual sovereignty. Still others of us enjoy taking turns dominating and being dominated. Sex is a sphere in which we can explore feelings of power and submission. S/M, advocates say, simply allows us to explore these feelings and fantasies within a safe, trusting, consensual exchange.

Does S/M reproduce unequal gender roles? Well, defenders say that it does involve roles of dominance and submission, but why must these be viewed as gendered—as masculine and feminine? Dominance and submission are not necessarily gendered experiences. Unlike cultural gender roles, S/M roles are individually negotiated and agreed upon, and they can be changed. More important, S/M roles do not typically extend beyond the sexual scene. S/M gives individuals a chance to experiment with roles and the associated feelings of power and powerlessness. Rather than reinforcing gender norms, its defenders argue, S/M undermines such roles because it approaches them as socially negotiated. S/M participants know that anyone can be dominant or submissive regardless of gender. Rather than S/M being antifeminist, then, it brings a greater awareness of the arbitrary, socially constructed character of gender roles.

Feminist critics of S/M disagree. They argue that we live in a society that divides people into dominant/submissive or active/passive roles that, like it or not, are linked to gender identities. Power, aggressiveness, and control are associated with men and masculinity in American culture, and men rule in virtually every major institution. By contrast, submission, passiveness, pleasing, and caretaking are expected of women, and these feminine traits are linked to roles and statuses that position women as less powerful than men. Accordingly, any social exchange that is organized around roles of dominance and submission or aggressivity and passivity carries gender meanings. S/M roles, these critics say, inevitably reinforce gender roles and inequality.[4] In the United States, men exercise power over women both through legal means (such as by occupying powerful social positions and roles) and through harassment, coercion, and violence. Physical force or its threat is a key way men control and dominate women. S/M expresses a culture that uses power and intimidation to sustain a male-dominant gender order. Indeed, critics argue, S/M eroticizes men's power; it makes men's dominance and women's submission sexy. S/M legitimates this unequal gender order by suggesting that women really want to be dominated and get pleasure from submission.

According to these critics, women are especially vulnerable to S/M. In a society that values women as caregivers and as objects of sexual desire, some women feel a sense of inner abuse and inferiority. S/M reinforces their low self-esteem and the feeling that their social subordination to men is somehow right or deserved. This is true even if women assume dominant S/M roles, since they are, in effect, acting as if they were men. There is, say critics, simply no avoiding the gendered character of S/M role playing and its entanglement in gender politics.

These critics have a point. Gender organizes much of modern society in a deep and pervasive way. Feelings, statuses, and social roles are often gendered or associated with masculine or feminine labels. It may not be possible to separate sexual role-playing from gender; however, this does not mean that S/M can be reduced to a narrowly gendered meaning. S/M can still be defended as an act of pleasure and self-expression. Practitioners repeatedly attest to its erotic and psychological power; they speak of experiences of considerable emotional release and expression. The voices of those who practice S/M should not be dismissed. But we should be mindful of the gendered associations of S/M in a society in which gender organizes personal and social life, and in which gender inequality is pervasive. S/M advocates must be more attentive to the potentially broader social and political significance of this practice. The defense of S/M should be linked to a critique of gender inequality and rigid gender roles.

What about objections to S/M on the grounds that it uses pain and humiliation? Does it not degrade the participants? Perhaps, but to the extent that S/M is consensual and pleasurable it should be tolerated. My own view is that, in general, if a specific sexual practice lacks any obvious victim, and if a strong case cannot be made for the presence of coercion, there is probably no justification for formal social control (that is, by the state or other institutions). This does not mean that such practices go without any regulation. There are effective informal controls, such as peer disapproval, ridicule, ostracism, and disrespect. And let us keep in mind, tolerating a practice is not the same as accepting it or making it into a social norm or ideal. As individuals, and as a society, we may tolerate many practices, but some of these lack state and institutional support (such as benefits and civil rights) and cultural respect. S/M, even if it is still the focus of conflict, should, at a minimum, be tolerated; it should not be the focus of state or medical social regulation. Its gendered meanings, however, should be thoughtfully scrutinized.

Chapter Fifteen
A RIGHT TO SEX WORK?

SEX WORK INVOLVES the exchange of sex for money. There are many different types of sex work, from stripping to porn acting to prostitution. The nature and conditions of sex work vary tremendously. It can be dangerous and exploitative, as in the case of street hookers, or it can be safe and playful, as in the case of male strippers at gay bars or straight clubs.[1] We will focus in this chapter on prostitution; prostitutes sell particular sex acts. We need to be mindful that the work conditions and income among prostitutes vary enormously. There are street walkers, high-class escorts, sex-show workers who are part of the tourist industry; both men and women can be prostitutes.

At the heart of this issue is the question of whether sex work is just another kind of work that should be regulated in terms of work conditions and worker rights, or whether it is different because it involves sex. Sex work raises a boundary dispute over the relationship between sex and commerce. If we permit graphic sexual images in pornography, magazines, advertisements, and movies, why not allow the buying and selling of sex acts?

The Victorian era may have celebrated sex only in marriage and for the purposes of procreation, but during that time there was a flourishing illicit sexual world that included prostitution. As cities became the center of industry and commerce in the nineteenth century, many Americans left the small towns and rural regions where they had been born and raised. Many of the new urban denizens were single men—alone and too poor or unsettled to marry. They created a demand for prostitutes. In particular, in port towns, mill towns, and coal mining towns, single men and married men who lived for long stretches of time alone sought out prostitutes.

America in the nineteenth century was male dominated. Men controlled the public sphere, the world of politics and paid work; women were expected to be wives, mothers, and caretakers for their husbands and children. Women did not have equal rights and were legally, socially, and often physically controlled by men. Women had few legitimate economic opportunities. Working-class and immigrant women sometimes looked to prostitution to survive or to help support their families. As many individuals were freed from the control of kin and church after they migrated to cities, prostitution flourished throughout the nineteenth century. For example, according to a contemporary observer, more than five hundred brothels operated in Chicago in 1860.[2]

Prostitution was never legal in America, but the laws against prostitution often went unenforced. However, during the waves of religious fundamentalism that periodically swept through America in the nineteenth century, moral crusaders campaigned against prostitution. Arrests were made, brothels were closed, and prostitutes and (rarely) their clients were publicly stigmatized.

Despite being illegal, and despite these crusades, brothels survived—in seaports, small towns in the West, and large cities in the East. Some people advocated that America follow the European practice of decriminalizing and regulating prostitution, but this offended Americans' sense of what was proper and decent. Criminalization and the abolition of prostitution were the chief aim of the moral crusaders, and most Americans supported their agenda.

Moral reformers found support in the women's movement, which criticized prostitution for its exploitation of women and for its double standard. Women were punished for providing a service, but men who purchased that service were typically not punished. By the late nineteenth century, suffragists, temperance groups, antiobscenity crusaders, such as Anthony Comstock, and a variety of business and government agencies all viewed prostitution as evil and sought its abolition.

Throughout the twentieth century, the U.S. government has backed the criminalization of prostitution. Today, it is estimated that more than ninety thousand arrests are made in the United States every year for prostitution. Nationwide, cities spend well over a hundred million dollars a year enforcing prostitution laws. Although most arrests occur in large cities, prostitution thrives in small and midsized cities as well. The aim of criminalization today is not abolition but containment. Police focus on confining prostitution to certain districts and preventing it from becoming visible in "respectable" society.[3]

With the exception of Las Vegas, the United States has not seriously considered alternatives to criminalization. The public has had little sympathy for legalizing prostitution. In the public mind, prostitution continues to be associated with crime, drugs, immorality, and social decadence.

In the 1980s, feminists entered the debate over sex work. As the women's movement expanded its focus from rights to sexuality, it turned to prostitution. Many feminists saw in prostitution another form of male domination: women sex workers are sexually used and commercially exploited by men. Groups such as WHISPER (Women Hurt in a System of Prostitution), founded in 1985, argued that prostitution reinforces male dominance. The world of prostitutes, they held, is one in which women are abused, violated, and degraded. Not all feminists, as we will see, share this viewpoint.

The debate became more complex with the emergence of sex-worker advocacy groups in the 1970s and 1980s. Paralleling civil rights groups and movements, advocacy groups such as COYOTE (Call Off Your Old Tired Ethics) sought rights and respect for prostitutes. They defended the right to engage in sex work, which they defined as a legitimate type of paid labor. They advocated decriminalization.[4]

Americans have long been divided over prostitution: society stigmatizes and criminalizes it but still tolerates it, and many people support it with their hard-earned wages. However, the social context of prostitution has changed. In the past few decades, sex has been brought fully into the world of commerce. Prostitution is now just one facet of a billion-dollar sex industry that is integral to American commercial and social life. From this perspective, the selling of actual sex may seem like a mere extension of the commercialization of sex. Blurring the line between using sex to sell goods and selling sex itself continues to stir public anxieties. Many Americans do not want that line crossed. But as a result of the commercialization of sex, many sex workers—and perhaps many Americans in general—now see sex as just one more good or skill to be sold. This defense of sex work gains credibility if sex and the need for sex are viewed as natural or as an ordinary part of life. Moralists once objected to women working or to blacks occupying certain jobs; objections to sex work is said by advocates to be a similar prejudice that should no longer guide social policy.

Is sex work different from other types of work? In many jobs, workers exchange the use of their bodies for wages. Blue-collar workers and professional athletes sell their physical strength and endurance; models and actors exchange their physical attractiveness for money. Is selling particular sex acts not similar to marketing physical strength or beauty?

Until recently, prostitution had few defenders and many critics. On the whole, critics view sex work as degrading and exploitative. For some critics, prostitution degrades the meaning of sex. Sex should be a special way people establish a loving intimate relationship. Moreover, sexual expression is said to stir up one's deepest, most intimate feelings. Exchanging sex for money not only degrades sex by betraying its spiritual and moral purpose but it also alienates both the buyer and seller from their true selves. Accordingly, there is a big difference, these critics argue, between selling an ability to do physical labor or an attractive self-presentation and selling sexual favors. The latter is dehumanizing and alienating.

Feminist critics underscore a telling point: the vast majority of sex workers are women. Their work degrades and exploits them as humans and as women. Sex work makes women into "whores" and "bad girls" lacking self-respect and social value. Feminist critics of sex work argue that most women do not choose to be prostitutes; they are forced into this work by poverty, limited opportunities for well-paying jobs, drug or alcohol addictions, a history of sexual abuse, or the need to support their families.

In addition, prostitution reinforces women's low self-esteem and inferior social status. Women sex workers service men, which reinforces a view of women as sex objects to be used and discarded. Moreover, most often men own the brothels and control women sex workers. The whole sex-work industry is dominated by men, and prostitutes are their victims, according to these critics.[5]

Those who defend sex work acknowledge that many sex workers are treated badly, are often poorly paid, and sometimes suffer physical abuse. Also, defenders would agree with critics that many women do not choose to be sex workers but are forced into it by circumstances. Some defenders of sex work would admit that, like porn, sex work is largely an industry run by men, for men, and that it reinforces men's social dominance. Some of these objections to sex work, however, would apply to many work environments. Women who work as airline attendants, receptionists, or models are also sexually objectified, typically paid badly, and exercise little control over their work conditions.

But to get to the heart of the matter, is the buying and selling of sex necessarily degrading? From the point of view of the client, defenders of sex work say it is not. Although most of us, including sex workers, approach sex as a way to express love or establish intimacy and families, many of us also value sex as a form of pleasure and self-expression. And though many of us value sex for pleasure in loving relationships, some of us also choose to pursue sexual pleasure in more casual, consensual relationships. So, in principle, a person who purchases sex just for pleasure is not necessarily degrading the act or him- or herself.

But is selling sex degrading for the prostitute? It is reasonable to assume if you are selling sexual favors regularly that the sex will lose some of its pleasurable qualities and become just work. Of course, this is no different from many jobs that are repetitive and lack either expressive value or a clear social purpose. The issue is whether selling sex ruins a prostitute's ability to also have sex for pleasure and for love. Some argue that it does not. Prostitutes are able to disassociate themselves from the act when they are at work and to experience sex as a means of pleasure or love outside of work. Like any professional, a sex worker thinks of certain feelings and behaviors as having one meaning at work and other meanings outside of work. A skilled worker learns to separate his or her true self from the social roles required at work. The flight attendant who has to be congenial day after day for money does not lose her or his ability to be friendly outside of work. Similarly, many physicians regularly examine naked bodies and learn to desexualize intimate contact that would in other contexts be considered sexual. But we would not say that the physician loses his or her capacity to be sexual. The physician, like the attendant, learns a role that makes it possible to gain some emotional distance from work-related feelings and behaviors.

Defenders of sex work hold, then, that sex is not necessarily an integral part of one's core self. Sexual feelings are like other emotions: we learn to give them meaning and to manage them. Sometimes we have to use an emotion or behavior that carries strong expressive meaning in an instrumental way. Sex work, like other types of work, involves skills—and one of its chief skills is to treat sex during work in an emotionally neutral way.[6]

Defenders of sex work concede one important point: women are the overwhelming majority of sex workers, and this both reflects and reinforces a society dominated by men. Women become sex workers in part because of limited economic opportunities for better-paying jobs, in part because of the flexible work schedules, and in part because of a culture that already values them for their sexual attractiveness. A defense of sex work based only on the idea that adults have the right to choose their work so long as it does not involve any obvious social harm is a weak argument. Individual freedom is not absolute; social and psychological pressures always constrain choices. Because women have fewer economic options than men because they are disproportionately among the poor, responsible for child care and support in households in which there is no other help, and are raised in a society that makes self-esteem dependent on attractiveness, sex work may still be a choice, but it is one made under constrained conditions.

Yet, it is misleading for critics to argue that all women who become sex workers are forced to do so. Many of our work choices are constrained and are not self-fulfilling. The mere fact that sex work involves limited choice is not an argument either for or against it. The moral status of sex work rests ultimately on how we view the nature of the work.

This debate is often polarized between critics who exaggerate the victimization of sex workers and advocates who emphasize the role of choice and skill. Personally, I am persuaded by the argument that sex work involves skill and that selling sex is not necessarily degrading. Sex workers can manage emotions stirred up during sex without surrendering a satisfying personal sexual life. However, sex work *is* exploitative to the extent that it is women who do the sex work while men control the industry, and as long as women's wages are low and the working conditions are dangerous or unhealthy. Any defense of sex work needs to be connected to a critique of men's dominance in the sex-work industry. In other words, the issues raised by sex work are labor issues: work conditions, worker rights, and gender inequality in America.

Chapter Sixteen
GAY MARRIAGE: IS AMERICA A CHRISTIAN OR LIBERAL NATION?

MARRIAGE IS NOT JUST about love and intimacy between two adults. It is an institution. Marriage is recognized by the state, and those who marry get specific rights and benefits such as the right to spousal support, to bring wrongful death suits, to be listed as social security beneficiaries, to get legally recognized divorces, and to claim full parental rights. In most states in America, only a man and woman can marry. The question raised by the gay marriage debate is whether the gender of a spouse should matter in determining who can marry. And, what role should the state have in regulating intimate choices, including marriage?

Gay marriage was not an issue in the 1950s and early 1960s when gays and lesbians began their struggle for social justice. It initially surfaced in public debate in the 1970s. As we saw in an earlier chapter, a more confident and assertive gay movement redefined homosexuality: it was no longer a stigma but was viewed as natural and good. The gay movement approached being gay or lesbian as a positive basis of identity and community.

By the mid-1980s, the gay movement sought full, across-the-board legal and social equality. Gays and lesbians wanted to be equal citizens. They pursued equality at work, in schools, in the military, and in the eyes of the law. They also demanded to be treated respectfully in their families, by mass media, and elsewhere.

Gay marriage became a key issue in the 1990s as part of the pursuit of social equality.[1] Without the right to marry, gays are second-class citizens. Also, many gays and lesbians were turning their attention to intimate relationships. The generation that came out in the late 1960s and 1970s was now middle-aged; like many straight Americans in their thirties, forties, and fifties, their attention often turned to creating families. Many gays and lesbians were in or sought long-term intimate relationships. It was inevitable that they would turn their political focus toward marriage. Furthermore, AIDS pushed the issue of the legal status of their intimate relationships into the center of their lives. The AIDS crisis forced many gays and lesbians to address concerns such as health coverage of partners, hospital visitation rights, inheritance, and residency rights. AIDS compelled many gays and lesbians to invest enormous amounts of time, energy, and resources into caring for their partners, which made the legal status of their relationships an urgent concern.

Despite unfriendly social conditions, gays have always formed long-term relationships. For example, scholars have uncovered a long and complicated history of gay and lesbian relationships in nineteenth-century America. Sometimes women passed as men to form straight-seeming relationships; sometimes men or women lived together as housemates but were really lovers; sometimes individuals would marry but still carry on romantic, sometimes lifelong, same-sex intimate relationships.[2] By the 1990s, many gay men and lesbians were in long-term relationships; the lives of these couples were emotionally, socially, and financially intertwined in ways that were similar to straight marriages. Indeed, through either adoption or artificial insemination, many gay and lesbian couples were adding children to their families.

Gay marriage has today become a frontline issue for gays and lesbians—and not only in the United States. Gay marriage has become a worldwide issue. Many societies have already enacted laws that permit gays to marry (for example, Denmark, Canada, South Africa, and Argentina). In Germany, Ecuador, and Finland, laws have been passed that offer some type of state recognition to gay relationships.

Gay marriage might not have gained political traction in the United States were it not for broader changes in the American family. We are all aware that today families come in many sizes and shapes. Although the nuclear family, with a breadwinner husband and a stay-at-home wife, might still be an ideal for many Americans, it describes only a minority of actual households. The reality is a dizzying variety of families—cohabiting couples, one-parent households, combined families, marriages without children, lifelong partners who do not live together, and so on. The variety of intimate arrangements, the reality that almost half of all marriages end in divorce, the uncoupling of motherhood from marriage, and the lessening of the stigma attached to being single have all diminished the social or moral authority of marriage. Still, make no mistake; marriage is not just one choice among others. The state supports marriage with a cluster of rights and benefits that no other intimate relationship is given. In addition, the right to marry continues to serve as a symbol of first-class citizenship. Many gays and lesbians want to marry, or at least want the right to marry, to become equal, respected citizens.

Changes in the social organization of intimacy have also contributed to raising doubts about the reasonableness of excluding gays from marriage. For most of our parents and grandparents, the organization of marriage was more or less fixed. Men were the breadwinners; their lives were focused on making a living. Women were wives and mothers; their lives were centered on domestic tasks. Within the household, men were expected to do "masculine" domestic activities (mow the lawn, take out the garbage, discipline the children), whereas women were responsible for "feminine" tasks such as cooking, cleaning, and child care. Gender shaped the very texture of intimacy. Men were supposed to initiate and direct sex; women were supposed to go along without showing too much interest or pleasure. Men made the big decisions (where to live or how to spend money); women arranged the social affairs of the couple. Today, many women work, have careers, and pursue interests outside the household; men are expected to perform household and child-care tasks. We can perhaps reasonably speak of a somewhat new ideal of intimacy: marriage as a relationship between equals in which decisions are openly discussed and household roles are negotiated. In short, gender is becoming less important in organizing marriage. The gender of those who marry would then seem to matter less.

The battle over gay marriage is being fought on two fronts. A war is being waged in the legal courts and in the court of public opinion between mostly gay and lesbian advocates of gay marriage and straight critics. Public opinion is still on the side of critics, but this is changing rapidly. There is also debate within the gay movement. Not all gays and lesbians think that pursuing marital rights is the right goal for a movement that once aspired to ideals of sexual liberation. Gay critics view marriage as inimical to a culture championing sexual variation.

Straight critics of gay marriage make several key points.[3] Heterosexual marriage, they say, has deep roots in history. As far back as we know, marriage has always been between a man and a woman. There is something seemingly natural and right about heterosexual marriage. Moreover, heterosexual marriage is a cornerstone of the Judeo-Christian tradition. As some critics quip, God made Adam and Eve, not Adam and Steve. America has a secular government and was founded on secular principles, but a majority of Americans identify themselves as Christian.

Marriage is also a cornerstone of American society. It provides a stable, positive, moral environment essential for shaping good American citizens. Critics ask, will young people acquire clear gender identities without heterosexual marriage? Boys look to their fathers to learn what it means to be a man; wives provide daughters with a clear notion of what it means to be a woman. Gay marriage would create gender confusion.

Critics also raise another issue: marriage has already been weakened by the ease and frequency of divorce, by the increase in rates of illegitimacy and single-parent families, and by families in which both parents work. Legalizing gay marriage would further undermine the stability and strength of this institution. Even more ominously, permitting gays to marry would open the door for all sorts of people to demand the right to marry—polygamists, children, friends, kin.

These objections express real anxieties on the part of Americans about the fragility of marriage. Such concerns should not be quickly dismissed. Marriage has been, and still is, according to virtually all social researchers, a cherished ideal for most Americans. Marriage is bundled with a number of hopes shared by many Americans—for a home, a family, and a sense of community. Instead of bringing additional change to this already weakened institution, critics say, we should find ways to strengthen it.

Advocates of gay marriage have offered forceful rebuttals to these criticisms. No one denies, they say, that heterosexual marriage has deep roots in history, though recent historical scholarship suggests that same-sex intimacies, including marriage, were not as exceptional as once believed.[4] Setting aside past realities, though, the question that must be addressed is this: should the past or tradition always serve as a guide for the present? Consider that racism and sexism also have deep roots in history and social customs. Most of us agree that tradition should not be followed blindly, but examined in light of contemporary thinking and values. After all, imperfect people shaped past practices and traditions. Possibly the historical prejudice against homosexuality is similar to prejudices against nonwhites and women. The battleground for debating the issue of gay marriage should be the present, not the past.

What about the Judeo-Christian disapproval of homosexuality? With all due respect, gay marriage advocates hold that, like other traditions, religious practices too have been made by ordinary individuals who often shared the prejudices of their time. Christian belief and tradition has changed many times in history. The question for Christians is whether gay marriage can be understood as consistent with the spirit of Christianity. Both pro and con arguments have been made in this regard; I'll leave this debate to the faithful. There is, in any event, a more compelling reason to be cautious about religious objections to gay marriage. America is not a Christian nation. Although Judeo-Christian traditions have shaped America, so too have non-Christian and secular traditions. America is, arguably, a secular nation. Our government does not officially recognize or promote any particular religion and does not enact legislation, including laws regulating marriage, that need be aligned to any specific faith.

So, appeals to the past, to religious and secular traditions alone, should not exclude the right of gays to marry. But opponents have advanced additional arguments. Some argue that gays and lesbians are psychologically and morally unable to form stable marriages. This argument cannot be taken seriously because it relies on stereotypes that have been exposed and dismissed by social scientific research. The argument that if you extend marital rights to gays and lesbians then all sorts of people and relationships will clamor for the same rights is also not persuasive, since gays are not challenging the institution of marriage as a consensual relationship between two adults. Gays and lesbians simply want the same right of access as heterosexuals.

What are the positive arguments for gay marriage? The key issue, say advocates, is the meaning of marriage today. Too often, critics of gay marriage assume that marriage has always had the same meaning and social organization. This is not the case. Marriage has changed considerably, even in the short history of the United States. Consider that not too long ago marriage was possible only between adults of the same race. Antimiscegenation laws, initially enacted in Maryland in 1661 and not declared unconstitutional by the Supreme Court until 1967, forbid marriage between whites and nonwhites, including blacks, Asians, and Native Americans. Or, consider that throughout most of American history, marriage was rigidly organized around gender roles. Until the twentieth century, women were the legal property of men; a wife could not own her own property and did not even have the right to her own wages. Marriage was thought to be fundamentally for the purpose of having children. Today, we recognize spouses as equal before the law, and gender roles are not enforced by the state. Many couples marry and remain childless by choice.

Marriage today has various meanings. For some, it is about creating a family; for others, it is about social and financial security. For many of us, marriage is fundamentally about love and forging an intimate life with another person. In this companionate ideal, individuals look to marriage to find a deep emotional, social, even spiritual union. In principle, gender plays less of a role in organizing marriage. Men and women share domestic duties; they attempt to negotiate a life together as equals. Spouses want to be respected and fulfilled as individuals. To be sure, social scientists have documented that gender still plays a considerable role in organizing intimacy. For example, women continue to do the lion's share of domestic tasks, including child care. But, today, individuals can demand that their unique wants and desires, regardless of their gender, be considered in the social organization of intimate relationships.

If marriage is about equal individuals forging an intimate, loving, mutually committed relationship, then the gender of the partners should be irrelevant. What should matter is whether the partners agree to marry, and whether they are caring, committed, respectful, responsible, and willing to communicate openly their respective needs and wants. Permitting gays and lesbians to marry will not change the institution of marriage but strengthen an ideal of this institution as a relationship of loving intimacy between equals.

I think that some people oppose gay marriage because they are threatened by this egalitarian ideal of marriage. This ideal, after all, mutes the role of gender. Some men may fear a loss of status and power, and some women may fear economic insecurity and the loss or devaluation of their chief identity as full-time wives and mothers. For women and men who are deeply invested in gender roles and identities or in marriages that are fundamentally about having children, gay marriage may be viewed as a threat not because it challenges heterosexual privilege but because it challenges a very specific and narrow idea of gender and the family.

As the gay movement has rallied around the issue of gay marriage, some gays and lesbians have voiced their own objections.[5] Unlike opponents who see in gay marriage a threat to marriage, some gay critics propose that marriage itself is a threat to individual choice and diversity. Today, marriage is the business of the state. It confers a cluster of special rights and social benefits on those who marry. State-backed marriage devalues nonmarital intimate choices. This has especially bad effects on minorities and the poor, who tend to marry less. Extending marital rights to gay men and lesbians would expand state control over citizens' private lives and reinforce the divide between marital and nonmarital intimacies. This is not an argument against the idea of marriage but against marriage as a state-sanctioned institution. These critics wish to make marriage into a civil institution. This would mean the benefits associated with marriage would have to either become individual rights (for example, universal health care) or be available to a range of intimate relationships.

The criticism of state-supported marriage strikes me as persuasive. I am sympathetic to the idea that the less government, the better, when it comes to regulating intimate choices between consenting adults. However, there is little likelihood that the legal status of marriage in the United States will change, at least in the foreseeable future. Straight Americans show little interest in dissolving the close tie between the state and marriage. Indeed, most political activity around marriage is centered on strengthening it. In addition, the evidence suggests that gays and lesbians overwhelmingly want the right to marry. If marriage is here to stay, at least for some time, gays should have that right. It is a matter of first-class citizenship. We are not talking about abstract rights but real benefits: health care, rights of residency, hospital visitation rights, inheritance rights, and many more. Moreover, giving gays and lesbians the right to marry would contribute to recognizing them as fully respectable, morally good citizens; this would translate into less prejudice and real improvements in the quality of their lives.

So for both moral and practical political reasons, I think it is important to defend the right of gays and lesbians to marry. Although I do not expect an end to state support of marriage anytime soon, I do anticipate the distribution of some marital rights to other intimate arrangements—those relationships that, in terms of their intimate ties, look a lot like marriage, that is, relationships involving long-standing emotional, sexual, social, and economic interdependence between two unrelated adults. These intimate unions merit state recognition. In fact, this is already happening. Many of the rights and benefits of marriage are now claimed by "domestic partnerships"—which are recognized in many cities, states, businesses, unions, and colleges—by "civil unions," and by common-law marriages, cohabitation, and single-parent households.[6] In the short run, the best way to promote intimate diversity in the United States is to expand the range of intimate relationships that are recognized by the state.

Epilogue

CONFLICTS OVER SEXUALITY are unlikely to end soon. Americans are divided over the meaning and purpose of sex. Is sex primarily about pleasure, love, marriage, or procreation? Should all sexual acts between consenting adults be tolerated, or are there certain acts that are inherently perverse and intolerable, even though they lack obvious victims? Should gays and lesbians be treated as equal citizens? What about bisexuals, transsexuals, sex workers, and transgendered individuals? Where do we draw the line between sexualities that are accepted and those that are rejected? On what basis do we say that selling sexual images is okay but selling real sex is not? And what exactly is the meaning of marriage today? Is it primarily concerned with companionship, love, family, or economics? Should it be a civil or state institution?

Unfortunately, Americans are often unable to discuss these issues in calm, thoughtful ways. Although talk shows and popular magazines convey the impression that Americans talk incessantly about sex and are sophisticated in their thinking about sex, the fact is that most of us grow up with little or no formal sex education. Few of us have frank, informative discussions about sex with our kin, teachers, or peers; indeed, many of us lack the kinds of information about the body and sexual technique that would allow us to become skilled, effective sexual agents. Is it any wonder that many of us find it awkward or are simply incapable of talking about our sexual preferences and concerns in thoughtful ways?

A measured and reasonable discussion of sex is made more difficult by the fact that sexual conflicts frequently raise non-sexual issues. The debate over the nature of homosexuality raises questions about gender roles, the meaning of marriage and the family, and the very meaning of being an American citizen. Pornography forces us to think about the status of women today. Many of us still associate being a woman with being a wife and mother; do we really want women represented in highly erotic and sexually aggressive ways, even if those representations were nonsexist? The sex-worker debate raises questions about the sphere of work. Should sex workers be recognized as workers who deserve certain rights and protections? How do we draw the line between sexual activities that belong in the sphere of work—and that therefore should be covered by a web of civil rights—and sexual activities that do not?

Sex disputes are especially vulnerable to becoming emotionally charged. They stir up deeply held beliefs and values. To make matters worse, sexual disputes sometimes get framed as a morality play of good versus evil or as a national drama populated by monsters and saviors. Think of the public response to child molesters or the recent sex scandals enveloping the Catholic Church. During sex panics, emotions squeeze out reason. To keep sexual conflicts in the realm of reason, we need to keep the discussion focused, as much as possible, on the issues immediately raised by a dispute. For example, rather than framing the debate over gay marriage as being about the very fate of Western civilization, we need to sort through the rather specific and limited concerns raised by extending marriage to gays—such as, how would it affect the institution of marriage, or what would be the likely effects on gender roles and child rearing? A focused discussion would help avoid quick judgments on issues that can have great impact on people's lives.

A calm, measured public discussion of sexual disputes has been seriously compromised by politicians who play on citizens' sexual fears for political gain. Politicians and a media geared to ratings often create a sense of moral panic around sex. For example, despite the weight of research and informed opinion, there are politicians who continue to attack homosexuals as child-molesting and family-destroying threats merely to present themselves as defenders of "family values." Or, despite little or no research to support their claims, some politicians blame pornography for causing child abuse and turmoil in families. In this way, a politician can promote him- or herself as a fighter for children, families, and a world free of the moral pollution of porn. The effects of such irresponsible political maneuvers is to demonize homosexuals and pornographers as moral monsters, while distracting the public from the real threats to children and family life—low-paying jobs, lack of financial and emotional support by fathers, absence of health care, growing family debt encouraged by a consumerist culture, and so on. Sadly, scapegoating sexual outsiders has become a cornerstone of politics and a sensationalist media.

To encourage a thoughtful public discussion of sexuality we need to avoid stirring up emotions needlessly by resorting to a rhetoric of national threat or social decline. Sexual disputes do raise broad concerns about the meaning and organization of families, gender roles, and private and public behavior, as well as about the role of the state. But we need to try to keep our focus on the narrowly sexual issues at hand and sort through them in

light of the relevant research and the potential social consequences of various views and agendas.

We need something else to promote a more rational culture
of sexual conflict: a social view of sexuality. Ordinary citizens,
public officials, and media spokespersons continue to approach
sex as a biological need or instinct with which we are born or en-
dowed by God. Many of us continue to try to draw rigid boundaries between good and bad sexual behavior in terms of what
we think is natural or normal. Heterosexuals are good, homosexuals are bad; marriage and monogamy are normal and right,
other intimate arrangements are wrong and dangerous. Such a
simplistic approach does not encourage a cautious, thoughtful
debate but motivates individuals to draw quick lines of good
versus evil. We need a more nuanced moral language of sexuality.

The revolution in sexual scholarship has provided a new way
of thinking about sex. If we think of sex as deeply social—if we
approach the meaning of sex, its social organization, its rules and
norms, and the divisions established between good and bad sexualities as products of social factors (for example, economics, gender, public discourses, media images, family, science)—we will be
forced to think harder about the politics and morality of sex.
Thinking of sex as social pushes us to consider what sorts of rules
should organize sexuality; it compels us to furnish arguments defending these rules instead of simply invoking nature or religion.
Public discussions of sexual morality will strike a more reasoned
tone when, instead of appealing to some absolute authority (nature or God), we must consider available research, people's actual
experiences, and the likely personal and social consequences of
varied forms of sexual control. All this means approaching sex as
a social construction.[1]

Notes

CHAPTER ONE   THE SCIENCE OF SEX

1. On the ideas and history of sexology, see Harry Oosterhuis, *Stepchildren of Nature: Krafft-Ebing, Psychiatry, and the Making of Sexual Identity* (Chicago: University of Chicago Press, 2000); and Jeffrey Weeks, *Sexuality and Its Discontents: Meaning, Myths, and Modern Sexualities* (London: Routledge, 1985).

2. Perhaps the best introduction to Freud's views on sexuality is his "Three Essays on the Theory of Sexuality" in *The Standard Edition*, vol. 7 (London: Hogarth Press, 1953).

CHAPTER TWO   SOCIAL THEORIES OF SEXUALITY

1. For Marxist approaches to sexuality, see Reimut Reiche, *Sexuality and Class Struggle* (London: New Left Books, 1979); John D'Emilio, "Capitalism and Gay Identity," in *Powers of Desire: The Politics of Sexuality*, eds. Ann Snitow, Christine Stansell, and Sharon Thompson (New York: Monthly Review Press, 1983); and David Evans, *Sexual Citizenship: The Material Construction of Sexualities* (London: Routledge, 1993).

2. Nancy Chodorow, *The Reproduction of Mothering: Pyschoanalysis and the Sociology of Gender* (Berkeley: University of California Press, 1978).

3. Adrienne Rich, "Compulsory Heterosexuality and Lesbian Existence," *Signs* 5 (1980).

4. Catherine MacKinnon, *Toward a Feminist Theory of the State* (Cambridge, MA: Harvard University Press, 1989).

5. Gayle Rubin, "Thinking Sex: Notes for a Radical Theory of the Politics of Sexuality," in *Pleasure and Danger: Exploring Female Sexuality*, ed. Carole Vance (Boston: Routledge and Kegan Paul, 1984).

CHAPTER THREE   SOCIAL CONSTRUCTIONISM

1. Ira Reiss, *Premarital Sexual Standards in America* (Glencoe, IL: Free Press, 1960) and *The Social Context of Premarital Sexual Permissiveness* (New York: Holt, Rinehart and Winston, 1967).

2. John Gagnon and William Simon, *Sexual Conduct: The Social Sources of Human Sexuality* (Chicago: Aldine, 1973).

3. Ken Plummer, *Sexual Stigma: An Interactionist Account* (London: Routledge, 1975).

4. Jeffrey Weeks, *Sex, Politics, and Society: The Regulation of Sexuality Since 1800* (London: Longman, 1981).

5. Jeffrey Weeks, *Sexuality* (London: Tavistock, 1986), p. 26.

6. Jeffrey Weeks, *Coming Out: Homosexual Politics in Britain from the Nineteenth Century to the Present* (London: Quartet, 1977).

7. Jonathan Ned Katz, *Gay American History* (New York: Crowell, 1976) and *Gay/Lesbian Almanac* (New York: Harper & Row, 1983).

8. Carroll Smith-Rosenberg, "The Female World of Love and Ritual: Relations between Women in Nineteenth-Century America," *Signs* 1 (1975).

9. Lillian Faderman, *Surpassing the Love of Men: Romantic Friendship and Love between Women from the Renaissance to the Present* (New York: William Morrow, 1981) and *Odd Girls and Twilight Lovers: A History of Lesbian Life in Twentieth-Century America* (New York: Columbia University Press, 1991).

10. John D'Emilio, *Sexual Politics, Sexual Communities: The Making of a Homosexual Minority in the United States, 1940–1970* (Chicago: University of Chicago Press, 1983).

11. George Chauncey, *Gay New York: Gender, Urban Culture, and the Making of the Gay Male World, 1890–1940* (New York: Basic Books, 1994).

12. Michel Foucault, *The History of Sexuality*, vol. 1, *An Introduction* (New York: Vintage, 1980).

13. Judith Butler, *Gender Trouble: Feminism and the Subversion of Identity* (New York: Routledge, 1990).

14. For example, see Kristin Esterberg, *Lesbian and Bisexual Identities: Constructing Communities, Constructing Selves* (Philadelphia: Temple University Press, 1997).

CHAPTER FOUR   HETEROSEXUALITY

1. On the history of heterosexuality, see Jonathan Ned Katz, *The Invention of Heterosexuality* (New York: Penguin, 1995).

2. On the changing meaning of heterosexuality as a response to shifts in gender roles, see Chauncey, *Gay New York*; and Kevin White, *The First Sexual Revolution: The Emergence of Male Heterosexuality in Modern America* (New York: New York University Press, 1993).

3. See Debbie Epstein and Richard Johnson, *Schooling Sexualities* (Buckingham, UK: Open University Press, 1998); and Mairtin Mac An Ghaill, *The Making of Men: Masculinities, Sexualities and Schooling* (Buckingham, UK: Open University Press, 1994).

4. Peggy Reeves Sanday, *Fraternity Gang Rape: Sex, Brotherhood, and Privilege on Campus* (New York: New York University Press, 1990).

5. Steven Seidman, *Beyond the Closet* (New York: Routledge, 2003).

Chapter Five   Gay, Lesbian, and Bisexual Politics in the United States

1. To further explore this view of sexual politics, see Foucault, *The History of Sexuality*, vol. 1; and Rubin, "Thinking Sex".

2. On heterosexuality as an institution, the classic statement is Adrienne Rich, "Compulsory Heterosexuality and Lesbian Existence," *Signs* 5 (1980). Also see Chrys Ingraham, *White Weddings: Romancing Heterosexuality in Popular Culture* (New York: Routledge, 2008).

3. On the idea of romantic friendships in nineteenth-century America, see Smith-Rosenberg, "The Female World of Love and Ritual;" and Jonathan Ned Katz, *Love Stories: Sex between Men before Homosexuality* (Chicago: University of Chicago Press, 2001).

4. On the history of homosexuality in early twentieth-century America, see Chauncey, *Gay New York*; Faderman, *Odd Girls and Twilight Lovers*; Elizabeth Kennedy and Madeline Davis, *Boots of Leather, Slippers of Gold: The History of a Lesbian Community* (New York: Routledge, 1993); and Jennifer Terry, *An American Obsession: Science, Medicine, and Homosexuality in Modern Society* (Chicago: University of Chicago Press, 1999).

5. Diana Frederics, *Diana: A Strange Autobiography* (1939; reprint, New York: Arno Press, 1975), p. 18.

6. See Allan Berube, *Coming Out under Fire: The History of Gay Men and Women in World War Two* (New York: Macmillan, 1990).

7. See Kennedy and Davis, *Boots of Leather, Slippers of Gold;* and Faderman, *Odd Girls and Twilight Lovers*.

8. On gay politics in the 1950s and 1960s, see D'Emilio, *Sexual Politics, Sexual Communities*; and Toby Marotta, *The Politics of Homosexuality* (New York: Houghton Mifflin, 1981).

9. On gay liberationism, see Dennis Altman, *Homosexual Oppression and Liberation* (New York: Avon Books, 1971); Martin Duberman, *Stonewall* (New York: Dutton, 1993); Stephen Engel, *The Unfinished Revolution: Social Movement Theory and the Gay and Lesbian Movement* (Cambridge, MA: Cambridge University Press, 2001); and Barry Adam, *The Rise of the Gay and Lesbian Movement* (New York: Twayne Publishers, 1995).

10. On the politics of lesbian feminism, see Alice Echols, *Daring to Be Bad: Radical Feminism in America, 1967–1975* (Minneapolis: University of Minnesota Press, 1989); and Shane Phelan, *Identity Politics: Lesbian Feminism and the Limits of Community* (Philadelphia: Temple University Press, 1989).

11. John Lee, "The Gay Connection," *Urban Issues* 8 (July 1979): 179–80.

12. For perspectives on the bisexual movement, see Elizabeth Reba Weise, ed., *Bisexuality and Feminism* (Seattle, WA: Seal Press, 1992); Marjorie Garber, *Vice Versa: Bisexuality and the Eroticism of Everyday Life* (New York: Simon & Schuster, 1995); Paula Rust, *Bisexuality and the Challenge to Lesbian Politics* (New York: Columbia University Press, 1995); and Naomi Tucker, ed., *Bisexual Politics: Theories, Queries, and Visions* (New York: Haworth Press, 1995).

13. Lisa Orlando, "Loving Who We Choose," in *Bi Any Other Name: Bisexual People Speak Out*, ed. Loraine Hutchins and Lani Kaahumanu (Boston: Alyson, 1991), p. 224.

14. Stephen Donaldson, "The Bisexual Movement's Beginnings in the 70s: A Personal Retrospective," in *Bisexual Politics*, ed. Tucker, p. 53.

15. Naomi Tucker, "What's in a Name?" in *Bi Any Other Name*, p. 246.

CHAPTER SIX   THE REVOLT AGAINST SEXUAL IDENTITY

1. Katherine Sender, "Queens for a Day: *Queer Eye for the Straight Guy* and the Neoliberal Project," *Studies in Media Communication* 23, no. 2 (2006): 131–51.

2. Ritch C. Savin-Williams, *The New Gay Teenager* (Cambridge, MA: Harvard University Press, 2005).

3. Ibid.

4. Ibid.

5. Jane M. Ussher and Julie Mooney-Somers, "Negotiating Desire and Sexual Subjectivity: Narratives of Young Lesbian Avengers," *Sexualities* 3 (2000): 183–200.

6. Clyde Smith, "How I Became a Queer Heterosexual," in *Straight with a Twist: Queer Theory and the Subject of Heterosexuality*, ed. Calvin Thomas (Urbana: University of Illinois Press, 2000), pp. 60–67.

7. Ibid.

8. Robert Heasley, "Crossing the Borders of Gendered Sexuality: Queer Masculinities of Straight Men," in *Thinking Straight: The Power, Promise and Paradox of Heterosexuality*, ed. Chrys Ingraham (New York: Routledge, 2005), pp. 109–130.

9. Robert Heasley, "Queer Masculinities of Straight Men," *Men and Masculinities* 7, no. 3 (2005): 310–20.

10. Ibid., p. 314.

11. Ibid.

12. Heasley, "Crossing the Boarders of Gendered Sexuality," p. 316.

13. Suzanne Pennington, "Who 'Wears the Pants'?: Bisexuals' Performances of Gender and Sexuality in Romantic Relationships" (master's thesis, Department of Sociology, Ohio University, 2006). [full-text online: www.ohiolink.edu/etd/senddf.cgi?acc_num=ohiou 1148520142]; and Suzanne Pennington, "Bisexuals' 'Doing Gender' in Romantic Relationships," *Journal of Bisexuality* 9, no. 1 (March 9, 2009).

14. Pennington, "Bisexual' 'Doing Gender' in Romantic Relationships."

15. Eli Clare, *The Marrow's Telling: Words in Motion* (Ypsilanti, MI: Homofactus Press, 2007).

16. Tam Sanger, "Trans Governmentality: The Production and Regulation of Gendered Subjectivities," *Journal of Gender Studies* 17 (2008): 41–53.

17. Ibid.

18. Jason Cromwell, *Transmen and FTMs: Identities, Bodies, Genders and Sexualities* (Chicago: University of Illinois Press, 1999), p. 126.

19. Ibid.

20. Ibid., p. 128.

21. Sanger, "Trans Governmentality," p. 46

22. Ibid., p. 49.

Chapter Seven   Changing Cultures of intimacy

1. Nancy Cott, *Public Vows* (Cambridge, MA: Harvard University Press, 2000).

2. Michael Grossberg, *Governing the Hearth* (Chapel Hill: University of North Carolina Press, 1985), p. 170.

3. Ariela Dubler, "Governing through Contract: Common Law Marriage in the Nineteenth Century," *Yale Law Journal* 107 (1998): p 1894–95.

4. Grossberg, *Governing the Hearth*, pp.107–108.

5. Margot Canaday, *The Straight State* (Princeton, NJ: Princeton University Press, 2010).

6. Stephanie Coontz, *Marriage, a History* (New York: Penguin, 2005), p. 226.

7. Anthony Giddens, *The Transformation of Intimacy* (Stanford, CA: Stanford University Press, 1992).

8. Jean Cohen, *Regulating Intimacy* (Princeton, NJ: Princeton University Press, 2002); Jane Singer, "The Privatization of the Family Law," *Winsconsin Law Review* 1992): 1442–1567.

9. Anna Marie Smith, *Welfare Reform and Sexual Regulation* (Cambridge, MA: Cambridge University Press, 2007).

CHAPTER EIGHT   THE PROMISE AND PERILS
OF CYBER INTIMACIES

1. Pamela Haag, "Death by Treacle," *American Scholar* (Spring 2012).

2. Ibid., p. 82.

3. Stephen Marche, "Is Facebook Making us Lonely?" *Atlantic Monthly* (May 2012).

4. Eric Klinenberg, *Going Solo* (New York: Penguin, 2012)

5. Sherry Turkle, *The Second Self* (Cambridge, MA: MIT Press, 1984); *Life on the Screen* (New York: Simon & Schuster, 1996); and *Alone Together: Why We Expect More from Technology and Less from Each Other* (New York: Basic Books, 2011)

6. Nancy Baym, *Personal Connections in the Digital Age* (Cambridge, MA: Cambridge Polity Press, 2010). Also see Howard Gardner and Katie Davis, *The App Generation* (New Haven, CT: Yale University Press, 2013).

7. Baym, *Personal Connection in the Digital Age*, p. 116.

8. Ibid, p. 119.

9. Ibid, p. 130.

10. Katelyn Y.A. McKenna, Amie S. Green, and Marci E.J. Gleason, "Relationship Formation on the Internet: What's the Big Attraction?" *Journal*

of Social Issues 58 (2002): 9–31. Cited in Baym, *Personal Connections in the Digital Age*, p. 129.

11. Darius K-S. Chan and Grand H-L. Cheng, "A Comparison of Offline and Online Friendship Qualities at Different Stages of Relationship Development," *Journal of Social and Personal Relationships* 21 (2004): 305–20. Cited in Baym, *Personal Connections in the Digital Age*, p. 131.

12. For a short sampling of research reports on relationships and digital media use, see Sarah M. Coyne et al., "I Luv U:): A Descriptive Study of the Media Use of Individuals in Romantic Relationships," *Family Relations* 60 (2011): 150–62; Jin Borae and Jorge F. Pena, "Mobile Communication in Romantic Relationships: Mobile Phone Use, Relational Uncertainty, Love, Commitment, and Attachment Styles," *Communication Reports* 23 (2010): 39–51; and Jonathan Pettigrew, "Text Messaging and Connectedness within Close Interpersonal Relationships," *Marriage and Family Review* 45 (2009): 697–716.

13. Baym, *Personal Connections in the Digital Age*, p. 138

14. Ibid., p. 141.

15. Linda Nicholson, "Let Me Tell You Who I Am: Intimacy, Privacy and Self-Disclosure," in *Intimacies: A New World of Relational Life*, ed. Alan Frank, Patricia T. Clough, and Steven Seidman (New York: Routledge, 2013).

CHAPTER NINE   YOUTH STRUGGLES TO NEGOTIATE
INDEPENDENCE AND INTIMATE SOLIDALITY

1. There is a growing body of research on hooking up. Consider Kathleen Bogle, *Hooking Up* (New York: New York University Press, 2008); Paula England, Emily Fitzgibbons Shafer, and Alison C.K. Fogarty, "Hooking Up and Forming Romantic Relationships on Today's College Campuses," in *The Gendered Society*, ed. Michael Kimmel and Amy Aronson (New York: Oxford University Press, 2008); and Elizabeth A. Armstrong, Laura Hamilton, and Paula England. "Is Hooking Up Bad for Young Women?" *Contexts* 9 (2010): 22–27.

2. Leila Rupp and Verta Taylor, "Queer Girls on Campus: New Intimacies and Sexual Identities," in *Intimacies*, ed. Frank, Clough, and Seidman; also see Lisa Diamond, *Sexual Fluidity* (Cambridge, MA: Harvard University Press, 2008); and Ritch Savin-Williams, *The New Gay Teenager* (Cambridge, MA: Harvard University Press 2005).

3. Kathleen Gerson, *The Unfinished Revolution* (Oxford, UK: Oxford University Press, 2010).

4. Ibid., p. 172

5. Ibid., p. 171

6. Kathryn Edin and Maria Kefalas, *Promises I Can Keep: Why Poor Women Put Motherhood before Marriage* (Berkeley: University of California Press, 2005).

7. Kathryn Edin and Timothy Welson, *Doing The Best I Can: Fatherhood in the Inner City* (Berkeley: University of California Press, 2013).

8. Ibid., p. 193.

CHAPTER TEN   INTO OUR BEDROOMS

1. John D'Emilio and Estelle Freedman, *Intimate Matters: A History of Sexuality in America* (New York: Harper & Row, 1988); and Linda Hirshman and Jane Larson, *Hard Bargains* (New York: Oxford University Press, 1998), pp. 87–88.

2. Rosiland Petchesky, *Abortion and Women's Choice* (Boston: Northeastern University Press, 1984).

3. D'Emilio and Freedman, *Intimate Matters*, p. 174.

4. Kristen Luker, "Sex, Hygiene, and the State: The Double-Edged Sword of Social Reform," *Theory and Society* 27 (1998): 615.

5. D'Emilio and Freedman, *Intimate Matters*, pp. 157–59.

6. Hirshman and Larson, *Hard Bargain*, p. 172.

7. Singer, "The Privatization of Family Law," pp. 1444–45.

8. Petchesky, *Abortion and Women's Choices*, p. 292.

9. William Eskridge, *Gaylaw* (Cambridge, MA: Harvard University Press, 1999), p. 18.

10. Ibid., p. 124.

11. Ibid.

12. For this section, I have drawn considerably on Rachel Moran, *Interracial Intimacy* (Chicago: University of Chicago Press, 2001).

CHAPTER ELEVEN   POPULAR CULTURE INTRODUCES THE NEW NORMAL CITIZEN

1. This section draws on Steven Seidman, *Beyond the Closet* (New York: Routledge, 2003).

2. Carrie Cokely, "'Someday My Prince Will Come': Disney, the Heterosexual Imaginary and Animated Film," in *Straight Thinking*, ed. C. Ingraham (New York: Routledge, 2006), p. 168.

3. Karin Martin, *Puberty, Sexuality, and the Self: Boys and Girls at Adolescence* (New York: Routledge, 1996), pp. 61–62.

4. Meenakshi Gigi Durham, "Girls, Media, and the Negotiation of Sexuality: A Study of Race, Class, and Gender in Adolescent Peer Groups," in *Sexuality and Gender*, eds. Christine Williams and Arlene Stein (Malden, MA: Blackwell, 2002), p. 336.

5. Amy Best, "The Production of Heterosexuality at the High School Prom," in *Straight Thinking*, ed. Ingraham.

6. Chrys Ingraham, *White Weddings*, 2nd ed. (New York: Routledge, 2008), p. 9.

CHAPTER TWELVE   HETEROSEXUALITY IN PANIC

1. This section is drawn from Steven Seidman, *Romantic Longings* (New York: Routledge, 2001) and *Embattled Eros: Sexual Politics and Ethics in Contemporary America* (New York: Routledge, 2002).

2. P. J. McGann, "Healing (Disorderly) Desire: Medical-Therapeutic Regulation of Sexuality," in *Introducing the New Sexuality Studies*, eds. S. Seidman, Nancy Fisher, and Chet Meeks (New York: Routledge, 2006), p. 373.

3. Dagmar Herzog, *Sex in Crisis* (New York: Basic, 2008), pp. 31–32.

4. Tina Vares and Virginia Braun, "Spreading the Word, but What Word Is That? Viagra and Male Sexuality in Popular Culture," *Sexualities* 9 (2006): 324.

5. Heather Hartley, "The 'Pinking' of Viagra Culture: Drug Industry Efforts to Create and Repackage Sex Drugs for Women," *Sexualities* 9 (2006): 363–78.

6. Herzog, *Sex in Crisis*, p. 18.

CHAPTER THIRTEEN   PORN WARS

1. On the history of pornography in nineteenth-century America, see Walter Kendrick, *The Secret Museum: Pornography in Modern Culture* (Berkeley: University of California Press, 1996); and D'Emilio and Freedman, *Intimate Matters*.

2. See David Pivar, *Purity Crusade: Sexual Morality and Social Control, 1868–1900* (Westport, CT: Greenwood, 1973); and Nicola Beisel, *Imperiled Innocents: Anthony Comstock and Family Reproduction in Victorian America* (Princeton, NJ: Princeton University Press, 1997).

3. D'Emilio and Freedman, *Intimate Matters*, p. 277.

4. For perspectives on the porn industry and the politics of porn in the 1980s and 1990s, see David Hebditch and Nick Anning, *Porn Gold: Inside the Pornography Business* (London: Faber & Faber, 1988); Lynne Segal and Mary McIntosh, eds., *Sex Exposed: Sexuality and the Pornography Debate* (New Brunswick, NJ: Rutgers University Press, 1993); Donald Alexander Downs, *The New Politics of Pornography* (Chicago: University of Chicago Press, 1989); and Eric Schlosser, "The Business of Pornography," *U.S. News and World Report*, February 10, 1997, pp. 42–50.

5. Andrea Dworkin and Catherine MacKinnon, *Pornography and Civil Rights: A New Day for Women's Equality* (Minneapolis: Organizing Against Pornography, 1988).

6. For an overview of the libertarian defense of porn, see Seidman, *Embattled Eros*. For the feminist defense of porn, see Varda Burstyn, ed., *Women against Censorship* (Vancouver, Canada: Douglas and McIntyre, 1985).

7. For the conservative critique of porn, see Phyllis Schaffly, ed., *Pornography's Victims* (Westchester, IL: Crossway Books, 1987).

8. On the feminist critique of porn, see Laura Lederer, ed., *Take Back the Night: Women on Pornography* (New York: William Morrow, 1980).

9. See Ann Russo, "Feminists Confront Pornography's Subordinating Practices," and Gail Dines, "Dirty Business: *Playboy* Magazine and the Mainstreaming of Pornography," in *Pornography: The Production and Consumption of Inequality*, ed. Gail Dines, Robert Jensen, and Ann Russo (New York: Routledge, 1998).

CHAPTER FOURTEEN   SADOMASOCHISM, OR,
THE PLEASURES OF PAIN

1. On the introduction of S/M into mainstream American culture, see Melinda Blau, "Ordinary People," *New York*, November 28, 1994, pp. 38–46; Lynn Chancer, *Sadomasochism in Everyday Life* (New Brunswick, NJ: Rutgers University Press, 1992); and P. Cross and K. Matheson, "Understanding Sadomasochism," *Journal of Homosexuality* 50 (2006): 135–66.

2. For an overview of sexual changes in twentieth-century America, see D'Emilio and Freedman, *Intimate Matters*, and Seidman, *Embattled Eros*.

3. Samois, *Coming to Power* (Boston: Alyson, 1982); and Pat Califia, *Public Sex: The Culture of Radical Sex* (Pittsburgh, PA: Cleis, 1994). For a gay male defense of S/M, see Geoffrey Mains, *Urban Aboriginals* (San Francisco, CA: Gay Sunshine Press, 1984).

4. See Robin B. Linden, ed., *Against Sadomasochism: A Radical Feminist Analysis* (San Francisco, CA: Frog in the Well, 1982). For general overviews of the S/M debate, see Seidman, *Embattled Eros*; and Lynn Chancer, *Reconcilable Differences: Confronting Beauty, Pornography, and the Future of Feminism* (Berkeley: University of California Press, 1998).

Chapter Fifteen   A Right to Sex Work?

1. For helpful sociological overviews of sex work, see Ronald Weitzer, ed., *Sex for Sale: Prostitution, Pornography, and the Sex Industry* (New York: Routledge, 2000); and Graham Scambler and Annette Scambler, eds., *Rethinking Prostitution: Purchasing Sex in the 1990s* (London: Routledge, 1997).

2. On the history of prostitution in the United States, see Christine Stansell, *City of Women: Sex and Class in New York, 1789–1860* (New York: Knopf, 1986); Joan Jenson, *Loosening the Bonds: Mid-Atlantic Farm Women, 1750–1850* (New Haven, CT: Yale University Press, 1986); and Ruth Rosen, *The Lost Sisterhood: Prostitution in America, 1900–1918* (Baltimore: John Hopkins University Press, 1982).

3. For overviews of the sociology and politics of prostitution, see Ronald Weitzer, "The Politics of Prostitution in America"; and Wendy Chapkis, "Power and Control in the Commercial Sex Trade," in *Sex for Sale* ed. Weitzer.

4. For a sampling of perspectives by sex workers, see Frederique Delacoste and Priscilla Alexander, eds., *Sex Work: Writings by Women in the Sex Industry* (Pittsburgh, PA: Cleis, 1987).

5. A review of feminist criticisms of prostitution is provided by Lori Schrage, *Moral Dilemmas of Feminism: Prostitution, Adultery and Abortion* (New York: Routledge, 1994).

6. For feminist arguments defending prostitution, see Gail Pheterson, ed., *A Vindication of the Rights of Whores* (Seattle, WA: Seal Press, 1989); and Wendy Chapkis, *Live Sex Acts: Women Performing Erotic Labor* (New York: Routledge, 1997).

CHAPTER SIXTEEN   GAY MARRIAGE

1. On the history of the gay marriage debate, see William Eskridge Jr., *Equality Practice: Civil Unions and the Future of Gay Rights* (New York: Routledge, 2002).

2. On gay relationships in American history, see Katz, *Love Stories*; and Smith-Rosenberg, "The Female World of Love and Ritual," pp. 1–29.

3. For a sampling of the arguments in the gay marriage debate, see Andrew Sullivan, ed., *Same-Sex Marriage: Pro and Con* (New York: Vintage, 1997); and Robert Baird and Stuart Rosenbaum, eds., *Same-Sex Marriage: The Moral and Legal Debate* (Amherst, MA: Prometheus Books, 1997).

4. See John Boswell, *Same-Sex Unions in Pre-modern Europe* (New York: Villiard Books, 1994); and Bernadette Brooten, *Love between Women: Early Christian Responses to Female Homoeroticism* (Chicago: University of Chicago Press, 1996).

5. For criticisms of gay marriage from a gay perspective, see Paula Ettelbrick, "Since When Is Marriage a Path to Liberation? *Out/look* (Fall 1989): 8–12; and Michael Warner, *The Trouble with Normal* (New York: Free Press, 1999).

6. See Eskridge, *Equality Practice*, ch. 6.

EPILOGUE

1. See Seidman, *Embattled Eros*; and Jeffrey Weeks, *Invented Moralities* (New York: Columbia University Press, 1995).

Index